BEYOND
REDUNDANCY

BEYOND REDUNDANCY

How Geographic Redundancy Can Improve Service Availability and Reliability of Computer-Based Systems

Eric Bauer
Randee Adams
Daniel Eustace

IEEE PRESS

A JOHN WILEY & SONS, INC., PUBLICATION

Published by John Wiley & Sons, Inc., Hoboken, New Jersey.
Published simultaneously in Canada.

For general information on our other products and services or for technical support, please contact our Customer Care Department within the United States at (800) 762-2974, outside the United States at (317) 572-3993 or fax (317) 572-4002.

Wiley also publishes its books in a variety of electronic formats. Some content that appears in print may not be available in electronic formats. For more information about Wiley products, visit our web site at www.wiley.com.

Library of Congress Cataloging-in-Publication Data
Bauer, Eric.
   Beyond redundancy : how geographic redundancy can improve service availability and reliability of computer-based systems / Eric Bauer, Randee Adams, Daniel Eustace.
      p. cm.
   ISBN 978-1-118-03829-1 (hardback)
  1. Computer input-output equipment–Reliability.   2. Computer networks–Reliability.
3. Redundancy (Engineering)   I. Adams, Randee.   II. Eustace, Daniel.   III. Title.
   TK7887.5.B395 2011
   004.6–dc22

                                                                      2011008324

oBook ISBN: 978-1-118-10491-0
ePDF ISBN: 978-1-118-10492-7
ePub ISBN: 978-1-118-10493-4

Printed in the United States of America.

10 9 8 7 6 5 4 3 2 1

To our families for their encouragement and support:
Eric's wife Sandy and children Lauren and Mark
Randee's husband Scott and son Ryan
Dan's wife Helen and daughters Christie and Chelsea

CONTENTS

FIGURES

TABLES

EQUATIONS

PREFACE AND ACKNOWLEDGMENTS

The best practice for mitigating the risk of site destruction, denial, or unavailability causing disastrous loss of critical services is to deploy redundant systems in a geographically separated location; this practice is called geographic redundancy or georedundancy. Enterprises deploying a geographically redundant system may spend significantly more than when deploying a standalone configuration up front, and will have higher ongoing operating expenses to maintain the geographically separated redundant recovery site and system. While the business continuity benefits of georedundancy are easy to understand, the feasible and likely service availability benefits of georedundancy are not generally well understood. This book considers the high-level question of what service availability improvement is feasible and likely with georedundancy. The emphasis is on system availability of IP-based applications. WAN availability is briefly mentioned where applicable, but is not factored into any of the modeling. The service availability benefit is characterized both for product attributable failures, as well as for nonproduct attributable failures, such as site disasters. Human factors are also taken into consideration as they relate to procedural downtime. Furthermore, this book considers architectural and operational topics, such as: whether it is better to only do a georedundancy failover for a failed element or for the entire cluster of elements that contains the failed element; whether georedundancy can/should be used to reduce planned downtime for activities such as hardware growth and software upgrade; what availability-related georedundancy requirements should apply to each network element and to clusters of elements; and what network element- and cluster-level testing is appropriate to assure expected service availability benefits of georedundancy.

This book considers the range of IP-based information and communication technology (ICT) systems that are typically deployed in enterprise data centers and telecom central offices. The term "enterprise" is used to refer to the service provider or enterprise operating the system, "supplier" is used to refer to the organization that develops and tests the system, and "user" is used for the human or system that uses the system. In some cases, "enterprise," "supplier," and "user" may all be part of the same larger organization (e.g., system that is developed, tested and operated by the IT department of a larger, and used by employees of the organization), but often two or all three of these parties are in different organizations.

The term network element refers to a system device, entity, or node including all relevant hardware and/or software components deployed at one location providing a particular primary function; an instance of a domain name system (DNS) server is a network element. A system is *"a collection of components organized to accomplish a specific function or set of functions"* (*IEEE Standard Glossary*, 1991); a pool of DNS servers is an example of system. A solution is an integrated suite of network elements that can provide multiple primary functions; a customer care center that may include functionality, such as call handling facilities, web servers, and billing servers, is an example of a solution. With improvements in technology and hardware capacity, the distinction between these terms often blurs, since a single server could perform all of the functionality required of the solution and might be considered a network element. The more general term "external redundancy" is used to encompass both traditional geographic redundancy in which redundant system instances are physically separated to minimize the risk of a single catastrophic event impacting both instances, as well as the situation in which redundant system instances are physically co-located. While physically co-located systems do not mitigate the risk of catastrophic site failure, they can mitigate the risk of system failures. External redundancy is contrasted with internal redundancy in which the redundancy is confined to a single element instance. For example, a RAID array is a common example of internal redundancy because the software running on the element or the RAID hardware assures that disk failures are detected and mitigated without disrupting user service. If each element requires a dedicated RAID array and an enterprise chooses to deploy a pair of elements for redundancy, then those elements could either be co-located in a single facility or installed in separate, presumably geographically distant, facilities. Both co-located and geographically separated configurations are considered "externally redundant," as the redundancy encompasses multiple element instances. Elements can be deployed with no redundancy, internal redundancy, external redundancy, or hybrid arrangements. This book discusses internal redundancy but focuses on external redundancy arrangements.

AUDIENCE

This book is written for network architects and designers, maintenance and operations engineers, and decision makers in IT organizations at enterprises who are considering or have deployed georedundant systems. This book is also written for system architects, system engineers, developers, testers, and others (including technical sales and support staff) involved in the development of systems supporting external redundancy and solutions considering system redundancy. This book is also written for reliability engineers and others who model service availability of systems that include external redundancy, including georedundancy.

ORGANIZATION

The book is organized to enable different audiences to easily access the information they are most interested in. Part 1, "Basics," gives background on georedundancy and service availability, and is suitable for all readers. Part 2, "Modeling and Analysis of Redundancy," gives technical and mathematical details of service availability modeling of georedundant configurations, and thus is most suitable for reliability engineers and others with deeper mathematical interest in the topic. Part 3 'Recommendations' offers specific recommendations on architecture, design, specification, testing, and analysis of georedundant configurations. The recommendations section ends with Chapter 15 which offers a summary of the material. Most readers will focus on Parts 1 and 3; reliability engineers will focus on Parts 2 and 3; and readers looking for a high-level summary can focus on Chapter 15, "Summary."

Part 1—Basics, contains the following chapters:

- *"Service, Risk, and Business Continuity"* reviews risk management, business continuity and disaster recovery in the context of service availability of critical systems.
- *"Service Availability and Service Reliability"* reviews the concepts of service availability and service reliability, including how these key metrics are measured in the field.

Part 2—Modeling and Analysis of Redundancy contains the following chapters:

- *"Understanding Redundancy"* factors redundancy into three broad categories: simplex (no redundancy), internal system redundancy, and external system redundancy (including co-located and geographically separated configurations). The fundamentals of high-availability mechanisms and modeling of availability improvements from internal redundancy are covered. Criteria for evaluating high-availability mechanisms are also given.
- *"Overview of External Redundancy"* reviews the key techniques and mechanisms that support failure detection and recovery that enable internal and external redundancy. This chapter also reviews the technical differences between local (co-located) and geographically separated redundancy.
- *"External Redundancy Strategy Options"* reviews the three fundamental system-level external redundancy strategies that are used today: manually controlled, system-driven, and client-initiated recovery. Case studies are given to illustrate how these techniques can be integrated to achieve highly available and reliable systems.
- *"Modeling Service Availability with External System Redundancy"* presents mathematical modeling of the service availability benefit of the three external redundancy strategies. First, a generic model that roughly covers all external redundancy strategies is presented to highlight the differences between the recovery strategies; then more practical strategy specific models are presented and analyzed.
- *"Understanding Recovery Timing Parameters"* details how key recovery-related timing parameters used in the mathematical modeling of the previous chapter should be set to optimize the recovery time for the various external redundancy strategies.
- *"Case Study of Client-Initiated Recovery"* uses a domain name system (DNS) cluster as an example of client-initiated recovery to illustrate the concepts and models discussed earlier in this section.

- *"Solution and Cluster Recovery"* considers how clusters of network elements organized into solutions delivering sophisticated services to enterprises and their customers can be recovered together, and discusses the potential benefits of cluster recovery compared to recovery of individual elements.

Part 3—Recommendations contains the following chapters

- *"Georedundancy Strategy"* reviews considerations when engineering the number of sites to deploy a solution across to assure acceptable quality service is highly available to users.
- *"Maximizing Service Availability via Georedundancy"* reviews the architectural characteristics that can maximize the service availability benefit of external system redundancy.
- *"Georedundancy Requirements"* lists sample redundancy requirements for enterprise IT organizations to consider when specifying critical services.
- *"Georedundancy Testing"* discusses how the verifiable requirements of the "Georedundancy Requirements" chapter should be tested across the integration, system validation, deployment/installation, and operational lifecycle phases.
- *"Solution Georedundancy Case Study"* discusses analysis, architecture, design, specification, and testing of a hypothetical solution.
- *"Summary"* reviews the feasible improvements in service availability that can be practically achieved by properly configuring solutions and redundant systems.

Since many readers will not be familiar with the principles of Markov modeling of service availability used in this book, a basic overview of Markov modeling of service availability is included as an appendix.

ACKNOWLEDGMENTS

The authors acknowledge Chuck Salisbury for his diligent early work to understand the service availability benefits of georedundancy. The authors are also grateful for Ron Santos' expert input on DNS. Bill Baker provided extensive comments and shared his valuable insights on this subject. Doug Kimber provided detail and thoughtful review, and the technical reviewers provided excellent feedback that led us to improve the content and flow of the book. Anil Macwan provided guidance on procedural reliability considerations. Ted Lach and Chun Chan provided expert input on several subtle reliability items. Michael Liem provided valuable feedback.

ERIC BAUER
RANDEE ADAMS
DANIEL EUSTACE

PART 1

BASICS

1

SERVICE, RISK, AND BUSINESS CONTINUITY

Enterprises implement computer-based systems to provide various information services to customers, staff, and other systems. By definition, unavailability of services deemed "critical" to an enterprise poses a significant risk to the enterprise customers or stakeholders. Prolonged unavailability of a critical system—or the information held on that system—can be a business disaster. For example, without access to logistics, inventory, order entry, or other critical systems, an enterprise may struggle to operate; a prolonged outage can cause substantial harm to the business, and a very long duration outage or loss of critical data can cause a business to fail.

This chapter introduces service criticality and the linkage to service availability expectations. Georedundancy and risk management in the context of critical computer-based services is covered, along with business continuity planning, recovery objectives, and strategies.

1.1 SERVICE CRITICALITY AND AVAILABILITY EXPECTATIONS

Different systems offer different services to users, and different services have different criticalities to the enterprises that own those systems and offer those services. Generally,

Beyond Redundancy: How Geographic Redundancy Can Improve Service Availability and Reliability of Computer-Based Systems, First Edition. Eric Bauer, Randee Adams, Daniel Eustace.
© 2012 Institute of Electrical and Electronics Engineers. Published 2012 by John Wiley & Sons, Inc.

services can be grouped into several categories by criticality; while the category names and exact definitions may vary from industry to industry, the fundamentals are likely to be fairly consistent. As a generic and well-documented example of service criticality, let us consider the service criticality definitions used by the U.S. Federal Aviation Administration (2008) (FAA) in FAA-HDBD-006A in the context of the United States' National Airspace System (NAS), which includes air traffic control. The FAA's formal criticality definitions are:

- *Safety Critical.* Service thread loss would present an unacceptable safety hazard during transition to reduced capacity operations.
- *Efficiency Critical.* Service thread loss could be accommodated by reducing capacity without compromising safety, but the resulting impact might have a localized or system-wide economic impact on [national airspace system] efficiency.
- *Essential.* Service thread loss could be accommodated by reducing capacity without compromising safety, with only a localized impact on [national airspace system] efficiency.
- *Routine.* Loss of this service/capability would have a minor impact on the risk associated with providing safe and efficient local [national airspace system] operations.

To clarify these definitions, "*provide aircraft to aircraft separation*" is deemed by the FAA to be efficiency critical, while "*provide weather advisories*" is essential, and "*provide government/agency support*" is merely routine. Different industries and enterprises may have somewhat different terminology and definitions, but the rough distinctions between safety critical, efficiency critical, essential, and routine services will apply to all enterprises.

Enterprises typically set service availability expectations based on the criticality of the services offered by those systems. The FAA's availability expectations by criticality are given in Table 1.1; many other enterprises will have similar quantitative expectations.

While few enterprises develop and operate "safety critical" systems, most enterprises will have several services that are deemed "efficiency critical" and all will support myriad "essential" and "routine" services. This book focuses on "efficiency critical" (nominally five 9's) services. This book also provides guidance useful for safety critical services, but safety critical services are likely to require further diligence beyond what is presented in this book.

1.2 THE EIGHT-INGREDIENT MODEL

Information services are typically implemented via integrated suites of computer systems and networking infrastructure. In addition to networking infrastructure, the computer software and hardware require other supporting infrastructure to operate. The eight-ingredient model—described in Rauscher et al. (2006) and illustrated in Figure

TABLE 1.1. FAA's Availability Expectations by Service Thread Criticality

Service Thread Loss Severity Category	Service Availability Expectation	FAA's Design Guidance
Safety critical	99.99999% (seven 9's)	"Because the seven 'nines' requirement is not achievable with a single service thread[1], a service that is potentially safety-critical must be supported by two independent 'efficiency critical' service threads."
Efficiency critical	99.999% (five 9's)	"...achievable by a service thread built of off-the-shelf components in fault tolerant configuration."
Essential	99.9% (three 9's)	"...achievable by a service thread built of good quality, industrial-grade, off-the-shelf components."
Routine	99% (two 9's)	

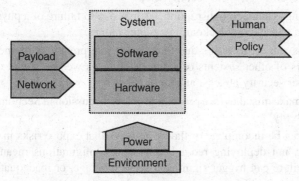

Figure 1.1. The eight-ingredient model.

1.1—gives a generic framework of the ingredients required for an information system to operate. The system itself consists of *software* that executes on *hardware*. The hardware requires electrical *power* to operate and must be maintained in an *environment* with acceptable temperature, humidity, dust, and corrosive gases, physically secured from theft and vandalism, and so on. The system relies on IP *networking* to communicate with other systems and users. Standard or application protocols are carried as *payloads* over IP networking to communicate with other systems and users. *Human* staff performs operations, administration, maintenance, and provisioning on the system. The humans are governed by enterprise *policies* that guide a huge range of activities that impact the system, such as policies for:

[1] The FAA sets these expectations based on "service threads' which are *"strings of systems that support one or more of the [national airspace system] capabilities. These Service Threads represent specific data paths (e.g. radar surveillance data) to controllers or pilots. The threads are defined in terms of narratives . . ."* (U.S. Federal Aviation Administration, 2008).

- redundancy configuration and dimensioning of system hardware;
- system operation and maintenance procedures, including how promptly security and stability patches are installed;
- required training and experience of staff;
- characteristics of the physical environment and networking infrastructure;
- security policy, including what security appliances protect the system from cyber security attack; and
- configuration and setting of network and application protocol options.

Each of the eight ingredients is subject to countless threats, such as:

- Software is susceptible to residual software defects.
- Hardware is subject to random hardware failures and wear out.
- Power is subject to outages, brownouts, surges, and sags.
- Environment is subject to temperature extremes due to air conditioning failure or fire, breach of physical security, etc;
- Networking is subject to disruption, such as due to failure of a physical transport link (a.k.a., "backhoe blackout") or router failure.
- Payload is subject to errors due to different interpretations of specifications by developers of other systems or software bugs, as well as denial of service and other cyber security attacks, and so on.
- Humans make mistakes (see procedural errors discussion in Section 2.2.3 "Outage Attributability").
- Policies can be incomplete or flawed in ways that expose risks in other ingredients (e.g., not deploying redundant system configurations means that critical system failure can trigger significant service outage, or inadequate training can cause humans to make mistakes).

It is often useful to consider attributability for events that can impact the eight ingredients. The telecommunications industry's quality standard TL 9000 defines three outage Attributability categories that are both useful and generally applicable: product attributable events, enterprise attributable[2] events and external attributable outage events.

- *Product Attributable Risk.* System suppliers are primarily responsible for identifying and managing risks to software and hardware components, as well as overall system integration, to assure that the system meets the reliability and availability specifications. The supplier is responsible for clearly communicating required system dimensioning and configuration to meet the expected engineered load with acceptable service quality, reliability, and availability. The supplier is

---

[2] This category is actually called "*customer attributable*" in TL 9000 standard. The label "customer attributable" contrasts nicely with the "supplier attributable" (now "product attributable") label.

also responsible for communicating required aspects of the expected power, environmental, networking, payload, human, and policy that should be addressed by the enterprise.

- *Enterprise Attributable Risk.* The enterprise is accountable for assuring that the right system configuration is deployed and continuously provided with high-quality electrical power and reliable networking in an acceptable environment. The enterprise should assure that the system, environment, and network infrastructure is competently operated by human maintenance engineers following suitable policies and procedures. Implicit in this statement is that enterprises are responsible for assuring that ingredients that are subject to external, often catastrophic, risk are appropriately mitigated. For example, while the enterprise is typically not responsible for commercial power outages, they are responsible for mitigating the service availability risk associated with threats to the power ingredient.

- *External Attributable Risk.* External factors can threaten service availability through both catastrophic and isolated incidents. Catastrophic events like earthquakes or tsunamis can physically damage or destroy: hardware; power distribution, transmission, or generation infrastructure; data center facilities or environment; networking facilities or equipment provided by service providers or the enterprise itself; and prevent human staff from safely accessing, operating, or repairing the system. Since enterprises are generally incapable of influencing the frequency, timing, nature, or magnitude of catastrophic events, enterprises must focus on mitigating the risk of external attributable events, including events that render physical sites temporarily or permanently inaccessible.

These outage Attributability categories are discussed in more depth in Section 2.2.3 "Outage Attributability."

1.3 CATASTROPHIC FAILURES AND GEOGRAPHIC REDUNDANCY

Failures are inevitable in the real world, and fault tolerant designs anticipate single-failure events and include mechanisms, policies, and procedures to mitigate single failure events with minimal service disruption. For example, hardware modules on fault-tolerant systems (i.e., with hardware redundancy) are often packaged in field replaceable units (FRUs) for blades, circuit assemblies, hard disk drives, fan tray assemblies, and so on, that can be promptly and efficiently replaced in the field with minimal service disruption. It is common for mean time to repair (MTTR) values to be specified for the time it takes an appropriately trained technician to complete the replacement or repair of a single failure.

Unfortunately, catastrophic failures occasionally occur, which simultaneously damage multiple components, modules, or even systems, and thus overwhelm the fault tolerant system design and supporting policies. These catastrophic events range from equipment and building fires to water damage from roof leaks, plumbing mishaps, and floods to physical equipment or building damage from roof collapse, earthquake, tornado, or hurricane, to terrorism, sabotage, and acts of war. Snedaker (2007) offers the following general list of catastrophic risks to consider:

Natural Hazards

Cold weather-related hazards
- Avalanche
- Severe snow
- Ice storm, hail storm
- Severe or prolonged wind

Warm weather-related hazards
- Severe or prolonged rain
- Heavy rain and/or flooding
  - Floods
  - Flash flood
  - River flood
  - Urban flood

Drought (can impact urban, rural, and agricultural areas)

Fire
- Forest fire
- Wild fire—urban, rural, agricultural
- Urban fire

Tropical storms
- Hurricanes, cyclones, typhoons (name depends on location of event)
- Tornado
- Wind storm

Geological hazards
- Landslide (often caused by severe or prolonged rain)
- Land shifting (subsidence and uplift) caused by changes to the water table, man-made elements (tunnels, underground building), geological faulting, extraction of natural gas, and so on

Earthquake

Tsunami

Volcanic eruption
- Volcanic ash
- Lava flow
- Mudflow (called a lahar)

Human-Caused Hazards

Terrorism
- Bombs
- Armed attacks
- Hazardous material release (biohazard, radioactive)
- Cyber attack
- Biological attack (air, water, food)
- Transportation attack (airports, water ports, railways)
- Infrastructure attack (airports, government buildings, military bases, utilities, water supply)
- Kidnapping (nonterrorist)
- Wars

Bomb
- Bomb threat
- Explosive device found
- Bomb explosion

Explosion

Fire
- Arson
- Accidental

Cyber attack
- Threat or boasting
- Minor intrusion
- Major intrusion
- Total outage
- Broader network infrastructure impaired (Internet, backbone, etc.)

Civil disorder, rioting, unrest

Protests
- Broad political protests
- Targeted protests (specifically targeting your company, for example)

Product tampering

Radioactive contamination

Embezzlement, larceny, theft

Kidnapping

Extortion

Subsidence (shifting of land due to natural or man-made changes causing building or infrastructure failure)

Accidents and Technological Hazards

Transportation accidents and failures
• Highway collapse or major accident
• Airport collapse, air collision, or accident
• Rail collapse or accident
• Water accident, port closure
• Pipeline collapse or accident

Infrastructure accidents and failures
• Electricity—power outage, brownouts, rolling outages, failure of infrastructure
• Gas—outage, explosion, evacuation, collapse of system
• Water—outage, contamination, shortage, collapse of system
• Sewer—stoppage, backflow, contamination, collapse of system

Information system infrastructure
• Internet infrastructure outage
• Communication infrastructure outage (undersea cables, satellites, etc.)
• Major service provider outage (Internet, communications, etc.)

Systems failures
• Power grid or substation failure
• Nuclear power facility incident
• Dam failure

Hazardous material incident
• Local, stationary source
• Nonlocal or in-transit source (e.g., truck hauling radioactive or chemical waste crashes)

Building collapse (various causes)

High-availability mechanisms and fault-tolerant designs address ordinary, non-catastrophic failure events. Catastrophic events that impact critical infrastructure ingredients and cannot rapidly be recovered locally are typically mitigated by having a redundant system at a facility that is physically separated from the primary facility by a far enough distance that the catastrophic event which impacts the primary site will not impact the geographically redundant site. Disaster recovery or other processes and procedures are used to assure that critical services can be promptly recovered to the geographically redundant (or georedundant) site following catastrophic failure.

1.4 GEOGRAPHICALLY SEPARATED RECOVERY SITE

Geographic redundancy, or simply georedundancy, refers to systems that are:

1. Deployed at a facility that is *geographically separated from the primary site*; that is, systems are generally deployed at an active, hot, warm, or cold recovery site or a service bureau. There may be a one-to-one mapping of active to recovery sites, or there may be many active sites that share a recovery site that must be configured for the site for which it is assuming service.
2. Fully installed and *maintained in a state of readiness* to begin emergency recovery actions promptly, that is, redundant systems are active or in hot, or at least warm standby.
3. Redundant systems are *engineered to carry sufficient traffic to support normal capacity* (or minimum acceptable) traffic loads when primary system or site is unavailable.

To mitigate the risk of site destruction or site inaccessibility, enterprises will often deploy a redundant set of core elements on a recovery site at a geographically remote location. Recovery site options are broadly classified as follows:

1. *Ad Hoc Site.* The enterprise can simply plan to find a new facility after a disaster occurs, and have the replacement equipment delivered and installed at that new facility. This ad hoc strategy naturally yields the longest service disruption following a disaster.
2. *Cold Recovery Site.* ISO/IEC 24762 (2008) defines cold recovery site as a facility *"with adequate space and associated infrastructure—power supply, telecommunications connections, environmental controls, etc—to support organization Information Communication Technology (ICT) systems, which will only be installed when disaster recovery (DR) services are activated."*
3. *Warm Recovery Site.* ISO/IEC 24762 (2008) defines warm recovery site as a facility *"that is partially equipped with some of the equipment, computing hardware and software, and supporting personnel, with organizations installing additional equipment, computing hardware and software, and supporting personnel when disaster recovery services are activated."*
4. *Reciprocal Backup Agreement.* Some governmental agencies and industries have mutual aid agreements to support each other in time of need (i.e., disaster recovery).

5. *Service Bureau.* Some companies offer processing capabilities for both ordinary and disaster recovery needs.

6. *Hot Site.* ISO/IEC 24762 (2008) defines hot recovery site as a facility *"that is fully equipped with the required equipment, computing hardware and software, and supporting personnel, and fully functional and manned on a 24 × 7 basis so that it is ready for organizations to operate their ICT systems when DR services are activated."*

Systems installed at hot sites or service bureaus can be maintained at one of the following levels of service readiness

- *Active.* A network element that is fully available and serving traffic is called "active."
- *Hot Standby.* A hot standby network element has its software installed and its data has been kept in synch with its mate and thus should quickly be able to assume service once its active mate has failed and disaster recovery has been activated. A hot standby network element can also be either automatically triggered into service or manually activated.
- *Warm Standby:* A warm standby network element generally has its software installed but will need data updates before it can assume service for a failed network element as part of disaster recovery. Generally, it takes less time to prepare it to take over as the active module than a cold standby element and has been configured to be the standby mate for a particular network element.
- *Cold Standby.* A cold standby network element generally does not have its software and data installed and as a result they must be installed and configured as part of disaster recovery before it can assume service for a failed network element. As a result, it takes the longest to become available. Sometimes, it is used as a spare for multiple network elements, and is thus installed once it is determined which element needs to be backed up.

Note that some enterprises or suppliers use portable disaster recovery facilities, such as staging equipment installed in trailers or shipping containers that can be promptly dispatched to a designated site following a disaster.

1.5 MANAGING RISK

Risk management is the process of identifying and analyzing risks, selecting appropriate mitigations to handle the risks, monitoring performance, and replanning as appropriate.

1.5.1   Risk Identification

Section 1.3, "Catastrophic Failures and Geographic Redundancy," enumerates the catastrophic risks that can confront a typical critical enterprise information system.

1.5.2   Risk Treatments

There are several broad categories of risk treatment:

- *Risk Avoidance.* Since best-in-class business processes are typically built around sophisticated and high-performance enterprise systems for service delivery, manufacturing, logistics, order entry, customer care, and so on, avoiding these systems means forgoing the business advantages that best-in-class processes enable. Thus, risk avoidance is not generally desirable for critical enterprise systems.
- *Risk Reduction.* The risk of unavailability of critical enterprise systems is reduced in two broad ways:
  - *reduce risk of critical failure*; and
  - *reduce risk of unacceptable service disruption* following critical failure.

    The risk of critical failure is reduced by assuring that the eight ingredients of Section 1.2 are consistently delivered with quality; for example, hardware and software should be developed using mature and high-quality processes. The risk of unacceptable service disruption is mitigated via:

    1. appropriate hardware and software redundancy;
    2. appropriate high-availability software to support automatic failure detection, isolation, and recovery; and
    3. manual recovery procedures to backup automatic mechanisms.

    Internal redundancy should mitigate most single hardware and software failure events, and external redundancy can mitigate virtually all hardware and software failure events. Geographically distributed external redundancy mitigates *force majeure*, external attributable risks of site destruction or denial covering power, environment, network, and human ingredients.
- *Risk Sharing.* Mutual aid arrangements are used in some industries and governmental sectors to share risks by having enterprises assist one another when addressing a disaster. While mutual aid arrangements are common for public safety and utilities, they may be impractical for most commercial endeavors because competitors are likely to be more interested in gaining customers and market share rather than aiding a competitor.
- *Risk Transfer.* Some companies offer disaster recovery service, such as hosting recovery sites or providing replacement equipment and facilities on short notice. It may be economically advantageous for an enterprise to contract for disaster recovery services, thus transferring some risk to a supplier. It may also be prudent to arrange for insurance coverage to hedge direct and indirect costs of major unavailability risks.

• *Risk Retention.* Some risks are retained by the enterprise itself as a normal part of business operations and policy. Usually, the enterprise retains the risk for minor or typical failures, such as failure of single-user devices, like laptops or smartphones.

For critical systems, enterprises often consider:

1. Internal redundancy to efficiently mitigate risk of hardware or software failures. High-availability systems are designed to withstand a single failure (e.g., failure of a single field replaceable unit or a single human mistake) without causing unacceptable service disruption. Unfortunately, hardware, power, environment, humans, and networking are vulnerable to catastrophic events like fire, earthquake, or sabotage that produces multiple failures that overwhelm traditional high-availability mechanisms.
2. Geographically distributed external redundancy to mitigate risk of a catastrophic event that renders a site destroyed, unavailable, or inaccessible.

In addition to geographically separated external redundancy, a well-thought-out and rehearsed business continuity plan is essential to assure that enterprises can promptly recovery from a disaster.

1.6 BUSINESS CONTINUITY PLANNING

Customers and users expect enterprises to assure that critical services are continuously available, and many information and communications services are even more important following a natural or man-made disaster. Thus, the earthquake or other *force majeur* event that impacts an enterprise site may also increase service demand as users attempt to learn more about the disaster and take action to mitigate their personal and professional risk of loss from the event. Diligent business continuity planning assures that customers and end users will experience minimal service impact due to catastrophic natural and man-made events.

Business continuity planning involves contingency planning for mitigating catastrophic risks, including disasters that compromise system hardware, environment, power, networking, or human access to those facilities. The best practice for well-run businesses and governmental organizations is to create continuity plans to assure that operations can promptly be recovered following a natural or man-made disaster. Business continuity is summarized in ISO/IEC 27002 (2005) as:

A business continuity management process should be implemented to minimize the impact on the organization and recover from loss of information assets (which may be the result of, for example, natural disasters, accidents, equipment failures, and deliberate actions) to an acceptable level through a combination of preventive and recovery controls.

The common motivations for business continuity planning are:

- Required to support service level agreements with internal and/or external customers.
- Required to support continuity and operations of just-in-time manufacturing, and mitigate risk of contractual penalties.
- Required to support strict and inflexible delivery-related penalties of products or services.
- Required by the industry, like Payment Card Industry Data Security Standard (PCI DSS), HIPAA Security Rule, ISO 27001, or BS25999.
- Demanded by shareholders to mitigate risk of business collapse following natural or man-made disaster.

The two aspects of business continuity planning are:

- *Preventive planning* seeks to minimize the risk of business disasters occurring. Preventive planning includes many commonsense items, like carefully selecting the locations for business facilities to minimize the risk of flooding and other natural hazards, physically securing the facility and assets, and screening staff and visitors to minimize the risk of human-caused business disasters. Preventive planning is outside the scope of this book.
- *Recovery planning.* Disaster recovery plans are formulated to assure that natural or man-made disasters are promptly addressed with minimal impact to the business. If a catastrophic event occurs, then a predefined disaster recovery plan can be activated to promptly recover services and operations. Geographic redundancy is often a key facet of recovery planning; this book considers geographic redundancy.

The exact value to the enterprise of business continuity planning will vary based on the nature of the service provided by the target enterprise systems. It should be noted that networking facilities and access equipment located outside of secured data centers, even outdoors, may be vulnerable to more hazards (and are more likely to fail) and will thus require special considerations.

1.7   DISASTER RECOVERY PLANNING

To assure prompt and appropriate recovery actions following a disaster, the best practice is to create a written disaster recovery plan that details the processes, policies, and procedures required to recover or to continue service after a site failure or other disaster. At the highest level, a disaster recovery plan generally begins with the following steps after a catastrophic event:

1. *Implement emergency action procedures* to protect the staff at the impacted site, and protect equipment and assets.

2. *Activate enterprise's emergency management team* to assess damage.
3. *Decide whether or not to activate disaster recovery plan*—an appropriate enterprise leader considers the assessment and recommendation of the emergency management team and decides whether to:
   • invoke disaster recovery plan and restore service onto recovery site; or
   • restore service onto affected primary site ASAP.

If the decision is made to invoke the disaster recovery plan and restore service onto the recovery site, then the following steps are generally executed:

1. *Issue formal disaster declaration* and notify the recovery site, all applicable personnel, and necessary suppliers.
2. *Activate and prepare the recovery site.* Required staff will travel to the recovery site, if necessary. If off-site system backups are held at a location other than the recovery site, then arrangements must be made to transport backups to the recovery site.
3. *Execute recovery activities* to prepare the recovery site, restore system data, etc. The procedures should be clearly documented and performed by trained staff.
4. *Recover service* onto recovery site systems.

A canonical disaster recovery scenario is illustrated in Figure 1.2.

Note that explicit human decision making and task execution are typical in traditional disaster recovery plans. In Section 5.5 "System-Driven Recovery" and Section 5.6 "Client-Initiated Recovery," this book will introduce two automatic recovery mechanisms that can compliment traditional manual disaster recovery procedures.

Eventually, the primary site will probably be repaired, service will be gracefully transitioned back to the primary site, and normal operations of the primary site will resume. Depending on system architecture and documented procedures, there may be a user visible service disruption when service is switched back to the primary site.

Disaster recovery planning is covered in detail in Toigo (2003), Gregory and Jan Rothstein (2007), Dolewski (2008), Snedaker (2007), and many other books and other resources.

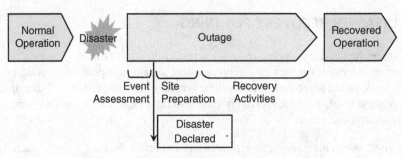

Figure 1.2. Canonical disaster recovery scenario.

1.8 HUMAN FACTORS

Disaster recovery and geographical redundancy—particularly manually controlled— have a distinct human aspect. A group of humans is usually following a documented procedure and plan (including a detailing of roles and responsibilities) to perform the recovery. The success of that operation is dependent on many aspects:

- How well trained the staff are on the procedures.
- How well documented and tested the procedures are.
- Complexity of the procedures (e.g., number of manual steps versus automation).
- Complexity of the system (e.g., number of components).
- Amount of coordination necessary among staff to perform the recovery.
- How well documented error scenarios and associated recovery techniques are in the event of a problem executing the procedure.
- Availability of tools to automate manual steps.
- How well the system detects, isolates, and reports problems.
- The level of increased stress due to schedule constraints and large number of human activities to be performed (Singh and Hannaman, 1992).

Failures experienced during the recovery process will further delay the system recovery. Failures introduced due to human error or faulty documentation are usually categorized as procedural. System unavailability time due to these types of failures is referred to as procedural downtime. Steps should be taken when implementing and testing geographic redundancy or disaster recovery to protect against procedural errors. Recommendations for addressing procedural errors are included in Section 11.3.2.

1.9 RECOVERY OBJECTIVES

The two key objectives for disaster recovery planning and execution are:

- *Recovery Time Objective* (RTO) is the target time between formal disaster declaration and when service is recovered onto the recovery site. The recovery time objective should be significantly shorter than the maximum tolerable downtime target.
- *Recovery Point Objective* (RPO) is the most recent point in time at which system state can be restored onto the recovery site. The recovery point objective characterizes the maximum acceptable data loss that the enterprise can sustain. The implication is that any sales, inventory, financial, provisioning, user, or other transactions which occurred after the recovery point objective but before the disaster are likely to be lost, so enterprises must set their RPO appropriately.

Figure 1.3 illustrates how RTO and RPO relate.

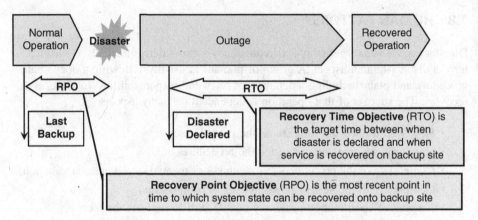

Figure 1.3. Recovery time objective and recovery point objective.

Different systems are likely to have different RTO and RPO targets. For example, efficiency critical systems directly supporting product manufacturing, service delivery, and other directly customer-impacting services are likely to have stricter targets than less real-time services like provisioning and payroll systems.

1.10 DISASTER RECOVERY STRATEGIES

There are several common strategies or patterns for disaster recovery of enterprise systems, and in 1992, these patterns were conveniently organized by the SHARE group (SHARE) into tiers of value offering better (i.e., shorter) RTO and RPO. These tiers are defined as ("Seven Tiers";Wikipedia):

- *Tier 0: No Off-Site Data.* Tier 0 enterprises have no disaster recovery plan and no saved data. Recovery time from disaster may take weeks or longer and may ultimately be unsuccessful.
- *Tier 1: Data Backup with No Hot Site.* Tier 1 enterprises maintain data backups offsite but do not maintain a hot site. Backup data must typically be physically retrieved (so-called pickup truck access method, PTAM), and thus significant time is required to access backup media. Since Tier 1 enterprises may not maintain their own redundant servers to recover service onto, time may be required to locate and configure appropriate systems.
- *Tier 2: Data Backup with a Hot Site.* Tier 2 enterprises maintain data backups as well as a hot site, and thus recovery times are faster and more predictable than in Tier 1.
- *Tier 3: Electronic Vaulting.* Tier 3 enterprises maintain critical data in an electronic vault so that backup data is network accessible to the hot site rather than requiring backup media to be physically retrieved and transported to the hot site.

- *Tier 4: Point-in-Time Copies.* Tier 4 enterprises maintain more timely point-in-time backups of critical data so that more timely backup data is network accessible to the hot site, thus reducing the RPO.
- *Tier 5: Transaction Integrity.* Tier 5 enterprises assure that transactions are consistent between production systems and recovery sites. Thus, there should be little or no data loss from a disaster.
- *Tier 6: Zero or Little Data Loss.* Tier 6 enterprises have little or no tolerance for data loss and thus must maintain the highest level of data consistency between production and recovery sites. Techniques like disk mirroring and synchronous I/O are generally deployed by Tier 6 enterprises to minimize RPO.
- *Tier 7: Highly Automated, Business-Integrated Solution.* Tier 7 enterprises automate disaster recovery of Tier 6 enterprises, thus shortening the RTO and with minimal RPO.

Each tier successively will support increasingly better recovery point or recovery time objectives but at an additional cost for the business. This must be taken into account during business continuity planning.

2

SERVICE AVAILABILITY AND SERVICE RELIABILITY

Enterprises spend money to deploy systems that provide valuable services to end users, enterprise staff, suppliers, or other systems. Two key operational characteristics of such a system are the service availability and service reliability delivered by the system. This chapter defines service availability, service reliability, and how both are measured.

2.1 AVAILABILITY AND RELIABILITY

2.1.1 Service Availability

Service availability characterizes the readiness of a system to deliver service to a user. Readiness of a system is commonly referred to as being "up." Mathematically, service availability is estimated as

$$\text{Service Availability} = \frac{\text{Uptime}}{\text{Uptime} + \text{Downtime}}$$

Equation 2.1. Service Availability Equation

Beyond Redundancy: How Geographic Redundancy Can Improve Service Availability and Reliability of Computer-Based Systems, First Edition. Eric Bauer, Randee Adams, Daniel Eustace.
© 2012 Institute of Electrical and Electronics Engineers. Published 2012 by John Wiley & Sons, Inc.

TABLE 2.1. Service Availability and Downtime Ratings

Number of 9's	Service Availability	Annualized Down Minutes	Quarterly Down Minutes	Monthly Down Minutes	Practical Meaning
1	90%	52,596.00	13,149.00	4383.00	Down 5 weeks per year
2	99%	5259.60	1,314.90	438.30	Down 4 days per year
3	99.9%	525.96	131.49	43.83	Down 9 hours per year
4	99.99%	52.60	13.15	4.38	Down 1 hour per year
5	99.999%	5.26	1.31	0.44	Down 5 minutes per year
6	99.9999%	0.53	0.13	0.04	Down 30 seconds per year
7	99.99999%	0.05	0.01	–	Down 3 seconds per year

Service availability is commonly expressed as the number of "9's" and "five 9's" is a common availability expectation for critical systems. Table 2.1 gives the maximum service downtime for common availability ratings.

2.1.2 Service Reliability

Service reliability characterizes the probability that service requests are fulfilled correctly with acceptable service quality and latency. Session-oriented services often explicitly measure both the probability of successfully initiating a session with service, commonly called accessibility, and the probability that a session delivers service with acceptable quality until the user initiates session termination, commonly called "retainability." A familiar example of accessibility and retainability is in the context of telephone calls:

- *Accessibility* is the probability that a correctly dialed telephone call alerts the correct callee and delivers ringback to the caller promptly. Accessibility can be generalized to be the ability to establish a session with any session-oriented service, such as establishing an Instant Message session;
- *Retainability* is the probability that the call maintains acceptable voice quality until one of the two parties explicitly disconnects the call. Retainability can be generalized as the ability to maintain service via an established session with acceptable quality for any session-oriented service.

Service reliability is also measured for transaction oriented systems or operations, such as successful database queries or updates, new subscribers provisioned, or web pages delivered.

As most system services are highly reliable and percentages very close to 100% (e.g., 99.9876% or 99.9123%) are awkward for many people to work with, it is common to measure service *unreliability* as defects per million operations, or DPM. DPM is easy to compute as:

$$DPM = \frac{Failed\ Operations}{Attempted\ Operations} \times 1,000,000$$

Equation 2.2. Defects per Million Equation

Service reliability percentages can be converted to DPM using

$$DPM = (100\% - Service\ Reliability) \times 1,000,000$$

Equation 2.3. Converting Service Reliability to DPM

For example, service reliability of 99.9876% converts to 124 defects per million (DPM) transactions while service reliability of 99.9123% translates to 877 DPM. Using service (un)reliability expressed in DPM, it is simple to see that 877 DPM (99.9123% service reliability) has seven times the rate of failed transactions as 124 DPM (99.9876%) because 877 divided by 124 is 7.07.

DPM is often computed on an hourly, daily, weekly, or monthly basis either directly from performance statistics maintained by the system or indirectly from usage statistics recorded by a monitoring system.

2.1.3 Reliability, Availability, and Failures

Service availability and reliability should nominally be perfect (100% available, 0.00 DPM) except for:

1. *Overload* because overload controls cause some service requests to be rejected when offered load exceeds the engineered capacity of available resources, thus impacting service reliability.
2. *Failures* which cause some service requests to fail, thus impacting service reliability metrics and possibly service availability metrics. Note that activation of service recovery procedures can occasionally cause service impact to be somewhat greater than the primary failure. An example is when a system must be restarted (which will impact all users) to clear a critical software problem that is only affecting some of the users.
3. Some *planned activities* like upgrade or reconfiguration may involve brief periods of downtime, thus possibly impacting service reliability and service availability metrics, particularly if they go beyond the boundaries of an agreed upon maintenance period.

The impact of failures on service reliability and service availability metrics is not obvious for two reasons:

1. *Failure Severity.* Failures are commonly classified by the magnitude of their service impact. A minor event may impact a single user's transaction or a single user's session or a single function offered by the system. A major event may impact multiple users or multiple functions. A critical event may impact most or all of a system's users.

2. *Failure Impact Duration.* Practical systems are designed to tolerate or "ride over" brief service disruptions. For example, networked systems often automatically retry or retransmit IP messages that were not properly acknowledged in a specified time. Successful operation of these robustness mechanisms generally minimizes the service impact of brief failure events. Service reliability metrics may be impacted during the brief window when a failure is automatically detected, isolated, and recovered, but very brief disruptions are generally excluded from service availability metrics.

The relationship between duration of service impact, service reliability metrics, and service availability metrics is graphically illustrated in Figure 2.1. If the service disruption following a failure is milliseconds long, then simple robustness mechanisms like timeout and retry logic will often "ride over" the event, and many enterprises and users will consider it a transient event rather than a service outage. If the duration of service disruption stretches to seconds, then some transactions are likely to timeout or be abandoned by users so that it might be considered a degraded service event, rather than a service outage. If the duration of service impact is more than a few seconds, then many enterprises will consider the service to be "down," and hence the service availability metric is impacted. The maximum acceptable service disruption latency after which an event causes service to be deemed unavailable varies based on the nature

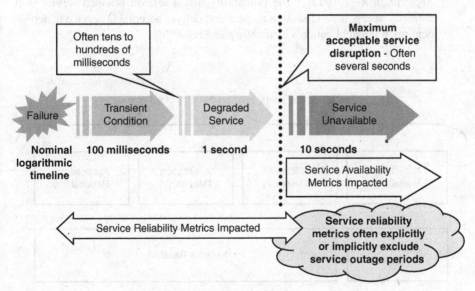

Figure 2.1. Canonical service impact timeline.

of the service delivered by the system, industry standards, enterprise policy, and other factors. Some user services may be impacted if the duration of service impact is longer than retry/retransmission or other robustness mechanisms can tolerate, and thus service reliability metrics are likely to be impacted for many events that are shorter than the maximum acceptable service disruption. For example, users are likely to abandon a telephone call if they do not hear ringback within a few seconds of dialing the last digit or pressing "send," and web surfers may abandon (or perhaps cancel and reload) a page if it does not finish loading after several seconds.

Note that while service reliability metrics are accurately measured when the system is "up," service reliability metrics are often not directly measured accurately by the target system when the system itself is "down." Thus, service reliability metrics often exclude periods when the system is deemed to be unavailable/down. This means that user service is impacted during periods of service unavailability and partially impacted by service reliability impairments when the system is nominally "up."

Availability and reliability also drive the overall quality of service experienced by users, as shown in Figure 2.2. Quality of a network-based service is largely driven by the following factors:

- *Network Availability.* The networking facilities and infrastructure that transport packets between the user and network elements implementing the system service must be available to connect users to applications.
- *Network Reliability.* The networking facilities must reliably deliver packets with acceptable quality (e.g., minimal packet loss, low latency, minimal jitter)
- *Application Availability.* The system offering the service or application must be available to serve users.
- *Application Accessibility.* The probability that a session oriented service will correctly accept a valid session request and deliver acceptable service is dependent upon the application's availability and reliability.

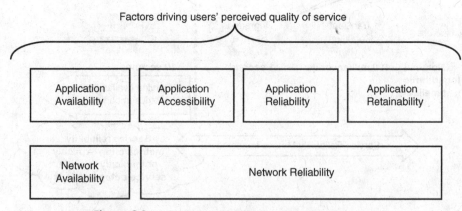

Figure 2.2. Reliability, availability, and quality of service.

• *Application Reliability*. The probability that a properly formed and authorized client request is correctly served with acceptable quality of service is primarily a function of the transactional reliability of the application.

• *Application Retainability*. The ability of an application session to remain fully operational with acceptable quality of service until normal session termination is driven by both the reliability and quality of service of the underlying network, as well as the application's availability and reliability.

While application accessibility and application retainability may not be applicable for stateless transaction-oriented services, network and application availability, and network and application reliability are directly applicable to a broad class of network based services. This book considers service or application availability and reliability; it does not consider the availability and reliability of IP-based networks.

2.2 MEASURING SERVICE AVAILABILITY

The key outage measurement concepts are:

• formal definition of total and partial outages;
• normalization units;
• minimum chargeable service disruption duration;
• outage attributability;
• systems and network elements; and
• treatment of planned events.

Both equipment suppliers and service providers operating telecommunications equipment have agreed to formal, standardized service outage definitions and metrics in TL9000 (QuEST Forum, 2006). These definitions can cover a broad class of computer based systems, and thus TL9000 (QuEST Forum, 2006) measurement concepts will be used in this book.

While service availability is typically defined as a function of uptime and downtime as was given in Section 2.1.1, "Service Availability," it is typically measured by considering outage time in a reporting period relative to planned operation time in that period. For example, January has 31 days, which is 44,640 minutes (which is 31 days times 24 hours per day times 60 minutes per hour). Service availability for a single system in January is computed as:

$$\text{Availability}_{\text{January}} = \frac{31 \times 24 \times 60 - \text{DownMinutes}_{\text{January}}}{31 \times 24 \times 60} = \frac{44,460 - \text{DownMinutes}_{\text{January}}}{44,460}$$

Thus, minutes of downtime, or outage time, drives service availability calculations. Hence, the factors that drive measurements of outage time directly drive service availability calculations.

2.2.1 Total and Partial Outages

Most enterprise systems are capable of both supporting multiple users simultaneously and offering multiple functions to users. Given the complexity and design of enterprise systems, events that impact some but not all functionality or some but not all users are often more common than events that totally disable all functionality for all users. For example, failure of a single software process on an enterprise server is likely to impact the users or function(s) supported by that process, while users served by other processes may be unaffected and functions offered by other processes may remain available.

The obvious measurement strategy for less than total outages is to prorate them based on the capacity or functionality lost. For example, if a failure impacts a quarter of a system's users (e.g., a storage failure that renders data for 25% of a system's users unavailable), then the event could be prorated as a 25% outage. If this failure took 1 hour to recover, then 60 minutes of outage multiplied by 25% capacity loss yields 15 minutes of prorated down time. Thus, partial capacity loss outages can be normalized into total system outages.

While prorating for percentage of capacity lost is fairly straightforward, prorating a partial functionality loss event is more complex because different enterprises and users may value specific functionality differently. Partial outage definitions are often both elaborate and precise. For example, consider TL 9000's partial outage definition for "application servers" (TL 9000 category 1.2.7), covering *"Equipment that provides IP based multimedia services"* like multimedia instant messaging systems:

- Loss of more than 5% of the IP-based multimedia services
- Loss of stable service sessions
- Total loss of one or more but not all services
- System congestion which impacts greater than 5% of all session set-up attempts
- 85% or more of the service subscribers experience a session delay of 3 seconds or greater for a period longer than 30 seconds
- Interface switchovers lasting longer than 60 milliseconds
- Total loss of one or more operations, administration and maintenance (OA&M) functions (default weight is 5%)
- Total loss of visibility from Element Management System (default weight is 10%)

In contrast, the TL 9000 total outage definition for applications servers is very simple:

Total loss of ability to provide IP-based multimedia services.

Best practice is for system suppliers and enterprises to clearly agree on how partial functionality loss events will be measured in advance, rather than attempting to agree on how to quantify service impairments and service-level agreement remedies after the fact.

Partial capacity loss outages are typically normalized against some unit to convert a concrete service impact (e.g., 17 users affected) into a percentage of capacity that can prorate the outage duration. Normalization units for enterprise systems are either based on the number of systems in service, number of provisioned users, or number of active users. Normalizing outages based on systems can be somewhat misleading if systems have different configurations and/or user loads that can overstate outages on small, lightly loaded systems and understate outages on large, heavily loaded systems. Normalizing on the number of provisioned users can understate the apparent user impact, because although only a fraction of provisioned users may be online at any point an outage is significant to them. Normalizing on the number of active users can overstate the customer impact of events that occur in off hours when traffic is very light.

Thus, it is common for sophisticated enterprises to explicitly track minutes (or seconds) of severely impacted service as absolute availability impact, and normalize it in reports to permit sensible month-by-month, quarter-by-quarter, and year-by-year comparisons. Normalized (un)availability or (un)reliability metrics are often tracked as key performance indicators against targets. Performance below target can lead to investigation and root cause analysis, followed by corrective actions. Sophisticated enterprises will tie performance of key service availability, reliability, and/or quality metrics of critical systems to compensation to assure that maintenance staffs are fully motivated to assure excellent performance of these key metrics.

2.2.2 Minimum Chargeable Disruption Duration

Failures are inevitable and real high-availability mechanisms must take a finite amount of time to detect and isolate a failure, initiate a failover or other recovery action, and restore user service. Typically, maximum acceptable service disruption latency is established, and system designs and configuration (e.g., protocol timeouts and retry strategies) are planned accordingly. For example, SONET/SDH standards stipulate that optical transmission systems shall recover service within 50 milliseconds of an optical cable break. Thus, if a fiber is cut and service is recovered in less than 50 milliseconds, then the event is not counted as a service outage.

Few applications require such rapid service recovery. TL 9000 specifies the following for application servers and other general elements:

- ". . . an *unscheduled* event must be longer than 15 seconds to be considered [an] outage"; and
- ". . . a *scheduled* event must be longer than 15 seconds to be considered [an] outage."

The minimum chargeable outage duration is often driven by the nature of the service itself and how users interact with it. For example, some applications like IP-TV have strict real-time service delivery requirements, and service is visibly impaired when these service delivery requirements are not met; other services like e-mail have softer real time service delivery requirements. Thus, the minimum chargeable outage duration for network elements in an IP-TV solution is likely to be shorter than the minimum chargeable outage duration for elements in an e-mail service.

2.2.3 Outage Attributability

It is useful to establish outage attributability rules so that suppliers and enterprises will agree on who is accountable for each outage. TL 9000 formally partitions outage attributability into three categories: product attributable, enterprise[1] attributable, and external attributable. These categories are defined as:

1. *Product Attributable Outage.* Some outages are primarily attributable to the design or failure of the system's software or hardware itself. The telecommunications industry defines product-attributable outages (QuEST Forum, 2006) as follows:

   An outage primarily triggered by

   a) system design, hardware, software, modules or other parts of the system,
   b) scheduled outage necessitated by the design of the system,
   c) support activities performed or prescribed by [a system supplier] including documentation, training, engineering, ordering, installation, maintenance, technical assistance, software or hardware change actions, etc.,
   d) procedural error caused by the [system supplier],
   e) the system failing to provide the necessary information to conduct a conclusive root cause determination, or
   f) one or more of the above.

2. *Enterprise Attributable Outage.* Some outages are primarily attributable to actions or inactions of the enterprise operating the equipment. The telecommunications industry defines this category (called "customer-attributable outage" in which "customer" refers to the enterprise operating the equipment) as follows (QuEST Forum, 2006):

   An outage that is primarily attributable to the [enterprise's] equipment or support activities triggered by

   a) [enterprise] procedural errors,
   b) office environment, for example power, grounding, temperature, humidity, or security problems, or
   c) one or more of the above.

---

[1] TL 9000 standard actually uses the term "customer" rather than enterprise, but to minimize confusion between TL 9000's usage of "customer" and common usage of "customer" to "user," this book will use the term "enterprise."

Procedural errors are further defined in TL9000 (QuEST Forum, 2006) as:

An error that is the direct result of human intervention or error. Contributing factors can include but are not limited to

a) deviations from accepted practices or documentation,
b) inadequate training,
c) unclear, incorrect, or out-of-date documentation,
d) inadequate or unclear displays, messages, or signals,
e) inadequate or unclear hardware labeling,
f) miscommunication,
g) non-standard configurations,
h) insufficient supervision or control, or
i) user characteristics such as mental attention, physical health, physical fatigue, mental health, and substance abuse.

Examples of a Procedural Error include but are not limited to

a) removing the wrong fuse or circuit pack,
b) not taking proper precautions to protect equipment, such as shorting out power, not wearing ESD strap, etc.,
c) unauthorized work,
d) not following Methods of Procedures (MOPs),
e) not following the steps of the documentation,
f) using the wrong documentation,
g) using incorrect or outdated documentation,
h) insufficient documentation,
i) translation errors,
j) user panic response to problems,
k) entering incorrect commands,
l) entering a command without understanding the impact, or
m) inappropriate response to a Network Element alarm.

3. *External Attributable Outage.* Some outages are attributable to external events beyond the control of either the enterprise operating the system or the system supplier. The telecommunications industry defines this category as follows (QuEST Forum, 2006):

Outages caused by natural disasters such as tornadoes or floods, and outages caused by third parties not associated with the customer or the organization such as commercial power failures, 3rd party contractors not working on behalf of the [system supplier] or [enterprise].

As the attributability taxonomy implies, the rate of product attributable outages is primarily driven by the quality and reliability of the system itself. The rate of enterprise attributable outages is primarily driven by the planning and operational quality of the IT department operating the system. The rate of external attributable events is primarily driven by external factors and mitigated by careful diligence and planning by the enterprise and system suppliers. Network failures are generally considered external attributable events as the network is usually configured and controlled by the enterprise.

Note that extreme and severe service outages—especially *force majeure* events—that expose an enterprise to grave and existential risk are commonly called disasters. Disaster recovery planning in general and geographic redundancy in particular is designed explicitly to mitigate the risk of *force majeure* and other external attributable outages.

2.2.4 Systems and Network Elements

A useful definition of a *system* is a suite of hardware and software that is integrated into a logical unit to appear to both end users and management systems and staff to be a single logical entity. People often associate "system" with hardware because it is far easier to visualize a physical server than intangible software. Networking and sophisticated middleware sometimes tend to blur the precise boundaries between one system and another; unfortunately, when measuring and predicting service availability and reliability, it is essential to crisply define boundaries so that impairments can be precisely attributed to the correct item. Thus, the telecommunications quality standard, TL 9000, uses the more concrete notion of *network elements* to frame service availability and other quality metrics. TL 9000 defines "network element" as follows:

> The Network Element must include all components required to perform the primary function of its applicable product category [e.g., router, application server, element management system]. If multiple [Field Replaceable Hardware Units], devices, and/or software components are needed for the NE to provide its product category's primary function, then none of these individual components can be considered an NE by themselves. The total collection of all these components is considered a single NE. Note: While an NE may be comprised of power supplies, CPU, peripheral cards, operating system and application software to perform a primary function, no individual item can be considered an NE is its own right (QuEST Forum, 2006).

When discussing an interface between two elements, one of the elements is the client (the element requesting a service) and the other is the server (the element providing the service). If an element has multiple interfaces, it could be the server on some interfaces and a client on others.

Solutions are comprised of one or more network elements, like firewalls, load balancers, application servers, database servers, element management systems, billing servers, provisioning servers, and so on. Solutions are covered in detail in Section 9.1, "Understanding Solutions."

2.2.5 Service Impact and Element Impact Outages

Differentiating network elements from systems enables one to more precisely measure service availability of complex services. As a simple example, consider a multi-engine commercial airplane. While one is primarily concerned with the availability of suffi-cient propulsion to keep the airplane flying, one is also very interested in the availability of each individual engine. After all, failure of one engine is a problem; loss of multiple engines is a disaster. This distinction is made via two distinct metrics:

- *Network Element Impact Outages* for failures where some or all network element functionality or capability is lost or unavailable for a period of time. For example, failure of a single engine on a multiengine airplane is logically a network element impact outage.[2] TL 9000 measures network element impact outages with "NE" metrics, such as NE04 for "*network element impact product attributable outage downtime.*"
- *Service Impact Outages* for failures where end user service is directly impacted. For example, failure of multiple engines on a multiengine airplane is likely to be a service impact outage because insufficient propulsion is available to safely maneuver and land the airplane. TL 9000 measures service impact outages with "SO" metrics, such as S04 for "*service impact product attributable outage down-time per* [Normalization Unit] *per year.*"

The subtle relationship of service impact and network element impact outages is best understood by considering these two metrics for both a simplex (standalone) and a redundant network element configuration. In standalone NE deployment, an outage of the element (assumed to be "B1") is both network element impacting and service impacting, as shown in Figure 2.3. "B1" delivers service until a critical failure of "B1" disrupts service. "B1" is down—and hence service is unavailable—until "B1" is repaired and service is restored. Thus, the duration of the network element outage is the same as the duration of the service outage.

If redundant NE's are deployed (assume "B1" and "B2"), then service impact downtime can be shortened by recovering service away from the unavailable NE "B1" to the redundant NE "B2," as is illustrated in Figure 2.4. When element "B1" fails,

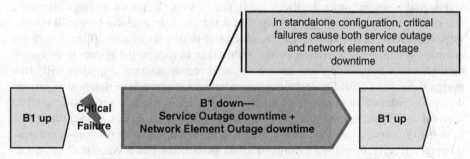

Figure 2.3. Outage downtime in standalone NE deployment.

[2] Obviously, jet engines are not actually "network elements," but they do make an easy to understand example.

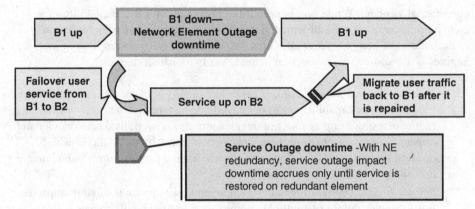

Figure 2.4. Outage downtime with redundant NE deployment.

users who were served by "B1" will experience a service outage until they are failed over onto "B2." Once users are restored to service on "B2," the service impact outage event is over; network element outage downtime continues to accrue until "B1" is restored to service. Even if the network element downtime for "B1" is the same in both the redundant example depicted in Figure 2.4 as in the simplex example depicted in Figure 2.3, the service downtime experienced by users is much shorter in the redundant configuration.

The key point is that although redundancy doesn't impact the time to repair a failed element, it does enable the service impact to be dramatically shorter than the time to repair the failed network element.

2.2.6 Treatment of Planned Events

Since enterprise information and communication technology systems often have designed service lifetimes of 3 or more years, it is likely that software will be patched and upgraded several times, hardware configurations may be grown as usage increases, and system configuration may be changed as demands of the business evolve. It is often far simpler for both the supplier and the enterprise to take the system offline to perform complex system reconfiguration events, rather than to require the system to be online throughout the system upgrade, growth, or other reconfiguration. Suppliers will often design their systems and maintenance procedures to minimize the duration of service disruption required to complete planned activities, but it is often very challenging to perform significant system reconfigurations without at least a brief service disruption to stable or transient sessions. Many readers will be familiar with occasional notifications they receive from their IT organizations announcing that a voice mail system or other enterprise system will be down for a few hours in an off-peak period to complete some planned maintenance activity. Thus, many enterprises will carefully plan maintenance events to occur in low-usage periods to minimize impact to users. As long as the service disruption is not longer or larger than expected, the service downtime is often excluded from service availability metrics. Likewise, recording of service reliability metrics is often suspended during planned maintenance activities.

Some critical systems require true 24/7/365 continuous availability, and hence planned service downtime is unacceptable at any time of the day. For critical systems, any impact beyond the expected service disruption may be recorded as service downtime and charged against service availability metrics. In these cases more complex system and service architectures are often deployed to permit graceful, non-service impacting migration of traffic from one unit or element to another to permit individual units or elements to be taken offline to perform and complete planned maintenance activities (e.g., restarting a processor or element to activate updated software). Service can then be gracefully migrated back to the updated unit so remaining units can be updated with minimal service impact.

2.3   MEASURING SERVICE RELIABILITY

Service reliability characterizes the probability that a properly formed service request will be properly executed by the system and correct results will be returned to the user with acceptable quality within the specified service delivery latency. Service reliability is generally measured using one or more of the following techniques:

1. Analysis of transaction or billing logs to compute the rate of incomplete, abnormal, or unacceptably slow transactions.
2. Service probes that send test traffic to the system and carefully measure the service provided.
3. Analysis of performance management data, such as comparing the number of various abnormal service error responses sent by the system against the number of normal responses.

Note that service reliability assessment inherently involves massive data sets of successful and abnormal or failed transactions; this contrasts with a much smaller number of generally well defined service outage events. Thus, while it is often reasonable to complete root cause analysis of every ticketed service outage, it is typically infeasible to deduce the root cause of every failed transaction. As a result, one cannot generally determine the exact cause of each defective transaction. For example, some transactions will fail due to momentary or brief overload while others will inevitably fail due to subcritical or minor software defects; messages will be lost, damaged, or delayed when traversing the access, backhaul, and wide-area networks, security devices, and other intermediate systems. As one can imagine, it is often not feasible to track every single lost network transaction due to a single spike in network traffic, or to a lightning strike that disrupted an access or backhaul network, or to a software defect. However, service reliability provides another way of gauging the robustness of a system and may indicate trends, such as increasing transaction failure rates, that could trigger further investigation or closer system monitoring to avoid an impending issue.

PART 2

MODELING AND ANALYSIS OF REDUNDANCY

3

UNDERSTANDING REDUNDANCY

Redundancy is a primary ingredient for achieving high service availability because it offers the opportunity to rapidly recover service onto an operational unit rather than accruing a longer service outage while failures on a standalone element are debugged, repaired, and service is restored. This chapter begins by categorizing redundancy into types that have key differences in their ability to improve service availability. How simple redundancy actually improves service availability is then considered both qualitatively and quantitatively via mathematical modeling. The chapter concludes with a discussion of criteria for assessing the relative merits of redundancy and high-availability schemes and mechanisms.

3.1 TYPES OF REDUNDANCY

Duplication of critical elements to improve availability is called redundancy. Note that simply because seemingly identical units are used in a system does not mean that the units are redundant; for example, although both the right wing and left wing of an airplane are essentially identical, they are not redundant because the plane will not fly

Beyond Redundancy: How Geographic Redundancy Can Improve Service Availability and Reliability of Computer-Based Systems, First Edition. Eric Bauer, Randee Adams, Daniel Eustace.
© 2012 Institute of Electrical and Electronics Engineers. Published 2012 by John Wiley & Sons, Inc.

without both of them. This book factors redundancy into two general categories: internal redundancy and external redundancy.

- *Internal redundancy* considers the hardware and software redundancy that is internal to and managed by a single system instance. The six-cylinder internal combustion engine in an automobile has six internally redundant cylinders that are integrated and appear as a single engine to both end users and mechanics. A mechanical failure that prevents one of the six cylinders from operating typically results in a loss of engine power but is not usually a critical failure rendering the engine—and hence the automobile—unavailable. The degenerate case of internal redundancy is a nonredundant system, such as a single light bulb.
- *External redundancy* considers a suite of internally redundant or nonredundant systems that are arranged in a pool to offer higher availability and/or capacity to end users or other systems. The headlamps on an automobile illustrate external redundancy because while each lamp is a distinct (nonredundant) element, they are configured to illuminate the same area so that if one lamp fails, then the second lamp provides adequate illumination. As a second example, an Internet service provider (ISP) may deploy multiple DNS servers based on the number of computers deployed in the network. Since each of the ISP's DNS server instances are essentially the same, if the solution is architected correctly, the load can be logically distributed across the server instances; in the event of a DNS server failure, traffic can be (re)directed to one of the operational servers. Note that redundancy does not always entail a one-to-one mapping. As in the DNS server example, there may be multiple copies to select from. External redundancy can be further factored into two logical categories:
- Co-located external redundancy is when redundant system instances are physically close together. For example, headlamps on an automobile or jet engines on a commercial airliner are examples of redundant systems that are physically co-located. Co-located enterprise systems are generally installed in the same data center or office, such as when a pool of rack mounted servers is installed in the same equipment rack.
- Geographically distributed external redundancy, or "georedundancy," is when redundant instances are physically separated, often by great distances. These solutions distribute systems far apart to minimize the risk that a disaster event like an earthquake or tsunami would devastate the solution and render service unavailable for an indefinitely long period. Some examples are a distributed pool of DNS servers or a distributed pool of web servers supporting the same web site.

Figure 3.1 summarizes this redundancy taxonomy for a single or multiple system(s) (or network element(s)). Section 3.1.1 discusses service availability of simplex configurations; Section 3.1.2 discusses service availability of redundant configurations.

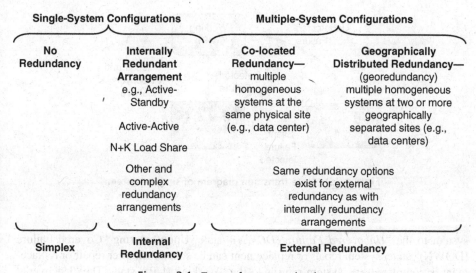

Figure 3.1. Types of system redundancy.

3.1.1 Simplex Configuration

Conventional systems are deployed simplex, meaning that a single non-redundant operational unit is available to provide service. A single, simple unit has two well-known operational states:

1. *Working*, or "up," in which the system is known to be operational
2. *Failed*, or "down," in which the system is known to be nonoperational, and presumably repair or replacement is planned.

In addition to these known states, there is also a third possible state in which the system is nonoperational but the system is incorrectly presumed to be operational. In this third state, the system is not delivering acceptable service or possibly not even available for service at all, but neither the system nor human operators are aware of the failure, and hence no automatic recovery, repair, replacement, or other mitigation actions has been started or scheduled. Reliability engineers refer to this undetected failure situation as an "uncovered failure" because the failure was not detected, or "covered," as it should have been. This unknown failure state is sometimes called a "silent failure" or a "sleeping failure" because the system has not automatically identified and recovered from the failure nor explicitly announced the failure to a human operator.

Behavior of a simplex system is illustrated in Figure 3.2. The system is normally in the *"Working (UP)"* state. Eventually, an inevitable failure event will occur. This failure can either be a covered failure that is promptly detected, thus bringing the system to the *"Covered Failure (DOWN)"* state, or an uncovered failure which brings the

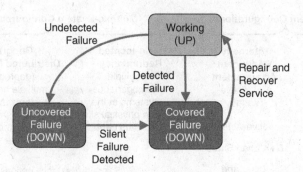

Figure 3.2. State transition diagram of simplex system.

system to the *"Uncovered Failure (DOWN)"* state. Upon entering "Covered Failure (DOWN)" state, system repair or replacement can be scheduled; after repair or replacement is completed, the system returns to the "Working (UP)" state. The "Uncovered Failure (DOWN)" state is more problematic because while the system is unavailable for service, the human operator is unaware of the failure, so repair or replacement will not be scheduled; the system remains in the "Uncovered Failure (DOWN)" state until the failure is recognized, at which point the system moves to the "Covered Failure (DOWN)" state and system repair or replacement can be scheduled; system returns to the "Working (UP)" state normally after system repair or replacement has been successfully completed.

Mathematical modeling can be used to estimate the time spent in each state of Figure 3.2 based on estimates of failure rate, repair and recovery latency, probability a failure is automatically detected, and time to detect a (silent) failure that was not automatically detected. Since service availability is defined as uptime divided by uptime plus downtime, availability of the simplex system of Figure 3.2 is computed as follows:

$$\text{Availability} = \frac{\text{Working (UP)}}{[\text{Working (UP)} + \text{Covered Failure (DOWN)} + \text{Uncovered Failure (DOWN)}]}$$

Equation 3.1. Availability of Simplex System Formula

Working (UP), CoveredFailure (DOWN), and UncoveredFailure (DOWN) represent the amount of time spent in each of those states.

Continuous-time Markov modeling is often used to solve this mathematically. Even without mathematical modeling, readers will recognize that service availability of simplex systems can be improved by improving one of four key characteristics:

1. *Reduce the failure rate*, thus minimizing the frequency of events that take system out of "Working (UP)" state.
2. *Shorten the repair time*, thus minimizing the time spent in the "Covered Failure (DOWN)" state.

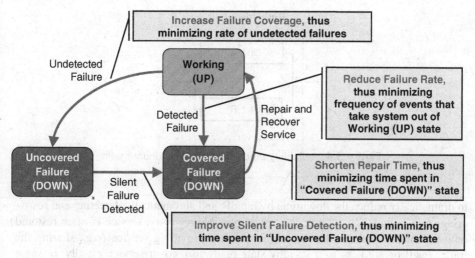

Figure 3.3. Availability improvement strategies for a simplex system.

3. *Increase the failure coverage*, thus maximizing the probability that a failure will take the system to the "Covered Failure (DOWN)" state from which repair activities can be promptly initiated.
4. *Improve silent failure detection*, thus minimizing the time the system remains in the "Uncovered Failure (DOWN)" state following undetected failures.

These availability improvement strategies for a simplex system are illustrated in Figure 3.3.

Since simplex systems inherently rely on manual repair or replacement activities to recover from hardware failures, the time spent in the Covered Failure (DOWN) state for each hardware failure event often ranges from about 30 minutes (assuming spare parts and a skilled maintenance technician are available on-site to initiate an emergency repair) to days to schedule a maintenance technician to diagnose the failure, acquire appropriate spare parts, and complete the repair. Thus, any hardware failure of a simplex system is likely to accrue significant service downtime. Manual recovery from software failures is often somewhat faster than manual recovery of hardware failures, since the problems are often able to be diagnosed and repaired remotely and thus not incur the travel or logistics time required to bring the technician or spare part to the system.

3.1.2 Redundancy

Because any failure of a simplex system is likely to cause many minutes or hours of downtime, hardware redundancy and high-availability infrastructure is often deployed

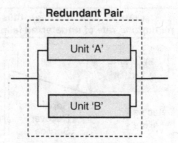

Figure 3.4. Reliability block diagram of redundant pair.

to dramatically reduce the downtime by rapidly and automatically detecting and recovering from failures. To achieve the fastest possible recovery, service is often restored onto redundant modules that are either actively providing service (e.g., sharing the traffic load) or are kept in a standby state ready to recover service rapidly. In some cases, the entire element may be duplicated, such as having two identical jet engines on an airplane. In other cases, each type of field replaceable hardware unit is duplicated, such as by arranging compute blades in pairs or load shared pools. Simple redundancy is visualized in Figure 3.4, showing a pair of elements in parallel; if at least one of the systems is available ("up"), then a request can traverse across one of the systems to deliver service. Real high-availability systems may be built by architecting redundant arrangements of all critical modules that seamlessly failover to a mate so that no single unit failure will produce a service outage.

Fundamentally, redundant pairs can either share the load across both elements (called "active–active") or have one unit actively serving load while the redundant unit waits in standby (called "active–standby"). In both of these cases, failure of a unit actively serving load (i.e., "active" unit in "active–standby" arrangements, or either unit in "active–active" arrangements) will impact service availability. The service impact can be simply modeled by considering four factors, as shown in Figure 3.5. While the example in Figure 3.5 gives an active–standby pair, the same factors apply to active–active redundancy arrangements. Note that *switchover* is when service is manually switched from the active unit to the standby unit; a *failover* (or takeover) is when the system automatically switches service from the active unit in response to an automatically detected failure of the active unit.

Downtime across this redundant pair of modules is driven by the following four system characteristics:

- *Critical failure rate* is the rate of service-impacting failure events. Note that reducing critical failure rate benefits both redundant and simplex configurations.
- *Failure coverage* is the probability that the system will rapidly detect and correctly isolate a critical failure to the appropriate recoverable module. Failures are typically detected by both real-time mechanisms like checksum validations, return codes from subroutines and processor exceptions, as well as periodic

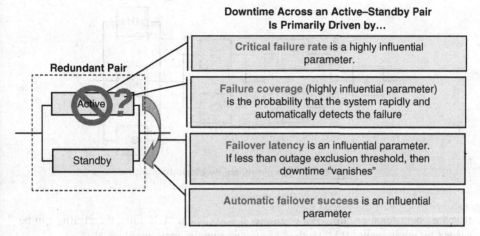

Figure 3.5. Service availability of active–standby redundant pair.

integrity checks or audits, such as verifying that sufficient heap memory and disk space remains available. Failure coverage is more influential on redundant systems than on simplex systems because automatic recovery latency is typically much, much shorter than silent failure detection time.

- *Failover latency* is the time it takes for the system to recover service onto the redundant "standby" unit. The objective is that the failover latency be no longer than the maximum acceptable service disruption latency so that the customer deems the failure a transient event rather than a service outage. Once that objective has been met, further reducing failure detection time plus failover latency below the maximum acceptable service disruption latency will not improve service availability metrics (because the downtime is already excluded), but should improve service reliability metrics by minimizing the window of compromised transactions.
- *Automatic failover success* is the probability that the automatic failover operation is successful, meaning that manual intervention is not required and the service is impacted for the nominal failure detection plus recovery time.

3.1.3 Single Point of Failure

The redundancy arrangement of a system is conveniently illustrated with a reliability block diagram (RBD). An RBD shows all components that are required to be operational for service arranged as a sort of daisy chain that carefully illustrates the redundancy configuration of each component. Figure 3.6 is an example RBD showing a single component instance "A" in series with a pair of components "B1" and "B2" in series with another pair of components "C1" and "C2" in series with a pool of components "D1," "D2," and "D3." The service offered by this sample system is available when there is a path from the left edge of the figure to the right edge via components

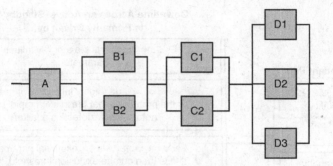

Figure 3.6. Sample reliability block diagram.

that are operational or "up." For example, if component "B1" fails, then traffic can be served by component "B2," so the system can remain operational or "up."

The objective of redundancy and high-availability mechanisms is to assure that no single failure will produce an unacceptable service disruption. When a critical element is not configured with redundancy—such as component "A" in Figure 3.6—that simplex element represents a *single point of failure* that will cause service to be unavailable until the failed simplex element can be repaired and service recovered. High-availability and critical systems should be designed so that no single points of failure exist.

3.2 MODELING AVAILABILITY OF INTERNAL REDUNDANCY

Redundancy alone is not sufficient to achieve high service availability; automatic mechanisms to detect failure and switch service to a redundant unit rapidly are required to leverage redundancy. The software and design that automatically shifts service away from failed units to maintain high service availability is generally called high-availability software or high-availability mechanisms. Continuous-time Markov models are commonly used to estimate service availability of various system architectures. This section reviews Markov modeling of traditional active–standby and active–active redundancy schemes controlled by a single high-availability mechanism. Chapter 6, "Modeling Service Availability with External System Redundancy," will cover modeling of external redundancy recovery, which is very different from the traditional, internal redundancy recovery approaches. This section first reviews traditional, internal redundancy modeling of active–active redundancy because it is the simplest configuration to consider. Internal active–standby redundancy is slightly more complicated due to its inherent asymmetric nature, and that is considered next. Modeling external redundancy is inherently more complicated because multiple autonomous (external) systems are involved in the recovery, and availability modeling must consider this complexity.

Figure 3.7 illustrates the sample redundant element we will consider; we will consider both active–active redundancy and active–standby redundancy, and compare both of those options to the service availability of a nonredundant deployment. P1 and

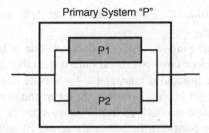

Figure 3.7. Sample standalone redundant system.

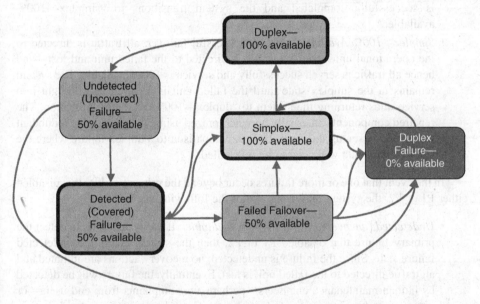

Figure 3.8. Active–active Markov availability model.

P2 are redundant units within a single system controlled by a high-availability architecture and/or infrastructure mechanism.

3.2.1 Modeling Active–Active Redundancy

Active–active redundancy means that traffic is evenly shared by two operational units, but full engineered traffic load can be served with acceptable quality by a single unit. Figure 3.8 gives a generic state transition diagram of active–active redundancy. States are shown as boxes and valid state transitions are shown with directional lines.

Consider first the three typical availability states (shown with bold borders) individually.

- *Duplex—100% Available.* Both P1 and P2 are fully operational and all user traffic is being served.
- *Detected (Covered) Failure—50% Available.* If one of the two active modules P1 or P2 experiences a covered critical failure, then the system transitions to this state in which one module is unavailable for service *until* the system is able to complete the failover actions necessary to revert the system to the "simplex— 100% available" state in which all traffic is served by the operational unit. Since traffic should have been distributed evenly across P1 and P2 before the failure, we assume that 50% of the traffic is still processed properly by the remaining operational module, but the remaining 50% of the traffic that should have been processed by the failed module is impacted until the automatic failover operation is successfully completed and the system transitions to "simplex—100% available."
- *Simplex—100% Available.* After a successful failover, all traffic is directed to the operational unit—thus no traffic is directed to the failed unit and lost—and hence all traffic is served successfully and service is 100% available. The system remains in the simplex state until the failed unit is repaired and brought into service, thus returning the system to "duplex—100% available" operation. The repaired component can usually be synchronized using its newly active redundant mate, thus lessening the repair time in comparison to a duplex failure where the software and data will need to be reinstalled.

In the event that one or more failures occur beyond the primary failure that disabled either P1 or P2, the system may enter one of the following states:

- *Undetected (uncovered) failure—50% available.* If the system fails to detect the primary failure that disabled P1 or P2, then the system enters the undetected failure state. Since the failure is undetected, no recovery actions are initiated and all traffic directed to the failed unit is lost. Eventually, the failure will be detected by human maintenance engineers—perhaps via complaints from end users—or via a secondary automatic failure detection mechanism. Once the failure is detected, the system transitions to the "detected failure (covered)" state described above and failover can be activated. Since every second of undetected failure represents 50% unavailability, it is important to minimize the percentage of uncovered failures.
- *Failed Failover—50% Available.* Failover operations are often complex, and since they are executed following failure of an active module, the system state when failover is attempted may be unexpected and thus may expose a residual software defect that prevents the failover from completing successfully, thereby preventing the traffic being directed to the failed module from being promptly shifted to the operational module. Typically, a failed failover is resolved by manual diagnostic troubleshooting by a maintenance engineer and execution of appropriate manual switchover or recovery actions. Inevitably, failed failovers add minutes or more of 50% downtime while the failed failover is detected, manually diagnosed, and suitable recovery actions are manually executed.

- *Duplex Failure—0% Available.* If the second module fails before the first module is repaired, then the system experiences a duplex failure and service is completely unavailable. While duplex failure events are rare, the duration of duplex failures is often quite long because at least one of the units must be repaired, including installation of software and data, before even simplex service can be restored.

Markov modeling enables one to mathematically compute the time spent in each of the states by knowing the rates of each state transition. Many texts detail how to solve Markov models, such as Trivedi (2001). To solve the model, one first estimates the rate of each state transition. For example, the transition rate between "duplex—100% available" state and "detected (covered) failure—50% available" is the product of:

- Critical failure rate (λ), which is assumed to be the same for both identical units P1 and P2
- Two (2) because a failure of either P1 or P2 will drive the system from the "duplex—100% available" state
- Failure coverage factor (C_A) which gives the probability that a critical failure is successfully automatically detected in nominal time

Figure 3.9 overlays mathematical formulas that estimate the rate of each state transition. Table 3.1 defines the input parameters and gives nominal parameter values. Solving the Markov model of Figure 3.9 with the input parameters of Table 3.1 predicts the relative time spent in each state shown in Table 3.2.

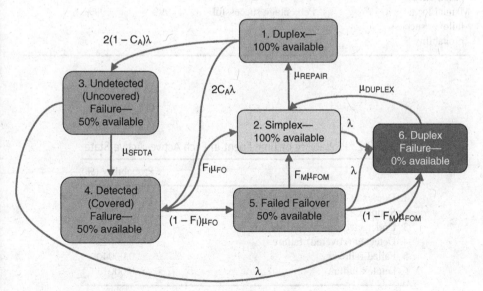

Figure 3.9. Active–active Markov availability model with formulas.

TABLE 3.1. Sample Input Parameters for Active–Active Model

Description	Symbol	Nominal Unit	Nominal Input	Modeled Input Value (Hourly Rates)
Failure rate	λ	System fails per year	4	0.000456308
Failure coverage factor of an active unit	C_A	Percentage successful	90%	90%
Automatic failover (or takeover) rate	μ_{FO}	Median minutes to complete automatic local failover	0.17	360
Manual failover rate	μ_{FOM}	Median minutes to complete manual local failover	30.00	2
Simplex failure repair rate	μ_{REPAIR}	Median minutes to complete manual repair	30.00	2
Duplex failure repair rate	μ_{DUPLEX}	Median hours to complete repair of simplex failure	4.00	0.25
Uncovered silent failure detection rate (active elements)	μ_{SFDTA}	Median minutes to detect silent failure of active elements	30.00	2
Automatic internal failover success probability	F_I	Percentage successful	99%	99%
Manual local failover success probability	F_M	Percentage successful	99%	99%

TABLE 3.2. Probability of Time Spent in Each Active–Active State

State	Probability (%)
1. Duplex	99.94899
2. Simplex	0.04561
3. Undetected (uncovered) failure	0.00456
4. Detected (covered) failure	0.00025
5. Failed failover	0.00046
6. Duplex failure	0.00013

Availability of the active–active configuration can be calculated as follows:

$$\text{Availability} = \frac{[\text{Duplex}_{\text{Probability}} + \text{Simplex}_{\text{Probability}} + 50\% * (\text{DetectedFailure}_{\text{Probability}} + \text{UndetectedFailure}_{\text{Probability}} + \text{FailedFailover}_{\text{Probability}})]}{\sum_{\text{AllStates}} \text{Probabilities}}$$

Equation 3.2.   Availability of Active–Active System Formula

where $\text{Duplex}_{\text{Probability}}$, $\text{Simplex}_{\text{Probability}}$, $\text{DetectedFailure}_{\text{Probability}}$, $\text{UndetectedFailure}_{\text{Probability}}$, $\text{FailedFailover}_{\text{Probability}}$, and $\text{DuplexFailure}_{\text{Probability}}$ are the portion of time spent in each of these states. Solving this equation using the results of Table 3.2 yields:

$$\text{Availability} = \frac{99.94899\% + 0.04561\% + 50\% * (0.00025\% + 0.00456\% + 0.00046\%)}{1}$$

$$= 99.99724\%$$

3.2.2   Modeling Active Standby Redundancy

Active–standby redundancy is logically simpler than active–active because one unit at a time is active and carries 100% of the traffic while the standby unit waits for the high-availability mechanism to promote it to "active" and direct traffic to it. However, the asymmetry between active and standby units increases the complexity of the model in two ways:

1. *"Standby down uncovered—100% available"* state is added to represent a silent or undetected failure on the standby unit. Although service remains 100% available, the system is actually simplex, so a failure of the active unit will cause a prolonged outage.
2. The failure states that were shown as "50% available" are 0% available for active–standby redundancy.

Both of these differences come from the simple fact that with active–active load shared redundancy, any failure impacts nominally half the traffic until the high-availability mechanism can successfully direct traffic away from the failed unit to the operational unit, while since the active unit in active standby carries 100% of the load and the standby unit carries 0% of the load, the model must differentiate failures of active unit from failures of standby unit. Figure 3.10 shows the Markov transition diagram for active–standby redundancy with mathematical formulas.

Because standby units are not carrying active traffic, the probability of detecting a failure on the standby unit may not be the same as the probability of detecting a critical failure on an active unit. Likewise, the typical time to detect a failure that was not successfully automatically recovered on a standby unit often is not the same as the time to discover undetected failures on active units. Table 3.3 summarizes the new parameters and offers normalized input values for those parameters.

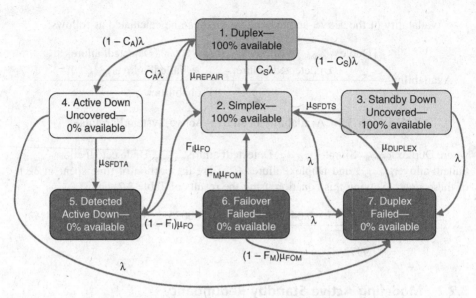

Figure 3.10. Active–standby Markov availability model.

TABLE 3.3. Sample Additional Input Parameters for Active–Standby Model

Description	Symbol	Nominal Unit	Nominal Input	Modeled Input Value (Hourly Rates)
Failure coverage factor of standby unit	C_S	Percentage successful	90%	90%
Uncovered silent failure detection rate (standby elements)	μ_{SFDTS}	Median HOURS to detect silent failure of standby elements	24	0.04

Table 3.4 solves the active–standby model of Figure 3.10 using the input parameters of both Tables 3.1 and 3.3.

Availability is the ratio of the sum of the time in "duplex—100% available," "simplex—100% available," and "standby down uncovered—100% available" states compared with total time. Note that when computing availability of active–standby model, service is either completely up (100% available) or completely down (0% available). Active–standby availability is computed as follows:

$$\text{Availability} = \frac{\text{Duplex}_{\text{Probability}} + \text{Simplex}_{\text{Probability}} + \text{StandbyDownUncovered}_{\text{Probability}}}{\sum_{\text{AllStates}} \text{Probabilities}}$$

Equation 3.2. Availability of Active–Standby System Formula

TABLE 3.4. Probability of Time Spent in Each Active–Standby State

State	Probability (%)
1. Duplex	99.84335
2. Simplex	0.04556
3. Standby down (uncovered)	0.10816
4. Active down (uncovered)	0.00228
5. Detected active down (covered)	0.00013
6. Failed failover	0.00023
7. Duplex failure	0.00030

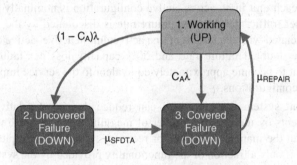

Figure 3.11. Simplex model with mathematical formulas.

Inserting the results from Table 3.4 into the availability equation produces:

$$\text{Availability} = \frac{99.84335\% + 0.04556\% + 0.10816\%}{100\%} = 99.99707\%$$

3.2.3 Service Availability Comparison

Just as mathematical modeling can be used to predict service availability of active–active in Figure 3.9 and of active–standby in Figure 3.10, mathematical formulas can be overlaid onto the simplex model of Figure 3.2 to produce Figure 3.11.

Using the same failure rates, recovery latencies, and other parameters of Tables 3.1 and 3.3 in the Markov models for simplex (Fig. 3.11) yields the probabilities shown in Table 3.5.

Table 3.6 gives a side-by-side comparison of predicted service availability for simplex (Fig. 3.11), active–standby (Fig. 3.10), and active–active (Fig. 3.9) systems. The table reveals two key insights:

1. Active–active redundancy offers only a small availability benefit over active–standby redundancy. This is fundamentally because of capacity loss prorating of outages in active–active configurations. Active–active configurations have

TABLE 3.5. Probability of Time Spent in Each Simplex State

State	Probability (%)
1. Working (up)	99.9749
2. Uncovered failure (down)	0.0023
3. Covered failure (down)	0.0228

twice as many elements carrying user traffic as active–standby configurations, and thus one of the two active elements in active–active is twice as likely to fail as the single active element in an active–standby configuration. However, because each unit in an active–active configuration is nominally carrying 50% of the user traffic, the doubled failure rate is discounted by the 50% capacity loss associated with the failure of one active unit in active–active configuration. Thus, the doubled failure rate and 50% capacity loss per failure essentially cancel out to become approximately equivalent to the service impact of active–standby configurations.

2. Redundant system configurations can reduce downtime relative to simplex deployments by more than an order of magnitude because failovers are much faster than the manual repair and/or recovery required by simplex systems. In addition, if only a fraction of the functionality provided by the system (e.g., loss of 50% capacity through loss of 1 of the active–active servers), a partial downtime (in this case 50%) can be declared rather than a 100% downtime. (A 10-minute downtime would only be recorded as 5 minutes.)

3.3 EVALUATING HIGH-AVAILABILITY MECHANISMS

Critical failure rate is obviously a highly influential factor in service availability. The high-availability mechanism controls automatic failure detection, isolation, and recovery, which enable redundancy to effectively mitigate the service downtime of each critical failure event. The efficacy, and hence benefits, of a high-availability mechanism can be evaluated based on how it addresses five vectors:

1. Recovery time objective (a.k.a., nominal outage duration)
2. Recovery point objective
3. Nominal success probability
4. Capital expense
5. Operating expense

Each of these vectors is considered separately, followed by a discussion section.

TABLE 3.6. Nominal Downtime Predictions for Different Redundancy Schemes

	100% Available			50% Available			0% Available			
	Duplex	Simplex	Uncovered Standby Down	One Down Covered	Uncovered One Down	Failed Failover	Covered	Uncovered	Failed Failover	Duplex Failure
Simplex system configuration (no redundancy)										
Probability by state		99.9749%					0.0228%	0.0023%		
Subtotal probability	99.9749%			0.0000%			0.0251%			
Prorated service availability	99.9749%			0.0000%						
Active–standby redundant system configuration										
Probability by state	99.8433%	0.0456%	0.1082%	0.0003%			0.0001%	0.0023%	0.0002%	0.0003%
Subtotal probability	99.9971%			0.0000%			0.0029%			
Prorated service availability	99.9971%									
Active–active redundant system configuration										
Probability by state	99.9490%	0.0456%		0.0003%	0.0046%	0.0005%	0.0001%			0.0001%
Subtotal probability	99.9946%			0.0053%			0.0001%			
Prorated service availability	99.9972%									

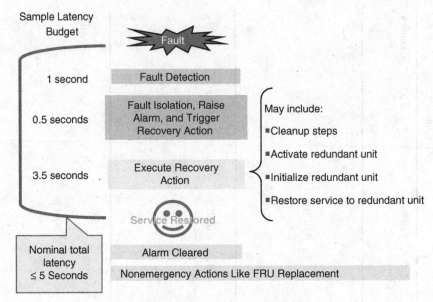

Figure 3.12. Outage duration.

3.3.1 Recovery Time Objective (or Nominal Outage Duration)

The duration of service disruption after critical failure is obviously a primary metric for any high-availability mechanism. Note that the outage duration for successfully detected, isolated, and recovered critical failures is generally easy to measure in the lab. Failures that are not properly detected, isolated, or recovered will inevitably have longer service disruption due to the need for human maintenance engineers and secondary/tertiary failure detection, isolation, and recovery mechanisms to operate. This is illustrated in Figure 3.12. The probability that the primary high-availability mechanisms operate successfully is explicitly considered as an evaluation criteria in Section 3.3.3.

Note that from a disaster recovery perspective, outage duration is the sum of the recovery time objective (RTO) and the time to assess the disaster and make the decision to activate the disaster recovery plan. This is illustrated in Figure 3.13.

3.3.2 Recovery Point Objective

Transactions can be impacted the moment a critical failure occurs, and thus database updates and other service-related changes may be lost. A key performance metric of any high-availability system is to what point in time relative to the moment of critical failure is the high-availability mechanism able to restore system state. For example, if service restoration for some failures calls for restoring system data from the most recent database backup, then the recovery point objective is the nominal or maximum time

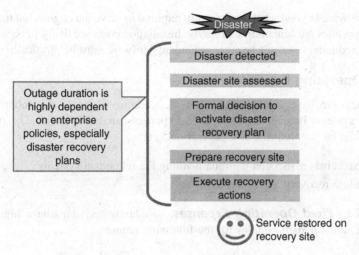

Figure 3.13. Outage duration for disasters.

from the last backup. If backups are done on a daily basis, then the nominal recovery point objective is 12 hours, and the maximum time is 24 hours.

Data replication or mirroring can significantly reduce (i.e., improve) recovery point objectives. One can even require individual database changes to be written to multiple hard disks before committing a transaction to assure essentially instantaneous recovery point objective performance.

3.3.3 Nominal Success Probability

The recovery time objective and recovery point objectives that are observed during testing and when recovering from most failures entail those recoveries where failure detection, failure isolation, and failure recovery (and perhaps disaster recovery plans) are successful. These automatic actions are inherently complex, and the critical failure— and perhaps cascaded secondary failures—increases complexity and thus the risk that the recovery action will not complete successfully in the nominal time.

Success probability of automatic high-availability mechanisms is improved by robust designs that are implemented with high quality and thoroughly tested in the same operational profile in which they will be used. Success probability of human procedures is improved by providing well-qualified, well-trained and highly motivated staff with well documented and thoroughly tested methods of procedure (MOPs).

Success probability can be estimated by simulating many critical failures and verifying actual performance of the high-availability mechanism.

3.3.4 Capital Expense

Redundancy has an obvious incremental capital expense compared with simplex deployment of the same system; essentially, the enterprise must acquire additional system hardware beyond what is minimally required to serve the engineered traffic load when all modules are functioning properly. Installation costs are likely to be somewhat higher for redundant systems because redundant hardware must be physically installed.

3.3.5 Operating Expense

Redundancy can have significantly different operating expenses than nonredundant (simplex) systems because failure-related expenses can be different. The operating expenses can be factored into two general buckets:

1. Fixed costs associated with maintaining the redundant systems
2. Failure recovery and repair expenses

3.3.5.1 Fixed Operating Expenses. Redundant systems have higher fixed costs than nonredundant systems for the following items:

1. *Real Estate.* Redundant units consume rack or floor space in an enterprise data center or other suitable facility. As data centers are often crowded, this space is generally considered very valuable.
2. *Power.* Redundant units consume power when they are online.
3. *Cooling.* Air conditioning consumes power to expel the waste heat produced by online systems. Thus, enterprises almost pay twice for the electric power used by systems: once to power the system itself, and once to power the air conditioner to expel the waste heat generated by powering the system. Redundant units that are online generate twice the cooling load of a simplex system.
4. *Operations and Surveillance.* Every unit must be configured, maintained, and monitored by both automated systems and human maintenance engineers. As part of maintenance, scheduled routine manual switchovers may be performed to ensure the health of the standby components and associated mechanisms.
5. *Maintenance Fees.* Ongoing software licensing and maintenance fees may be higher for redundant systems than for simplex systems.

3.3.5.2 Failure Recovery and Repair Expenses. Failure recovery and repair expenses for internally or externally redundant systems should be significantly lower than for simplex units or systems because it should be possible to recover service to a redundant system quickly, and perhaps without human intervention; after service has been recovered to redundant unit, then repair of the failed unit can be completed promptly, but on a nonemergency basis. If a simplex system fails, then service is unavailable until the system is repaired, and thus repairs are more likely to be performed on an emergency basis with higher costs for urgent response times, overtime pay, and so on.

3.3.6 Discussion

By their nature, availability of critical systems is important to the enterprise. Every hour or minute—or perhaps even second—of unavailability impacts the enterprise in one or more of the following ways:

- *Direct Loss of Revenue.* Unavailability of critical systems can cause direct loss of sales and revenue.
- *Payments for SLA Failure.* Failing to meet service level agreement (SLA) commitments can trigger financial remedies that must be paid by the enterprise.
- *Lost Employee Productivity.* Unavailability of a critical system may cause an assembly line, logistics center, or other facility to stop, and thus employees are unable to be productive. Employees must generally be paid during the outage, and may need to work overtime to clear the backlog of work that accumulated while the system was unavailable.
- *Loss of Good Will.* If enterprises are unable to deliver goods and services to customers on the schedule agreed with the quality expected, then the users will be disappointed, inconvenienced, and perhaps even angered. Users may then deem the enterprise to be unreliable and thus may implicitly discount the value of services offered by the enterprise. That implicit discounting of the value of goods and services offered by an enterprise due to poor quality, reliability, or availability often prompts users to investigate competitors with a goal of switching to better value with a competitor offering better quality, reliability, or availability.

Shortening recovery time objective directly impacts these costs. Note that for many systems, the recovery time objective need not be driven to 0 seconds because rare brief, transient service disruption may be acceptable to customers.

In contrast to recovery time objectives, recovery point objectives have much more tangible impact on most enterprises. Essentially, the recovery point objective defines how many seconds, minutes, or hours of productivity or business is lost when service is recovered because all data changes in that period are lost. For instance, a recovery point objective of 12 hours for an inventory control system means that all inventory changes 12 hours prior to a failure event are likely to be lost, and thus the enterprise presumably expects to manually audit inventories to resynchronize that recovery point with actual inventories. For an order entry or billing system, all orders or billing records that occurred more recently than the recovery point objective of the failure will be lost. These recovery point objective costs thus fall into several categories:

- *Direct Loss of Revenue.* Billing or other records that have been lost, and hence customers can not practically be billed for some (or all) goods or services delivered in that period.
- *Costs to Reenter Lost Data.* Some systems rely on manual data entry or other mechanisms that entail reentering of all the changes that were executed after the actual recovery point. These costs are then directly related to the length of the recovery point.
- *Costs to Resynchronize Data with Actual.* In many cases, it is infeasible to reenter the changes after the recovery point because records of those changes are not available and/or not in a usable form. In this case, a manual or automatic procedure must be executed to resynchronize the recovered data with the actual

or real-world data. For example, if inventory was consumed or material was moved after the recovery point, then that update must be applied to the recovered data, or a service failure will occur in the future when decisions are made based on incorrect decisions about levels or physical location of inventory.

• *Cost of Lost Data.* In some cases, it may be infeasible to recover some data; for example, it may be infeasible or impractical to reenter all data, so the loss of some data may simply be considered a total loss to the enterprise.

Different enterprises have different tolerances for risk of suffering a service outage or temporary (or permanent) loss of critical data. Different systems have different risks of suffering ordinary, repairable failures. Different physical sites, different enterprises, and other factors impact the risk of suffering natural or man-made disasters that produce catastrophic failures. Enterprises must balance their tolerance for these risks against capital and operating expense to select an appropriate redundancy and high-availability strategy for each of their critical systems.

4

OVERVIEW OF EXTERNAL REDUNDANCY

External redundancy fundamentally involves deploying a redundant system to improve availability. The redundant system may be physically co-located, deployed at a geographically remote site or a combination of both. Geographically distributed redundancy has the added benefit of minimizing the impact of a site disaster. As most critical systems are designed with internal redundancy to meet high-availability expectations, a key architectural question is how the additional redundant system interacts with or supplements the primary system's internal redundancy. This chapter presents a conceptual model for external recovery and delineates the salient technical differences between co-located redundancy and geographical redundancy.

4.1 GENERIC EXTERNAL REDUNDANCY MODEL

External redundancy inherently involves systems in a solution of multiple systems interacting to detect, isolate, and recover from failures. While this is conceptually similar to internal redundancy described in Chapter 3 "Understanding Redundancy," external redundancy is inherently more complicated because, unlike internal

Beyond Redundancy: How Geographic Redundancy Can Improve Service Availability and Reliability of Computer-Based Systems, First Edition. Eric Bauer, Randee Adams, Daniel Eustace.
© 2012 Institute of Electrical and Electronics Engineers. Published 2012 by John Wiley & Sons, Inc.

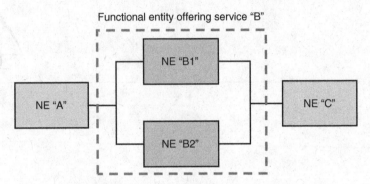

Figure 4.1. Generic high availability model.

redundancy, there is generally not a single logical controller that directs the high-availability activity. Instead, each network element acts largely autonomously, but redundancy is enhanced through communications with other elements or controllers that may facilitate recovery actions for failures that are not as easily detected on the network element itself.

Since high-availability mechanisms controlling external redundancy must address the same fundamental problems as internal redundancy, we use a simple model ignoring internal redundancy to highlight the linkages between each of the elements. Figure 4.1 illustrates the generic model that will be analyzed. This model considers service "B," which is offered by redundant "B1" and "B2" network elements (also referred to as servers). Network element "A" represents a client consumer of service "B," and network element "C" represents another network element in the service delivery chain. For example, network element "A" could be a computer, network element "B" could be a redundantly configured web server, and network element "C" could be a database server; thus, element "B1" manages traffic between database server "C" and computer "A." An actual end-to-end solution might include many logical instances of this canonical model, and "A" and/or "C" might actually be instances of redundant network elements themselves. Each of these elements is assumed to be a discrete computer or system, and the lines connecting them are communications channels (such as Ethernet, Wi-Fi, or CDMA/GSM/LTE); thus, all of the information exchanged between these elements could be inspected via an appropriately configured network analyzer.

Assume that network element "A" requests a service which requires a functional entity (or system) offering service "B" and support of network element "C." Based on the response to a DNS query, configuration data, or some other mechanism, network element "A" opts to associate with network element "B1," and "B1" establishes a linkage with network element "C" to deliver service on behalf of network element "A." The stable service delivery path is illustrated via a bold line in Figure 4.2.

If there is no logical element "C," then element "C" need not be considered, and the model degenerates as shown in Figure 4.3.

Now assume element "B1" fails, as shown in Figure 4.4. As element "B1" is now unavailable, traffic from "A" no longer flows to "C," and reverse traffic for "C" to "A"

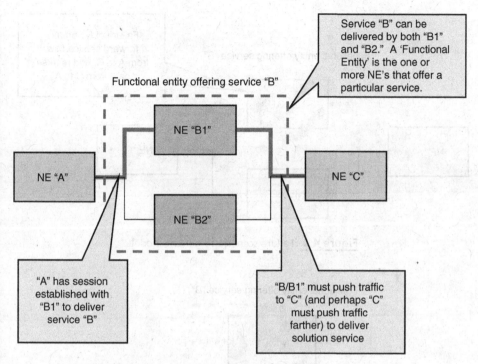

Functional entity offering service "B"

Service "B" can be delivered by both "B1" and "B2." A 'Functional Entity' is the one or more NE's that offer a particular service.

NE "A"

NE "B1"

NE "B2"

NE "C"

"A" has session established with "B1" to deliver service "B"

"B/B1" must push traffic to "C" (and perhaps "C" must push traffic farther) to deliver solution service

Figure 4.2. Stable service delivery path across generic model.

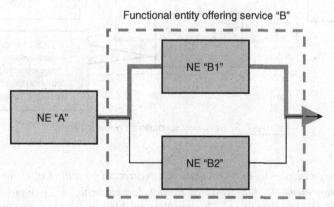

Functional entity offering service "B"

NE "A"

NE "B1"

NE "B2"

Figure 4.3. Degenerate generic model without element "C."

is likewise blocked. Ideally, high-availability mechanisms should "instantly" rearrange service to the configuration illustrated in Figure 4.5, in which forward traffic from "A" is routed to "B2" and then to "C," and reverse traffic from "C" returns via "B2." Eventually, service should be gracefully switched back onto "B1" after the element has been repaired and is ready for service. The fundamental high-availability problem is

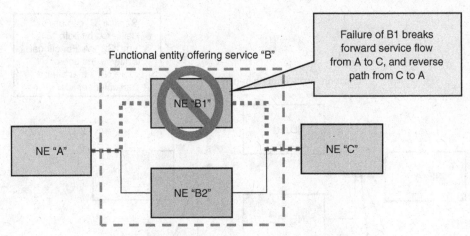

Figure 4.4. Failure scenario in generic model.

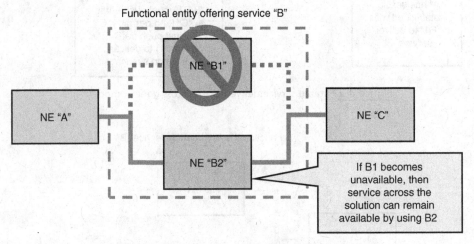

Figure 4.5. Recovery scenario in generic model.

how can service be rapidly and automatically redirected on failure of element "B1" so that redundant element "B2" restores service for element "A" without causing an unacceptable service disruption? The corollary problem is *how can service be gracefully switched back from a fully operational "B2" to "B1" without causing an unacceptable service disruption?*

This fundamental problem leads to several architectural questions:

1. How is the failure of element "B1" detected, and by which element?
2. Which entity triggers the recovery action?
3. How is traffic from element "A" redirected from "B1" to "B2" after failure?

Functional Entity offering service "B" using load sharing

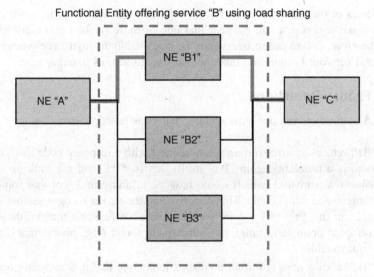

Figure 4.6. Generic high availability model with load sharing.

4. How much service context (if needed) is available to "B2" when traffic is redirected from "B1" (or when redirected from "B2" to "B1")?
5. Is "C" able to maintain any needed service context on behalf of element "A," or will switching service to "B2" (or "B1") necessitate restarting service across "C"?
6. How is service eventually migrated back from "B2" to "B1" after repair of "B1"?

Each of these fundamental questions is considered separately.

Note that the generic model can be extended to consider a load shared pool of elements offering service "B"; Figure 4.6 illustrates an example with three elements offering service "B." Although the load shared model may require a more elaborate procedure to distribute service load across the multiple operational elements both before and after failure, the fundamental technical redundancy control problems are the same as for the simple A/(B1 + B2)/C model.

The following sections review the generic failure detection and recovery steps of:

- failure detection,
- triggering recovery action,
- traffic redirection,
- service context preservation, and
- graceful service migration.

Note that the figures in this section do not explicitly show the IP network that is used to transmit messages between "A," "B1," "B2," and "C." While we are concerned about failures of the servers, we need to consider that the underlying network can also fail, and make it appear to an element that one or more of the other elements have failed. Therefore, failure and recovery must be designed to distinguish between element failures and network failures and take the appropriate actions in either case.

4.1.1 Failure Detection

Clients (A) can determine that their server ("B1") has failed when either:

1. "B1" returns an error response to a request with a response code that indicates there is a problem within "B1" itself; that is, "B1" did not indicate that the request was invalid (which would indicate a failure in A), or that some other element was unavailable. This occurs when the server recognizes that it has a problem that prevents it from servicing requests (e.g., an internal database is corrupted or an audit fails), or a subsequent server (e.g., an external database) is unavailable.
2. "B1" sends a message to all its clients indicating that it is currently unable to service requests due to an internal problem or a problem with a subsequent server.
3. "B1" does not respond to a request at all. This occurs when the server has completely failed (e.g., its power has failed or an application process has hung).

In the first and second cases, the client knows immediately that the server has failed. In the third, the client has to wait at least a few seconds (depending on the protocol) before it can conclude that the server has failed. Therefore, as long as a primary server is out of service, a few seconds of delay is added to every service request or transaction.

A common solution to this problem is for each client to periodically send a heartbeat message to "B1" to see if it is still operational. If "B1" responds to the heartbeat, then it is marked operational; and if it doesn't respond, then it is marked out of service and "A" must register with another server ("B2"). With this technique, the client is only vulnerable to transactional failure or increased latency for failures that occur after the last successful heartbeat. After detecting a failure, the client can continue to periodically heartbeat "B1," so that when it becomes available again, "A" can register back with "B1" after their next successful heartbeat.

Heartbeating can also be used by an alternate server to determine if the primary server is still operational. An alternate server should not make itself active until it is certain that the primary server has failed and is not likely to recover by itself. Therefore, the alternate should not activate until at least a few heartbeats have been missed. For example, if heartbeats are sent every 60 seconds, it might wait until three consecutive heartbeats have failed (3 minutes have elapsed since the last successful heartbeat) before going active.

Note that a loss of heartbeats does not necessarily mean that the primary server has failed; the problem might be that the alternate server has lost connectivity to the network. Therefore, the alternate server should try to access several other hosts (e.g., by pinging them), to verify that it has connectivity. It is not sufficient to ping another host on its own subnet, since the entire subnet could be isolated. If another host in the primary server's subnet responds to a ping, then we can be reasonably confident that the network is not the problem, and that the primary server is really down. However, in the event of a major disaster, the primary server's entire subnet might be down. Therefore, it is best to ping a host that is on a remote subnet in another location. If the verification check fails, then the alternate server should not attempt any recovery action since the primary server might be operational. The alternate server should periodically check its connectivity status, and when it finds it has connectivity again, restart timing for heartbeats.

Some protocols have a specific message sequence for heartbeating; in others, a request that does not change any session states (such as a request for status) may be used. With the SIP[1] protocol, the OPTIONS request is commonly used. When a server receives the OPTIONS, it should return a 200 OK response describing which optional capabilities it supports. The sender might not really care about these capabilities, it only cares about whether the server responds or not. When a server is in a standby state, it can return a failure response (such as a 503 Service Unavailable) to indicate that although it is operational, it is not processing requests. Similarly, Diameter[2] uses the device-watchdog-request (DWR) and device-watchdog-answer (DWA) messages for heartbeating. TCP has a configurable keepalive capability. Note that the default timeout for the TCP keepalive is 2 hours, so if it is to be used as a high-availability mechanism for redundant connections, then shorter timeouts should be configured.

Another alternative is to assign a separate network element, such as an element management system (EMS), to be responsible for external failure detection and recovery. The EMS heartbeats each of the servers, and if it detects that the primary server has failed, it activates the secondary server. It can also tell the clients to "quarantine" the primary server; that is, to stop sending requests to that server.

A service assurance, operation support, or management system can deduce that element "B1" is nonfunctional from anomalous service performance or throughput metrics. Service assurance products or other throughput monitoring mechanisms can detect so called "dreaming failures" in which an element reports that it is operational but is not actually providing useful service. Dreaming failures are generally much rarer than so called "sleeping failures" or uncovered failures in which an element simply "sleeps" and fails to respond to heartbeats and queries.

In summary, anomalous behavior of "B1" can fundamentally be detected by one or more of the following entities:

- "B1" can often detect and report its own failures and send protocol messages to other elements (e.g., "A," "B2," "C") to inform them.

[1] SIP (Session Initiation Protocol) is a signaling protocol for establishing sessions between users, such as VoIP (Voice over IP) calls, multimedia conferences, or chat sessions. It is defined in IETF RFC 3261 and enhanced by many other RFCs.

[2] Diameter is a protocol used for AAA (authentication, authorization, and accounting) functions. It is defined in IETF RFC 3588.

- "B2," "A," or "C" may detect failure of "B1" via expiration of a heartbeat timer or other failure of a high-availability/synchronization protocol mechanism.
- An element or network management system (not illustrated in generic model figures) can detect failure via alarms or nonresponsiveness or expiration of protocol timers for simple network management protocol (SNMP) or other management operations.
- A service assurance system may detect a failure through service performance analysis.

Note that a failure is likely to be detectable via most or all of these mechanisms, although the failure latency may vary. Often failures do not instantly identify exactly which module failed. For example, the expiration of a protocol timeout could indicate either the failure of the other network element or the failure of networking facilities linking the two elements, or perhaps other distinct failure scenarios. In addition, some failures will automatically be recovered by various facilities and mechanisms within individual elements or the solution itself; for example, if a single IP packet is lost or corrupted, then networking hardware, drivers, and/or protocols (such as TCP or SCTP, but not UDP) are likely to retransmit the packet. Thus, it is often necessary and appropriate to correlate individual failure events to identify and isolate the failed unit before triggering a recovery mechanism to bypass that failed unit.

4.1.2 Triggering Recovery Action

As explained in the previous section, a single failure event may cause many failure detection mechanisms to eventually activate. Judgment is thus required to:

1. *Identify the true primary cause of the failure.* This function is often called fault correlation when performed automatically and debugging or troubleshooting when performed manually. If the true primary cause is incorrectly identified, then corrective actions based on that misidentification are likely to be ineffective. Misidentification of the primary cause of a failure is often called "diagnostic failure."

2. *Determine if a failover is necessary to restore service.* Some transient failures can simply be tolerated (a.k.a., "ridden over") via automatic retry and other mechanisms, but nontransient (i.e., persistent) failures often require explicit recovery action. The appropriate recovery actions might include reestablishing a service session, restarting a software process, failing service over to a redundant entity, restarting an entire system, and so on. The goal is to select the recovery action that will mitigate the true primary root cause of the failure with the minimal overall service impact to all system users. Recognize that while there is an infinite set of possible failures, only a much smaller set of recovery actions is supported, and thus it is possible that supported recovery actions may impact service for users who were not (yet) affected by the primary failure.

3. *Trigger correct failover or recovery action.* Enterprises often have policies governing decisions to execute recovery actions that impact user service. For

example, while restarting a laptop to clear a software problem impacts only the laptop user, restarting a critical enterprise system can impact tens, hundreds, or thousands of users. Highly available systems are designed to automatically detect, isolate, and recover from failures to minimize service disruption, so high-availability systems will automatically trigger failover or recovery actions that should have brief and acceptable service impact. Decisions to restart entire systems or activate a disaster recovery plan to manually switch service to a system on a recovery site typically require explicit approval from appropriate decision makers in the enterprise since the impact is usually great.

4.1.3 Traffic Redirection

Having decided to activate a recovery action, traffic from "A" must be redirected from failed element "B1" to the operational element "B2." There are fundamentally five redirection strategies:

1. Traffic redirection via configuration
2. Traffic redirection via quarantine
3. Traffic redirection via DNS
4. Traffic redirection via intermediate system
5. Traffic redirection via IP mechanism

Each of these options is discussed separately.

4.1.3.1 Redirection via Configuration. Network elements can be explicitly configured with the addresses of multiple servers, and thus can retry traffic to a pre-defined secondary server if the primary server is unavailable. Enterprises will often explicitly configure systems to carefully balance or distribute the load across those systems in a way that assures acceptable service quality when all elements are operational and to simplify management of the overall network. For example, if an enterprise has one system instance of "B1" in the eastern region of a country and a second instance "B2" in the western region, then the enterprise may configure client systems in the eastern part of the country to use "B1" as their default primary system and "B2" as their alternate system, while client systems in the western part of the country use "B2" as their default primary system and "B1" as their alternate. This mechanism could be extended to support multiple systems distributed across multiple regions, with clients using a system in their local region primarily, and a system in a different region as their alternate.

4.1.3.2 Traffic Redirection via Quarantine. Quarantine is a mechanism that indicates to the clients which servers are unavailable. This technique works best when the availability of the servers is monitored by a separate system, such as a network management system. When any server ("B1," "B2") fails, it is "quarantined" by the monitoring system, and when it recovers, it is unquarantined. The list of quarantined servers is sent to all the clients to alert the clients not to send any requests to the servers on the quarantine list. Whenever a new client initializes, it should query the monitoring system for the current quarantine list.

4.1.3.3 Traffic Redirection via DNS.

4.1.3.3 Traffic Redirection via DNS. The DNS (domain name system) supports a mechanism for querying a database for the purpose of translating a domain (such as http://www.yahoo.com) into records that contain a set of parameters about the host computers associated with the domain, such as IP addresses and relative priorities. For example, an "A" record contains the IPv4 address of a host computer in the domain, and an "AAAA" record contains an IPv6 address. When a client wants to send a message to a computer in a domain (e.g., send an HTTP GET message to http://www.yahoo.com), it first sends the domain name to a DNS server in a query, and the DNS server returns a response with an "A" or "AAAA" record identifying an IP address. This is more flexible than provisioning IP addresses in every client; as servers are added, deleted, or moved, it is simpler to just update the records in the DNS server than to update all the clients. Also, it's easier to remember a domain (which should be a meaningful name) than a 32-bit or 128-bit IP address. DNS is defined in IETF RFCs 1034 and 1035.

When a network element uses the $N + K$ load sharing scheme, its clients need to be able to distribute their requests evenly among the available elements. A simple technique is to assign a domain name for the pool of elements (the servers), create a set of DNS "A" (or "AAAA") records for this domain (one record for each server), configure the DNS server to return the "A"/"AAAA" records in round-robin order, and configure the clients to query the DNS server with the servers' domain name on every request. Round-robin means that the DNS server will rotate the order of the records in each response, so that over time, each server will be equally likely to be first on this list. This will cause the initial requests from the clients to distribute their requests among all the servers. If the initial server does not respond to the request, the clients will reattempt with the next server. This technique has a few deficiencies:

- *If one of the servers fails, then the next server on the list will end up processing twice as many requests as the other servers.* It will be picked whenever it is at the top of the list, and it will also be picked whenever the failed server is at the top of the list.
- *The clients have to send a DNS query on every request.* Clients typically have the ability to cache the responses they receive from the DNS server so they can save processing resources by not repeating the query on every request. However, if a client reuses the same record, it will always send its requests to the same server over and over again. The query must be done on every request in order to send the queries to the servers in round-robin order.
- *The technique lacks flexibility.* To support georedundancy, the $N + K$ servers would be distributed across multiple locations. The clients might be distributed among the same locations. Rather than distributing all the requests across all the servers, latency and bandwidth can be minimized by distributing requests among

the local servers first, and only using servers in remote locations when the local servers are not available.

SRV (SeRVice) records (defined in IETF RFC 2782) can address these deficiencies. An SRV record contains a priority and a weight, along with the domain of a particular server (a single "A"/"AAAA" record maps the server's domain to the server's IP address). If a DNS server returns multiple SRV records (instead of simple "A"/"AAAA" records), then the client should pick the server with the lowest priority value. If multiple SRV records have the same priority, the client should distribute its requests among the servers according to the weights in the records.

In order to give priority to local servers, a separate domain name must be defined for each location. For location "X"'s domain, the SRV records for the servers in location "X" should have the lowest priority value (and equal weights), and the SRV records for the servers in the other location should have a higher priority value. Similarly, for location "Y"'s domain, the SRV records for the servers in location "Y" should have the lowest priority. The clients in (or near) location "X" would use location "X"'s domain, the clients in (or near) location "Y" would use location "Y"'s domain, and so on.

With this configuration, clients will normally distribute their requests evenly among the local servers, and will automatically begin distributing requests among the remote servers if all the local servers fail. If a single local server fails, the clients in that location should evenly distribute their requests among the remaining local servers, so no server will receive an unusually high level of traffic. The clients can cache the SRV records for a reasonable amount of time, since the clients are responsible for doing a (weighted) round-robin distribution, rather than the DNS server.

For example, suppose the solution has elements in two locations: one in the eastern region of the country and the other in the western region. The clients in the east should primarily send their HTTP requests to servers in the east, and clients in the west should primarily use western servers. The format of an SRV record is:

```
_Service._Proto.Name TTL Class SRV Priority Weight Port Target
```

And the format of a DNS "A" record is:

```
Name TTL Class A Address
```

We could create the following records in DNS:

```
_http._tcp.east.abc.com 60 IN SRV 10 1 80 east-site.abc.com.
                        60 IN SRV 20 1 80 west-site.abc.com.
_http._tcp.west.abc.com 60 IN SRV 10 1 80 west-site.abc.com.
                        60 IN SRV 20 1 80 east-site.abc.com.
west-site.abc.com 60 IN A 10.0.0.1
                  60 IN A 10.0.0.2
east-site.abc.com 60 IN A 10.0.1.1
                  60 IN A 10.0.1.2
```

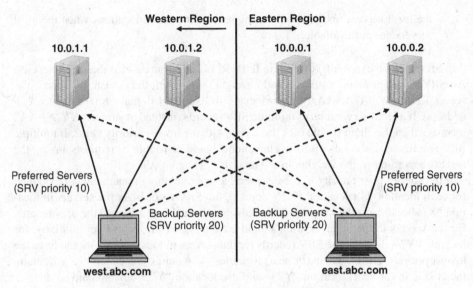

Figure 4.7. Georedundancy using DNS SRV records.

Clients in the western region would be provisioned with server fully qualified domain name (FQDN) west.abc.com and clients in the eastern region would be provisioned with east.abc.com. As shown in Figure 4.7, western clients would normally send their requests to one of the servers in the western region, but would send them to the eastern region servers if the western region servers were unavailable. The eastern region clients would do the opposite.

One problematic scenario can still occur with this technique: What if several, but not all, of the servers in a region fail? In this case, the local clients will still distribute all their requests among the remaining servers, but since there are only a few of them still running, they could get overloaded. It would be preferable to send at least some of the requests to another region. Some options are:

- When the servers are in overload, they should process as many requests as its resources will support, but reject any additional requests. The rejection response that it sends back to the client should contain an indication that the server is overloaded. This indication should trigger the client to reduce the number of requests it sends to that server. If a client is getting overload responses from all the local servers, then it will have to begin sending requests to remote servers.
- Each client can limit the number of requests they send to each server, such as no more than 10 requests per second, or no more than 100 simultaneous persistent sessions. Then if a client has reached its limit for all the local servers, then it will begin sending requests to remote servers. This option works best if there are only a few clients.

Servers can use DNS dynamic update to adjust the weight in the SRV records to balance the load among them. Heavily loaded servers can adjust the weight so that they are picked less often for new requests, and lightly loaded servers can adjust their weight to increase their new requests. However, one drawback to this technique is that to force the servers to adjust their load rapidly, the time to live (TTL) timer has to be set to a low time period (maybe 1 minute or less).

SRV records can also be used to support active-standby redundancy strategies. In this case, two SRV records are needed: one with the URI of the primary server (and a low priority value), and a second one with the URI of the alternate server (and a higher priority value).

4.1.3.4 Traffic Redirection via Intermediate System.
Intermediate systems like load balancers can expose a single fixed IP address to client systems ("A") and intelligently direct traffic to a specific server instance ("B1," "B2," etc) based on business logic. A load balancer can heartbeat all the servers to monitor the health of the servers. These heartbeats can also request the resource usage of each server, so that the load balancer knows which servers are already very busy and which can take on more requests. Common business logic is for the load balancer to distribute most new service requests to lightly loaded, operational server instances and avoid sending any server requests to failed servers.

4.1.3.5 Traffic Redirection via IP Mechanism.
Traffic can be redirected using two common IP protocol mechanisms:

- *Floating IP address* (also known as Virtual IP address). A pair of servers supporting active-standby redundancy can share an IP external address. If the active server fails, the alternate sends gratuitous ARP (Address Resolution Protocol, see IETF RFC 826) replies to take over the shared address. With this mechanism, the failover is transparent to the clients; they continue to send requests to the same address, but the requests are routed to the alternate server. However, this mechanism can only be used if both servers are on the same subnet, and remote sites are normally on different subnets to avoid routing broadcast traffic across the WAN. Therefore, floating IP addresses are only applicable for co-located redundancy, not geographical redundancy.
- *Multicasting.* Multicasting enables several system instances to receive the same IP datagram. A client sends a request to an IP multicast group address. The network sends a copy of the request to each of the servers that have registered to receive packets to that group address. The servers that are not too busy to process the request send a response to the client. Typically, the client will choose the first server that responds, and then sends subsequent transactions for the request directly to that server.

4.1.4 Service Context Preservation

Service context preservation is required to satisfy the service recovery point objective. In a perfect world, all session and service context from "B1" would be instantly available on "B2" from the moment "B2" was activated and both "A" and "C" could seamlessly continue service with "B2," so that the failover would be undetectable to the end user. This means that active sessions are maintained without interruption, pending transactions are completed, and users are not bothered with requests to reenter security credentials or otherwise acknowledge the failover.

Since IP traffic will have been redirected from "B1" to "B2," some network context information (e.g., IP address) will change, and some low-level protocol recovery and resynchronization with "A" will be necessary. This resynchronization should be rapid, automatic, cause minimal service disruption (e.g., minimize the impact to pending transactions), and not bother the user with warning messages to be acknowledged or requests to reenter security credentials. Ideally, this means that "B2" maintains:

- Context on all active sessions
- Context on all pending transactions
- Context on all resources allocated and used on behalf of "A," such as with "C."

In addition to synchronizing "B2" with "A," it is often necessary for "B2" to resynchronize with "C" so that "C" does not eventually detect failure of "B1," and gracefully terminate any active or pending services being provided on behalf of "B1." Imperfect service context preservation will cause service impacts such as:

- Failed transactions or requests
- Disconnected or lost sessions
- Inability to support subsequent requests for persistent sessions
- Prompts for users to reenter security credentials
- Prompts to acknowledge a failure or reconfiguration
- Service outage for end users
- Recent provisioning, configuration or other actions to be "lost" when system data is restored from last backup

4.1.4.1 *Data Replication.* Data can be classified into three types:

- *Persistent data* is provisioned into the system through a Graphical User Interface (GUI) or command line interface, either on the network element itself or through a provisioning system. This data is not generally changed through processing of requests from customers; it can only be changed by manual action by the system owner. Examples of persistent data are network element configuration data (IP addresses / domain names, timer values, etc.), tables needed to process requests (routing table, charging rate table, etc.), and the items for sale on a web site (including their descriptions, available sizes/colors, and price).
- *Semi-persistent data* is data that is not provisioned, but seldom changes. Examples are services that are configurable by a subscriber (e.g., call forwarding, speed dial numbers, passwords), a user's portfolio on a financial web site (how many

shares of each stock or mutual fund are owned by a customer), and account information on a web site (credit card number, shipping address, email address, etc.).

- *Volatile data* is constantly updated as sessions and service requests are processed. Examples are transaction state (waiting for database response, waiting for input from customer, etc.), signaling information that is needed for the duration of the call (SIP/HTTP transaction IDs), and a customer's current shopping cart on a web site.

Generally, persistent data does not need to be dynamically synchronized between the network elements. As data is added or modified on the provisioning system, it is downloaded to the active and standby call processing elements (or the pool of load shared elements) simultaneously. If one of the elements is out of service, then the provisioning system should either deny the database change, or record the update and retry when the element recovers. If the provisioning system itself is geographically redundant, then this data needs to be replicated in the standby system.

Each of the elements should store its persistent data in persistent storage (e.g., a hard disk), so that it is maintained through a minor failure (such as a power failure). Periodically (daily or weekly), the data should be backed up so that if the storage device is destroyed in a disaster, then the element can be restored (although the data might be slightly out-of-date). It might be desirable for the provisioning system to periodically audit the data on network elements to check for data corruption.

It is desirable to replicate volatile data, but this is often not practical. For example, when a request is being processed, it can go through many states as various databases are queried, the customer is prompted for data, and services are invoked. Attempting to replicate the service data at every change in state could require an enormous amount of bandwidth between the active and standby elements, and use a significant amount of processing time on the active element that could be better utilized processing more requests. Therefore, state data is only synchronized via replication during relatively long-lasting states. For example, in a VoIP or wireless network switch, the call state data might only be replicated:

- When the call is answered and moves in to the relatively stable, talking state.
- When a mid-call service is activated, such as call transfer or 3-way calling.
- When the call is released. (In this case, the replicated data in the standby element can be dropped.)

As a result, only stable (answered) calls are preserved when a call processing element does a redundant failover. Transient (preanswer) calls are lost.

Some network elements, such as database servers or media servers, process requests too quickly to justify replication of session data. If an element queries a database, and the database server fails, then it is simpler for the element to just query another database than for the database server to handoff the request to another server. Similarly, if an application server requests a media server to play an announcement, and the media server fails, then the application server should just reattempt the request with another media server.

It is more critical to replicate semi-persistent data. A user configures this information with the expectation that the data will be the same the next time they attempt to use the service, which could be days or months later. Fortunately, since this data does not change often, the bandwidth needed to replicate the data between elements is generally small.

Data replication is primarily used in active–standby or active-active configurations. It is more difficult in architectures with multiple active servers ($N + K$ load sharing), since if one server fails then its clients can failover to any of the other servers. If session context needs to be preserved in this case, then it can be stored in a central database. In the event of a server failure if a client recovers to another server, that server can query the central database for the client's session context information in order to successfully provide service to the client.

4.1.5 Graceful Service Migration

Eventually the failed "B1" will be repaired or replaced and made operational. If the unit is in active–active or load sharing redundancy, then it is essential that the operational unit can resume serving traffic with no service disruption to existing or new traffic. If the unit is in active–standby redundancy, then it should be possible to restore the repaired or replaced unit to "active" status with little impact on new or existing traffic. To minimize this impact, restores are done during periods of low traffic (e.g., at night).

4.2 TECHNICAL DISTINCTIONS BETWEEN GEOREDUNDANCY AND CO-LOCATED REDUNDANCY

The major benefit of georedundancy over co-located redundancy is that it can recover service when a disaster impacts an entire site. However, there are also some disadvantages to georedundancy:

- *Communications bandwidth is inherently lower between geographically separated systems.* Physical factors like signal loss, dispersion, and interference become more significant as distance increases, thus making long-haul transmission far more complicated than communications within a single room or site. To maintain acceptable transmission reliability, bandwidth is limited as distance increases. Even when high bandwidth links are available between distant geographic locations, the monthly line charges can be very expensive, and thus communications charges can impose a practical financial limit on the maximum affordable bandwidth. In contrast, very high-speed local area networks are less expensive.
- *Communications latency is inherently higher.* It takes light more than 3 milliseconds to travel 1000 kilometers and more than 5 milliseconds to travel 1000 miles.

In addition to the physical propagation latency due to the speed of light, data must pass through more intermediate systems like routers, multiplexors, and long-haul transmission systems that add more latency than for local area communications within a single room or data center. This communications latency may make it impractical to require synchronous data updates on both systems for performance-critical systems. Thus, some data may be maintained via near real time synchronization mechanisms rather than the strict real-time synchronous writes that are often used for critical data on locally attached mass storage. This communications latency directly contributes to service latency seen by users, thus affecting the quality of experience.

Lower communications bandwidth and higher communications latency constrain and complicate system and solution designs. For example, while real-time data mirroring can work well for co-located systems, mirroring data across a bandwidth-limited communications link quickly becomes impractical as system usage grows. Likewise, the higher communications latency to geographically remote systems reduces throughput of synchronous transactions and communications. While periodic data updates can be carried over more affordable long haul connections than real-time data updates, nonreal-time data synchronization creates a window of vulnerability in which data changes that occur after the data synchronization but before the disaster will be lost when the georedundant system is activated. This window of vulnerability may be similar to the window that exists between scheduled database backups. If a database is restored, then any changes since the time of the last backup will be lost.

Another potential disadvantage is that mechanisms for sharing IP addresses between modules typically require elements to be on the same subnetwork, so this option is not generally viable for georedundant deployments. This implies that clients must be capable of detecting which module is currently active.

4.3 MANUAL GRACEFUL SWITCHOVER AND SWITCHBACK

Sometimes, it might be useful to switchover to a redundant element even though the active element has not failed, for example, to perform a growth procedure on system hardware or update the element's software. Therefore, a procedure is needed to manually take the active element out of service and redirect traffic to a redundant element. Recall from Section 4.1.4.1, "Data Replication," that even with data replication, some in-progress transactions might be lost. To minimize the service impact, the procedure could be executed at night, during a period of low traffic.

However, a better approach would be to add steps to the procedure to:

1. Force new requests to be processed by a redundant server.
2. Periodically check the number of concurrent requests being processed by the server, and wait until all the requests have been completed before proceeding with the procedure.

The technique for step 1 depends on the technique used for distributing traffic to the element. For example, if DNS is used, then the SRV/A record for the element could be removed from the DNS database. If a load balancer is used, then the element could be taken out of the load balancer's load distribution table.

Step 2 requires a tool to determine how many requests are currently being served by the element. Well-designed systems typically have such tools to support debugging; in particular, tools to output state data for existing requests.

After a primary element has recovered from failure or from a manually induced switchover, it is often necessary to switch traffic back to the element. This may be done by following a similar strategy as the manual graceful switchover described above, or by simply reading the associated SRV/A record for the system to DNS.

5

EXTERNAL REDUNDANCY STRATEGY OPTIONS

Chapter 3, "Understanding Redundancy," described strategies for internal element redundancy; in this chapter, we begin to explore external redundancy. Several external recovery strategies have been implemented in commercial products, but these are all variants of three basic strategies, which we call manually controlled, system-driven, and client-initiated. This chapter introduces the basic strategies and describes application examples of each of them.

5.1 REDUNDANCY STRATEGIES

The following external redundancy schemes are commonly used:

1. *Active-Standby.* Two systems are deployed—one is designated as the "active" unit, and the other as the "standby" unit. Normally, the active unit provides service for all of the traffic, but if the active module fails, then the standby unit takes over service for users. The standby unit must be configured with sufficient capacity to support the full engineered traffic load from the active unit. Standby units can be maintained at varying degrees of readiness to restore service; these degrees of standby readiness are classified as follows:

Beyond Redundancy: How Geographic Redundancy Can Improve Service Availability and Reliability of Computer-Based Systems, First Edition. Eric Bauer, Randee Adams, Daniel Eustace.
© 2012 Institute of Electrical and Electronics Engineers. Published 2012 by John Wiley & Sons, Inc.

- *Hot Standby.* A hot standby network element has its software installed and its data has been kept in synch with its mate and thus should quickly be able to assume service once its active mate has failed and disaster recovery has been activated. Typically, all persistent data, semi-persistent data, and possibly some volatile session context data, is automatically replicated from the active unit to the hot standby unit to enable service to be restored onto the "hot" standby unit quickly with minimal service disruption. A hot standby network element can be either automatically triggered into service or manually activated. Usually, some sort of heartbeat message is periodically sent between the active and standby units (either the active sends a heartbeat to the standby or the standby sends a heartbeat to the active and expects to receive an acknowledgment). If the standby unit detects that the active has stopped processing heartbeats, then it makes itself active and traffic is redirected to it. Alternatively, manual failover could be used if the RTO requirement is not too strict and/or the enterprise wants to consciously decide when to trigger a georedundant failover.

- *Warm Standby.* A warm standby network element generally has its software installed but will need data updates before it can assume service for a failed network element as part of disaster recovery. Generally, it takes less time to prepare it to take over as the active module than a cold standby element and has been configured to be the standby mate for a particular network element.

- *Cold Standby.* A cold standby network element is generally not powered on and does not have its software and data installed. Before a cold standby unit can restore service from a failed active unit, the standby must be powered on, the operating system and platform software must boot up, persistent data must be loaded from a backup copy (usually, volatile data is lost), and the application must be completely started up. This procedure might take a few hours to complete. A manual failover procedure is required. Sometimes a cold standby is used as a spare for multiple network elements and thus cannot be installed until it is determined which element needs to be backed up.

2. *Active–Active.* Two units are deployed, each capable of serving the entire engineered service load. Both of these units are fully operational and carrying traffic during normal operation; typically, half of the traffic load will be carried by each unit. When one of the active units fails, traffic previously served by the failed unit can be carried by the other unit. Active–active can offer two advantages over active–standby arrangements:

- *Better service during normal operations* because each active unit should be running at no more than 50% of full engineered capacity, and thus service latency may be somewhat lower than on active/standby systems on which the active unit routinely serves more traffic

- *Lower risk of uncovered or silent failure* because it is generally simpler to detect failures of units that are actively delivering service than on standby units that are essentially idle.

3. *N + K Load Sharing.* In many cases, it is most cost-effective to share the engineered load of a system across a pool of identical modules. If "N" identical modules are required to carry the engineered load, then "K" extra modules can be deployed so that the system can withstand up to "K" simultaneous (i.e., unrepaired and/or unrecovered) element failures with no loss of capacity. Service load is evenly distributed across all operational elements in the pool of N + K identical modules. A common example of N + K load sharing is engines on multiengine aircraft; if "N" engines are required to takeoff, maneuver, and land, then N + 1 engines are used to mitigate the risk of engine failure on takeoff. Note that active–active is the degenerate case of N + K (1 + 1) load sharing. An N + K load-sharing scheme has several advantages. Since all of the network elements are generally active, once a failure of a network element has been detected by a client or by a load-sharing device, messages can be directed to any of the remaining network elements. The best candidates for this type of redundancy are services that do not support long-lived transactions that need to maintain state information and do not require registration to a particular module, thus allowing any of the modules to provide service. Each of the network elements may also have some level of internal redundancy, but the primary redundancy mechanism is external. Load-shared systems have a flexibility advantage in that generally, the elements can be either co-located or geographically distributed.

5.2 DATA RECOVERY STRATEGIES

The choice of redundancy strategy is primarily influenced by the RTO requirement, but the recovery point objective (RPO) requirement dictates the choice of data recovery strategy. The most common data recovery strategies are:

- *None.* Data is not synchronized between elements or backed up at all. This is acceptable for applications that process short-lived requests that can be retried. For example, consider the print jobs spooled by a print server. While it is theoretically possible to backup all print jobs, their transient nature and the overall unreliability of the printing process itself (e.g., paper jams, image quality issue) means that users are likely to be prepared to resubmit failed or lost jobs rather than expecting those jobs to be restored from backups.
- *Data Backup on Physical Media.* A backup of the data is generated periodically (usually, once a day) and stored on backup media (e.g., a hard disk or compact disk). The backup should be in a remote location, so that if the primary server's location is lost due to a disaster, the data can still be recovered at another site. Since the backup is on physical media, there is inherently a logistical delay in transporting the physical backup media to the target system. While the delay can be small for backups held on the site hosting the target system, logistical

delays inherently increase as geographically separated recovery sites move farther apart. Due to the infrequency of the backups, this strategy is appropriate for persistent data, and possibly semi-persistent data, but is not appropriate for volatile data.

- *Data Backup to Networked Vault.* Data can be backed up to a networked storage device rather than to physical media. While there is likely to be a small logistical delay in initiating a restoration from a networked backup, the bandwidth to the networked backup device will limit how quickly the entire data set can be downloaded, thus limiting RTO. Backups can be generated more frequently when using a storage device, such as once an hour, which may be fast enough to support volatile data for some applications.

- *Data Replicated to a Remote Server.* The same data is replicated on both servers. Whenever data is modified on the primary server due to client requests, the primary server sends updates to the alternate server so that the alternate is prepared to immediately take over service and preserve active requests if the primary fails. It might not be practical to send every single data change to the remote server; instead, the primary might wait until a request has reached a relatively stable state or the length of a request has exceeded a threshold before backing up the request's state data.

- *Data Synchronized on a Remote Registry.* Similar to replication on a remote server, but the primary server sends updates to a remote database, called a registry. This option is primarily used in load-shared architectures, because when a server fails, its requests are distributed across all the other servers. Since any server can backup any other server, it is not practical to keep the databases in all the servers synchronized. But if each server stores all its data in the registry, then any server can take over any request by reading the registry.

- *Data Stored in the Client.* Client data is stored in the client itself, so that if the primary server fails, the alternate server can retrieve the data from the clients. If the interface between the client and server is HTTP (B is a web server), then the servers can store and retrieve data in the client using cookies.

5.3 EXTERNAL RECOVERY STRATEGIES

The strategies listed in Section 5.1, "Redundancy Strategies," can be reduced into three fundamental options for controlling the external recovery process:

1. *Manually Controlled Recovery.* Human maintenance engineers first recognize that an active element has failed and then manually coordinate recovery by redirecting traffic to an alternate element. Relying on manual actions results in a recovery time that is usually too long for critical applications, but since it is the simplest recovery strategy to implement, it is often used for supporting functions. Active/cold standby schemes often use manually controlled recovery to manually power on systems and bring applications to full operational readi-

ness. Likewise, any recovery that relies on physical backup media stored off-site to recover data will require at least some manual control.

2. *System-Driven Recovery.* The systems themselves (named "B1," "B2," "C" in Fig. 4.1) automatically control recovery. The health of the primary element is monitored via some sort of heartbeat messages. When it is determined that the primary element has failed, its traffic is automatically redirected to an alternate element by either the alternate or the failed element. The recovery time is typically much faster than with manually controlled recovery. System-driven recovery is typically used with the Active/Hot-Standby, Active/Warm-Standby and Active-active schemes.

3. *Client-Initiated Recovery.* The client system ("A" in Fig. 4.1) drives recovery to a redundant server. When a server fails, the client is often the first to know when the server does not respond to requests or returns failure messages. The client can quickly reconnect to an alternate server and begin sending its requests there. Note that this option does not actually repair/recover the failed server, but it is the fastest strategy for restoring service from the client's point of view. To maximize the benefit of client-initiated recovery, it is primarily used when multiple servers are simultaneously active—that is, the active–active and $N + K$ load-sharing schemes.

Robust escalation strategies generally attempt to recover from a failure at the lowest level possible, such as a task or process restart, and escalate to a module reboot if that does not work, and then to a redirection to another network element if the failure is more catastrophic. Many network elements have internal redundancy mechanisms that will attempt to handle the majority of the failures through process restarts and blade failovers to lessen the impact of the failure. Failure to another network element may be the next level of defense for a network element failure that could not be successfully addressed by the internal mechanisms. This redirection to another network element may be triggered by either a system-driven or a client-initiated recovery action.

Each type of external recovery is described in the following sections.

5.4 MANUALLY CONTROLLED RECOVERY

Manually controlled recovery is the simplest external recovery scheme. While automatic fault and alarm software may detect and isolate the failure to "B1," a human maintenance engineer decides if, when, and how to execute a switchover to a redundant system and eventual switchback to "B1" after it has been repaired. Typically, less additional software needs to be developed for manually controlled recovery than for automatically controlled redundancy: just the ability to make backups of the database, to restore the database from backup, and to redirect traffic from one system to another. If the active element fails, then manual procedures must be executed to restore the standby element's database and bring it into service. Even when automatically controlled recovery is supported, manual procedures are also needed in case the automatic recovery fails. They can also be used to switchover to an alternate element to reduce the risk when a complex maintenance procedure needs to be performed on the primary elements (e.g., a software upgrade or hardware repair), or to periodically switchover to a standby server to verify it is still operational.

Manually controlled recovery is only practical for elements with a long RTO (e.g., at least eight hours), due to the time needed to:

1. Manually detect or recognize that the primary element has failed.
2. Assign a maintenance engineer and wait for him/her to prepare to perform the manual procedures (including traveling to the failed site, logging into the system, accessing the procedure documents, etc.).
3. Confirm the system failure and determine that the primary element cannot be restored quickly, and that the alternate element should be activated.
4. If necessary, restore the database on the alternate element with the latest backup from the primary element. This time can be reduced if the alternate element is routinely kept in sync with the primary element via frequent data replication.
5. If necessary, start the service processes on the alternate element. This time can be reduced if the processes are kept running on the alternate element all the time, so that only a single command is needed to bring it to the active state.
6. Manually redirect traffic in the network to communicate with the alternate element. This time can be reduced if the other elements can automatically detect that the primary element has failed and switch to the alternate element (see client-initiated redundancy below).
7. Monitor the new element until service is stable to verify successful recovery.

The next step is to repair the failed primary element, but since service has been recovered to a redundant element, the repair of the failed primary element can be executed on a nonemergency basis.

Automatic failure recovery (system-driven or client-initiated) is usually preferred over manual recovery, since it supports faster failover, but it carries some additional risks:

- Failures of the underlying communications network might make it appear that a remote element is down when it is really up. This can trigger unnecessary failovers that can make the problem worse.
- Software cannot be designed to anticipate every type of possible failure, so it might take the wrong action for some types of failures, such as inappropriate failovers or failovers to the wrong element.

Therefore, some customers only allow manual recovery, so that only a human being (who presumably has a full understanding of the current situation) can decide if, and when, a failover should be attempted.

5.4.1 Manually Controlled Example: Provisioning System for a Database

In order to offer as much processing power as possible in query processing, provisioning of new data is often moved to a separate network element, called a provisioning system. This standalone element might have sufficient resources to provide a user-friendly GUI (graphical user interface) to the users, whereas the database itself might only be able to provide a simple command line interface. As the users update the data through the GUI, the provisioning system has sufficient resources to check that the data is syntactically correct and consistent with the existing data (e.g., it may reject a request to modify the parameters of a service if the subscriber does not pay for the service). The provisioning system only sends an update to the database element if the update is valid. Only minimal resources are used on the database element for database updates, so that most of its resources are available for responding to requests from its clients.

The database element is considered to be the "master" copy. If the provisioning system loses its copy of the data, it can always restore it by up-synching the data from the database element. The RTO might still be an issue for some provisioning system, since a failure of the system cause service to new users to be delayed, which could impact revenue. Also, the time to up-synch the data might be significant. Nevertheless, manually controlled redundancy can be appropriate for provisioning systems with a sufficiently long RTO.

5.4.2 Manually Controlled Example: Performance Management Systems

A large solution might need several instances of each type of network element. As the traffic grows, additional elements will need to be added to the solution. In order to accurately determine when and how many new elements are needed, the elements themselves can keep count of the number of requests they process. All the elements send their counts and their system resource usage (central processing unit [CPU], memory, buffer, occupancy, etc.) to a centralized performance management system. This performance management system compiles the data and reports it in graphs or charts that help the network engineers determine bottlenecks where the solution is running short of capacity. Decisions to grow the solution are made after studying the performance data over a range of several weeks or months. So although the data is valuable, the total loss of a few days of data is not significant. With both a long RTO and RPO, manually controlled redundancy can be used.

5.5 SYSTEM-DRIVEN RECOVERY

System-driven recovery entails recovery at the network element level; the alternate element can be co-located or geographically separated from the primary element. High-availability mechanisms exist in the system that monitor the network elements, and when a failure is detected, the high-availability mechanism diverts traffic away from the failed element to another network element that is set up to assume the traffic on behalf of the failed network element. Failures can be detected and negotiated by the network elements ("B1" and "B2") themselves (e.g., through heartbeating) or by a separate module. The advantage of the former is that there is no need for another module; all detection and arbitration is handled between the mates. The disadvantage is that a situation referred to as "split brain" could occur in which a loss of communication between the modules causes both sides to believe the other has failed and each tries to be the active module. To minimize the risk of a split brain condition, when the standby element detects the loss of heartbeats, it should ping another element in the solution to ensure it is still connected to the network, increasing its confidence that the active element is really down. Otherwise, manual recovery may be required to reunite the "split brains."

System-driven recovery can also be managed through a separate module (e.g., a load balancer or element management system) that heartbeats with the mated modules, detects any failure with an active module and directs traffic away from the failed module to a redundant one. The other advantage of including a monitoring module is that the "split brain" scenario should not occur since a third party is monitoring the modules and negotiating the traffic according to their availability. One disadvantage is the need/cost for a separate module (which itself should be redundant).

With system-driven recovery based on an active/hot-standby configuration, the standby element can be automatically activated when the active element fails. Normally, heartbeats are exchanged either between the active and standby elements or between the active element and a separate monitoring element. When the active fails, the failure can be detected by the loss of the heartbeats. When a few consecutive heartbeats are lost, the standby server can be activated quickly, often before the system operator even realizes that there is a problem. Using heartbeats, system-driven recovery can support an RTO as short as a few minutes. However, as will be explained in Section 11.2.1, "Internal Versus External Redundancy," the RTO should not be set too short, since it is preferable to give the primary element some time to recover on its own before switching over to the alternate location because successful internal recovery is often less impactful to users than system-driven external recovery.

System-driven recovery can also support a short RPO through the use of data replication. Whenever its internal data changes, the active element can send updates to the standby element so that it can keep its own internal data in sync. Then, if the active fails, the standby can immediately take over processing of the active requests. However, keeping all the data in sync constantly (RPO = 0) may use an excessive amount of system resources (CPU time, bandwidth). It may be more practical to buffer the updates and send several seconds of updates at a time. Thus, the RPO can be made as short as necessary, but there is a trade-off between RPO and system resources.

After a system-driven failover, the "A" and "C" elements must automatically switch to the new server "B2." Any of the techniques described in Section 4.1.3, "Traffic Redirection," may be considered, depending on the capabilities of the A, B, and C elements.

5.5.1 System-Driven Recovery Examples

System-driven recovery is most commonly used in the following cases:

- When the clients do not support client-initiated recovery.
- When the clients and servers are owned by different enterprises and the owner of the servers needs to keep their internal topology private.
- When a complex registration or procedure is used, and there is a concern that excessive resources could be used if clients switch between servers too often.

A high-availability distributed database is an example of an application that might use system-driven recovery. A large database is too big to fit on a single pair of disk drives, so it is split up among several pairs (e.g., records that start with letters A through F are on disk pair 1, records that start with letters G through M are on disk pair 2, etc.). Each database query needs to be directed to the active disk of the disk pair that supports the record being retrieved.

If there are many clients, or if the clients are owned by a different enterprise, then it would be undesirable to put this complexity into the clients. A better solution is to place a front-end server between the clients and the disks. The clients would query the front-end server, and the front-end server would check an internal index table to see which disk pair has the requested data. The front-end server would also periodically heartbeat all the disks so that it always knows which ones are available, and only send queries to those.

Besides simplifying the complexity of the clients, this technique has the added benefit of increasing flexibility of the database. Over time, the number of G-M records might increase such that they need to be split up into separate disk pairs. This only requires a change in the front-end server's index table—the clients are not impacted.

5.6 CLIENT-INITIATED RECOVERY

Client-initiated recovery actions depend on the actions of the client ("A" in generic redundancy model). If the client detects a failure of a network element "B1," such as via a request timeout or explicit error response, then client "A" chooses a different network element "B2." This is usually supported by a standards-based protocol (e.g., SIP) that provides guidance on detecting a failure based on message parameters (e.g., exceeding timeout and maximum retry counts) or message return codes (e.g., SIP return code 503 Service Unavailable). Client-initiated configurations also require a means for selecting an alternate network element. This can be facilitated by preprovisioned data or by an outside source, such as domain name system (DNS).

The benefit of client-initiated recovery is that it may be a more direct means for the client to detect and recover from failures of its interfacing network elements. Client-initiated recovery is more effective than system-driven recovery in some cases of "uncovered" failures, such as defects that prevent "B1" from satisfying requests but do not prevent it from sending heartbeats to "B2" or the monitoring system. These types of failures would not trigger system-driven recovery to failover, but since clients do not get responses to their service requests, that will trigger them to failover to an alternate server.

Some potential disadvantages of client-initiated recovery are:

- *Behavior may vary based on the client*, which might be owned by a different company than the enterprise that owns the servers. For example, a web server pool has no control over functionality in the web browsers that are accessing the servers.
- *Timely failure detection and recovery depend on continuous monitoring of the network elements by the clients*, and an efficient means of detecting a failure of the network element and choosing an alternate network element/path to follow in the event of a failure. This is an issue in cases where requests are sometimes sent to a client. If the primary server has failed, and the client does not recognize this and switch to an alternate, these requests will be lost.
- *Client-initiated recovery does not facilitate the recovery of the failed network element*; it just improves the availability of the service from the client's point of view. This is not actually a disadvantage, but a note that client-initiated recovery merely mitigates a server failure; the failed system must eventually be repaired and returned to service.
- *If "B1" and "B2" run active-standby, then system-driven recovery is still needed* in conjunction with client driven recovery. If the redundant server is in standby rather than active, then something must trigger the standby to promote itself to become active; typically that trigger is a system-driven recovery mechanism.

5.6.1 Client-Initiated Recovery Overview

Traditional high-availability systems strive to automatically recover from failures with minimal disruption to the client or system user. Alternatively, the client can become an active part of the recovery process to overcome some of the deficiencies of traditional high-availability mechanisms that were covered in Chapter 3. This section offers a canonical model of client-initiated recovery, reviews the key architectural techniques supporting client-initiated recovery, and presents the key parameters and evaluation criteria for client-initiated recovery.

As the ultimate service consumer, element "A" is uniquely positioned to assess whether or not service is being acceptably delivered. In particular, even in the case of a silent or uncovered failure of "B1," element "A" is likely to detect the failure no later than the next attempted use of element "B1." Combining theoretically perfect failure coverage of "B" with the service state and context held by "A" potentially enables "A" to proactively participate in the high-availability process, and, as will be shown in Chapter 6 "Modeling Service Availability with External System Redundancy," potentially achieves service availability improvements that are infeasible for traditional high-availability strategies.

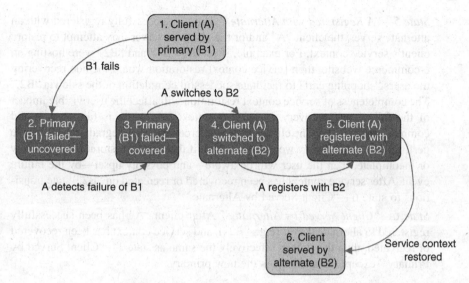

Figure 5.1. Client-initiated recovery scenario.

Consider the generic client-initiated failure recovery scenario is illustrated in Figure 5.1:

- *State 1—"Client Served by Primary."* In normal operation, client "A" is served by primary server "B1." When the primary server "B1" fails, the client is initially unaware of the failure and thus transitions to state 2—"Primary Failed—Uncovered."

- *State 2—"Primary Failed—Uncovered."* "B1" has just failed but the client is not yet aware of the failure. The client will remain in this state until it sends a request to "B1" and receives an explicit failure response indicating profound server failure or does not receive any response from the server at all. The client will retry requests that yield no responses, but eventually the client will deem the server to be unavailable, and thus transition to state 3—"Primary Failed—Covered."

- *State 3—"Primary Failed—Covered."* Client "A" now recognizes that server "B1" is unavailable, so it now selects an alternate server (e.g., "B2"). The alternate server is often either preconfigured for the client or picked from the responses provided by DNS. Having selected an alternate server, A attempts to register with that server, thereby transitioning to state 4—"Client Switched to Alternate."

- *State 4—"Client Switched to Alternate."* Having selected an alternate server (e.g., "B2"), the client contacts that server, negotiates an acceptable protocol version, presents identification and authentication credentials, and awaits confirmation of successful registration (which would trigger transition to state 5—"A Registered with Alternate").

- *State 5—"A Registered with Alternate."* Having successfully registered with an alternate server, the client "A" and/or the alternate server may attempt to restore client's service context. For example, if servers "B1" and "B2" were hosting an e-commerce website, then service context restoration would include recovering the users "shopping cart" to facilitate successful completion of the sale via "B2." The completeness of service context restoration will affect the user visible impact of the failure and recovery. If service context restoration is fast enough and complete enough, then the client may only perceive a brief degradation in service performance (e.g., a slow webpage refresh); if the context restoration is too slow or incomplete, then the user will be aware—and possibly upset—by the failure event. After service context has been recovered or recreated on "B2," state transitions to state 6—"Client Served by Alternate."
- *State 6—"Client Served by Alternate."* After client "A" has been successfully registered to alternate server (e.g., "B2"), and service context has been recovered or recreated, then the state is effectively the same as state 1—"Client Served by Primary," except the alternate is the new primary.

5.6.2   Failure Detection by Client

Most application protocols use some form of request/response message exchange in which one party sends one or more messages, and the other party sends a response or acknowledgment. Responses to requests can often broadly be classified into four categories; SIP [RFC3261] protocol messages are used as examples:

- *Normal responses* signifying that "B1" behaved as specified. For example, consider the following "normal" responses to SIP messages.
  - Successful 2xx responses like 200 OK
  - Provisional 1xx responses like 180 Ringing. Defined as: *"The UA receiving the INVITE is trying to alert the user"* (Internet Engineering Task Force, 2002).
  - Redirection 3xx responses like 301 Moved Permanently. Defined as: *"The user can no longer be found at the address in the Request-URI, and the requesting client SHOULD retry at the new address given by the Contact header field"* (Internet Engineering Task Force, 2002).
  - Request Failure 4xx responses that indicate user-related problems like:
    - 400 Bad Request. Defined as: *"The request could not be understood due to malformed syntax. The Reason-Phrase SHOULD identify the syntax problem in more detail, for example, 'Missing Call-ID header field'"* (Internet Engineering Task Force, 2002).
    - 401 Unauthorized. Defined as: *"The request requires user authentication. This response is issued by UASs and registrars, while 407 (Proxy Authentication Required) is used by proxy servers"* (Internet Engineering Task Force, 2002).
    - 404 Not Found. Defined as: *"The server has definitive information that the user does not exist at the domain specified in the Request-URI. This status*

is also returned if the domain in the Request-URI does not match any of the domains handled by the recipient of the request" (Internet Engineering Task Force, 2002).

These responses indicate that the request was formatted improperly or sent to an invalid destination.

○ Other request-specific failure responses such as:

- 501 Not Implemented. Defined as "The server does not support the functionality required to fulfill the request. This is the appropriate response when a UAS does not recognize the request method and is not capable of supporting it for any user. (Proxies forward all requests regardless of method.)" (Internet Engineering Task Force, 2002).

- 505 Version Not Supported. Defined as "The server does not support, or refuses to support, the SIP protocol version that was used in the request. The server is indicating that it is unable or unwilling to complete the request using the same major version as the client, other than with this error message" (Internet Engineering Task Force, 2002).

- 513 Message Too Large. Defined as "The server was unable to process the request since the message length exceeded its capabilities" (Internet Engineering Task Force, 2002).

- 600 Busy. Defined as "The callee's end system was contacted successfully but the callee is busy and does not wish to take the call at this time. The response MAY indicate a better time to call in the Retry-After header field. If the callee does not wish to reveal the reason for declining the call, the callee uses status code 603 (Decline) instead. This status response is returned only if the client knows that no other end point (such as a voice mail system) will answer the request. Otherwise, 486 (Busy Here) should be returned" (Internet Engineering Task Force, 2002).

- 603 Decline. Defined as "The callee's machine was successfully contacted but the user explicitly does not wish to or cannot participate. The response MAY indicate a better time to call in the Retry-After header field. This status response is returned only if the client knows that no other end point will answer the request" (Internet Engineering Task Force, 2002).

- 606 Not Acceptable. Defined as "The user's agent was contacted successfully but some aspects of the session description such as the requested media, bandwidth, or addressing style were not acceptable" (Internet Engineering Task Force, 2002).

• Failure responses signifying that "B1" experienced a critical or major failure and is unable to provide service, such as the following SIP failure responses:

○ 500 Server Internal Error. Defined as "The server encountered an unexpected condition that prevented it from fulfilling the request. The client MAY display the specific error condition and MAY retry the request after several seconds. If the condition is temporary, the server MAY indicate when *the client may retry the request using the Retry-After header field*" (Internet Engineering Task Force, 2002).

○ 503 Service Unavailable. Defined as "*The server is temporarily unable to process the request due to a temporary overloading or maintenance of the server. The server MAY indicate when the client should retry the request in a Retry-After header field. If no Retry-After is given, the client MUST act as if it had received a 500 (Server Internal Error) response*" (Internet Engineering Task Force, 2002).

- *Proxied Failure Responses.* Some protocols allow "B1" to explicitly differentiate failures of downstream elements (e.g., "C") from failures of "B1" itself, for example, the following SIP failure responses:

○ 502 Bad Gateway. Defined as "*The server, while acting as a gateway or proxy, received an invalid response from the downstream server it accessed in attempting to fulfill the request*" (Internet Engineering Task Force, 2002).

○ 504 Server Time-out. Defined as "*The server did not receive a timely response from an external server it accessed in attempting to process the request. 408 (Request Timeout) should be used instead if there was no response within the period specified in the Expires header field from the upstream server*" (Internet Engineering Task Force, 2002).

○ 408 Request Timeout. Defined as "*The server could not produce a response within a suitable amount of time, for example, if it could not determine the location of the user in time. The client MAY repeat the request without modifications at any later time*" (Internet Engineering Task Force, 2002).

- *No response* at all within the specified timeout period.

In the absence of a client-detection mechanism, these responses lead "A" to do one of the following:

- *Continue Normally.* Normal responses lead "A" to continue with normal processing.
- *Retry Request to "B1".* The first mitigation for no response to a request is to retry the request to the same server. This occurs when IP messages are occasionally lost or corrupted in transmission or discarded due to overflow. If the transport layer does not support restransmissions (e.g., UDP), then the upper layer protocol should include an automatic retry mechanism that enables messages to be retransmitted to mitigate risk of occasional packet loss or corruption.
- *Present Profound/Catastrophic Error to User.* Some fundamental service failures must simply be mapped to an appropriate user response. For example, there is normally little point in retrying a request that was rejected with "404 Not Found." The user should be informed that the request was invalid, so that they can modify it.

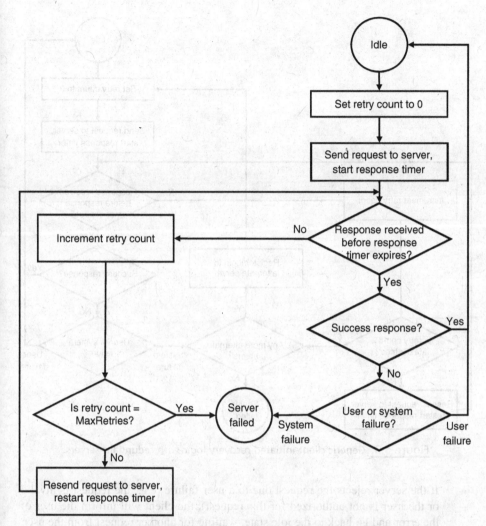

Figure 5.2. Typical client processing logic for standalone server.

This is illustrated for simple clients in Figure 5.2. When the client needs to request a server to perform some service, it sends a request and expects to receive a successful response. However, one of the following failures can occur:

- If the server does not respond, the client will attempt retransmission logic. Typically, the client will retransmit the original request up to a small maximum number of retransmission times (MaxRetries in the figure). When the maximum number of retransmission attempts is exceeded, the client will enter a profound error state.

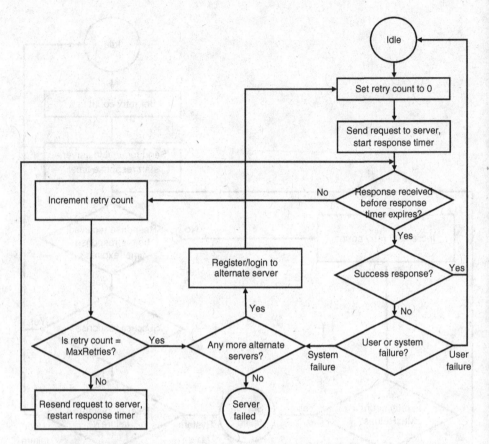

Figure 5.3. Generic client-initiated recovery logic with redundant servers.

- If the server rejects the request due to a user failure (e.g., the request is invalid or the user is not authorized for this request), the client will inform the user of the error and go back to the idle state, waiting for another request from the user.
- If the server responds that the request is valid, but it cannot support the service at this time, the client will enter a profound error state.

In an externally redundant solution, the client ("A") has the additional option of attempting to work around the failure of the primary server ("B1"), by retrying the failed operation to a redundant server ("B2"). Figure 5.3 overlays this client-initiated recovery logic onto the typical client processing logic of Figure 5.2.

The fundamental differences in the client-initiated recovery logic of Figure 5.3 compared with the typical client logic of Figure 5.2 are as follows:

- System failure responses and retransmission failures prompt the client to select an alternate server rather than either retry the request to the primary server or simply declare a profound error.

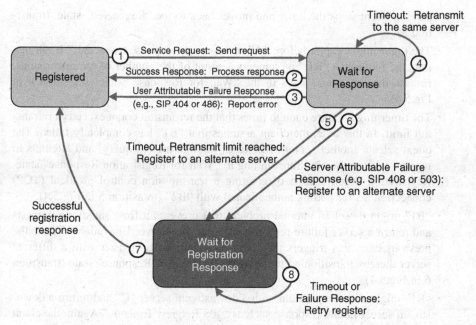

Figure 5.4. Session states seen by a SIP client "A" in client-initiated recovery.

- Having selected an alternate server, the client connects to it, sends the failed request to it, and restarts retransmission processing.
- If the client successfully engaged with the alternate server, future service requests will be sent to it.

Depending on the specific application and supported protocol, numerous variants of the generic client-initiated recovery logic can be employed. For example, some applications and protocols may permit a client to maintain active sessions with multiple servers (e.g., "B1" and "B2") simultaneously.

Client-initiated recovery can also be considered from the perspective of state as seen from client "A." Figure 5.4 illustrates the state machine of "A" in client-initiated recovery of SIP service.

Normally, client "A" is in the "Registered" state, that is, it is registered with a server "B1." When the user attempts to use a service, "A" sends a request to "B1" (transition 1 in Fig.5.4), moves to the "Wait for Response" state, and starts a timer. From this state, the following events can occur:

- "B1" might successfully satisfy the request and return a success response. In this case, the client stops the timer, moves back to the "Registered" state, and waits for the user to attempt another service. (transition 2 in Fig.5.4)
- "B1" might detect that the request cannot be satisfied due to an error by the user/client. It returns a user-attributable failure response (e.g., 404 Not Found),

and the client stops the timer and moves back to the "Registered" state. (transition 3)

- The timer might expire before "A" receives any response from "B1." It retransmits the request to "B1," increments a count of the number of retransmissions, restarts the timer, and stays in the "Wait for Response" state (transition 4 in Fig.5.4).
- The timer might expire enough times that the retransmit count exceeds a retransmit limit. In this case, the client assumes that "B1" has completely failed. The client selects another server "B2" (e.g., through a DNS query) and attempts to register with it, thereby transitioning to "Wait for Registration Response" state. Registration might consist of creating a transmission control protocol (TCP) connection and/or getting authenticated with "B2" (transition 5 in Fig.5.4).
- "B1" might detect an internal problem that prevents it from satisfying requests and return a server failure response such as "503 Server Unavailable." Like the previous case, this triggers the client to attempt to re-register with a different server thereby transitioning to "Wait for Registration Response" state (transition 6 in Fig.5.4)
- "B1" might detect a problem with a downstream server "C" and return a downstream server failure response such as "408 Request Timeout." Again, the client should attempt to reregister with a different server (transition 6 in Fig.5.4).

When "A" attempts to register with "B2" in "Wait for Registration Response" state, the following events can occur:

- "B2" might successfully register "A" and return a success response. The client moves back to the Registered state and waits for the user to request a service. If the recovery to "B2" has occurred fast enough, it might be able to retry the original request with "B2" if the user hasn't already abandoned the request. Otherwise, the client will just wait for the user to attempt another request (transition 7 in Fig.5.4).
- The timer might expire before "A" receives any response from "B2." The client can retransmit the request to "B2," or if the number of retransmissions exceeds a limit, attempt to register with "B3" (if available) or alternate between the servers. Alternately, the registration might fail, perhaps because the alternate server is too busy or unavailable, in which case the client can select a second alternate and attempt to register to that server (transition 8 in Fig.5.4)

Some protocols do not require the clients to do any registration. An example is DNS, where the clients can query any server without going though an authentication procedure. In this case, the third state for registration is not required, and the state machine simplifies to Figure 5.5.

The major change is that in the cases of the retransmit limit reached and a server attributable failure response, the client can simply retransmit the request to an alternate server and stay in the "Wait for Response" state. When the alternate server returns either

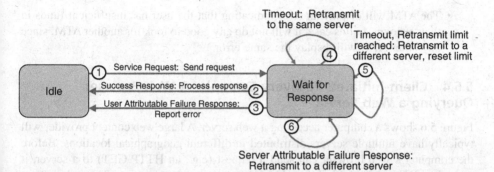

Figure 5.5. Session states seen by "A" in client-initiated recovery without registration.

a success response or a user-attributable failure response, the client can process the response and go back to the idle state, waiting for the next service request from the user.

5.6.3 Client-Initiated Recovery Example: Automatic Teller Machine (ATM)

A simple example of client-initiated recovery is a person trying to withdraw money from an ATM. On this interface, the person is the client, and the ATM is the server. There will be additional servers behind the ATM, such as a security server that verifies the user's account number and a database server that knows how much money is in the user's account.

The user will insert an ATM card and press buttons or a touch-screen to enter their password and specify how much they would like to withdraw. One of the following will happen:

- The user will successfully retrieve their cash.
- The ATM will either not accept the card or will not respond when any of the buttons are pushed. In this case, the user will probably wait for a few seconds (running a response timer in their brain with a value set to how long they think it typically takes an ATM to respond, plus a few seconds), and then retry. The user might try a few times, and then conclude that the ATM is out-of-order and walk down the street looking for another ATM.
- The ATM will display an error indicating that it is out-of-order or out of cash. Again, the user will look for another ATM. The recovery action is the same as in the previous case, except that since the ATM is displaying an explicit error response, the user will determine that it is unavailable quicker than if it just did not respond.
- The ATM might find that either the security server or the database server is down. It should check if there is another one available, possibly in a geographically remote location. If it finds one and uses it, the user will not notice that anything was wrong, as long as the failover is quick.

- The ATM will display an error indicating that the user has insufficient funds in their account. In this case, it will not do any good to look for another ATM, since any other ATM will display the same error.

5.6.4   Client-Initiated Recovery Example: A Web Browser Querying a Web Server

Figure 5.6 shows a computer accessing a web server. A large web content provider will typically have multiple servers distributed in different geographical locations. Before the computer's web browser can send a request (e.g., an HTTP GET) to a server, it must do a DNS query to find the address of an external web server. The web content provider's DNS server would return a set of A/AAAA records with the addresses of the web servers. These would be returned in round-robin order, that is, the records will be rotated before every response so that requests from clients are load shared among the servers. The browser would send its request to the first address in the list it receives in its response.

Using the terminology of the generic georedundancy model, the computer is the "A" element, the web servers are the "B1," "B2," . . . elements. The web servers might access a distributed database that stores the content; a database instance would be the "C" element. If a web server fails, then the browser will not receive any response for

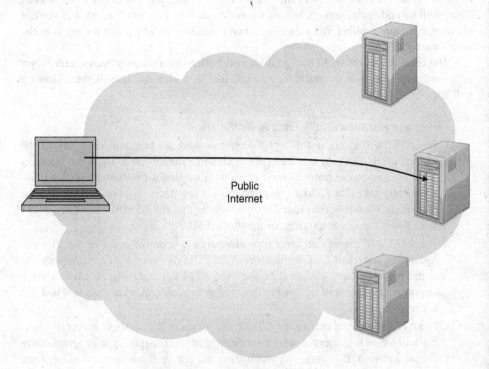

Public
Internet

Figure 5.6. Browser query to web server.

its request. In this case, the web browser could automatically reattempt the request to a different web server, although basic browsers are more likely to just display a failure message and require the user to retry the request. Since the web server A/AAAA records are processed in round-robin order, the second request will go to a different web server (the second address it received in the response to the original DNS query), and will likely be successful.

If a web server is operational but its database is down, the server has an option. It could send an explicit error response to the computer, which might take the form of a web page that explains that the database is down. In this case, the user could retry the request and the browser would send it to an alternate web server as in the previous case. A second option would be for the server to connect to a different database instance, so that it can send the requested content to the client. The second option is preferred since the failure of the "C" element would be transparent to the user (except that it will take a little longer for the server to respond).

5.6.5 Client-Initiated Recovery Example: A Pool of DNS Servers

DNS clients are an excellent application for client-driven recovery, since the traffic can be load-shared among many servers, and requests are short-lived so no service context information needs to be preserved when a server fails. A case study of DNS as an example of client-initiated recovery is presented in Chapter 8, "Case Study of Client-Initiated Recovery."

6

MODELING SERVICE AVAILABILITY WITH EXTERNAL SYSTEM REDUNDANCY

This chapter considers how to model the service availability benefit of external redundancy. The chapter begins by explaining why the simplistic availability model of redundant systems is generally inappropriate for critical enterprise systems and presents a generic Markov model of recovery for external system redundancy. This model is solved for manually controlled, system-driven and client-initiated recovery strategies. The modeling and analysis in this chapter applies to both geographically distributed and co-located redundant systems; for convenience, this chapter will refer to "georedundant" systems for both options to simplify comparison with internal system redundancy.

6.1 THE SIMPLISTIC ANSWER

The simplest estimate for service availability across a pair of elements is the sum of the probability that each element (e.g., "B1," "B2") is available minus the probability that both elements are up, which must be excluded to avoid double counting. Mathematically, this is expressed as Billinton and Allan (1992):

Beyond Redundancy: How Geographic Redundancy Can Improve Service Availability and Reliability of Computer-Based Systems, First Edition. Eric Bauer, Randee Adams, Daniel Eustace.
© 2012 Institute of Electrical and Electronics Engineers. Published 2012 by John Wiley & Sons, Inc.

$$\text{Availability}_{\text{Pair}} = 2 \times \text{Availability}_{\text{Element}} - \text{Availability}_{\text{Element}}^2$$

Equation 6.1. Simplistic Redundancy Availability Formula

This equation predicts that a pair of 99.9% elements (each with almost 9 hours of annualized unplanned service downtime) will have a service availability 99.9999% (six 9's), which is 32 seconds of service downtime per year. As a simple illustration of the unrealistic assumptions associated with this equation, readers should consider the difficulty of achieving less than 32 seconds of personal computer downtime per year by using a pair of laptop or desktop personal computers. Technically, achieving 32 seconds of downtime requires the following unrealistic assumptions:

1. Instantaneous detection of all failures with 100% accuracy
2. Instantaneous and flawless identification of the failed element so the proper recovery action can be initiated
3. Instantaneous and flawless service restoration onto the redundant element

While this simplistic model offers a theoretical upper bound on the service availability of a georedundant deployment, it does not predict a feasible or likely value for service availability.

6.2 FRAMING SERVICE AVAILABILITY OF STANDALONE SYSTEMS

If, as shown in Chapter 3, "Understanding Redundancy," adding internal redundancy to a system reduces downtime by more than an order of magnitude compared with simplex configuration, then how much incremental downtime improvement is feasible when georedundancy supplements internal redundancy? This can be addressed by reviewing each of the partially and totally down states which accrue downtime and considering if and how georedundancy can reduce time in that down state. This chapter will consider the same generic system redundancy arrangement discussed in Chapter 4, "Overview of External Redundancy," and illustrated in Figure 4.1—Generic High Availability Model. For convenience, that diagram is repeated as Figure 6.1, in which "A" represents the client network element that obtains service "B" from either system instance "B1" or system instance "B2." An element "C"—and "D," "E," "F," and so on—could be used by "B" to deliver service to client "A," but those subsequent elements are not considered in this chapter. Chapter 9, "Solution and Cluster Recovery," discusses service availability considerations for solutions and clusters of elements. The analysis and modeling in this chapter considers availability of service "B" seen by "A," especially when system instance "B1" experiences a failure.

Consider the scenario in which NE "B1" supports internal redundancy and an identical redundant element instance "B2" is added; in that case, how much downtime of the primary element "B1" can feasibly be mitigated by "B2"? For simplicity, this example will assume that primary element "B1" is active and redundant element "B2"

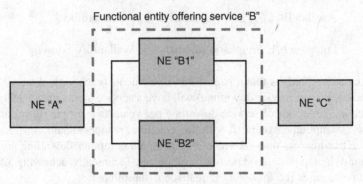

Figure 6.1. Generic high availability model.

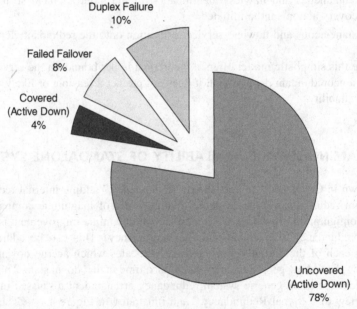

Figure 6.2. Sample unavailability contribution for active–standby redundancy.

is in standby, rather than having load distributed across both "B1" and "B2." The example further assumes that "B1" is configured with internal active–standby redundancy; the assumption of active–standby redundancy simplifies the example by eliminating the need to consider prorating capacity loss for failures within element "B1." The example assumes the active–standby example and modeling results from Section 3.2.2, "Modeling Active Standby Redundancy"; Figure 6.2 visualizes the downtime predicted in Table 3.4 of Section 3.2.2 "Modeling Active Standby Redundancy." Note that since service is not impacted in the "standby down uncovered" state, time spent in state 3 of Figure 3.10 is not counted as downtime. Below, we consider the feasibility of mitigating each category of predicted downtime for network element "B1" via recovery to redundant element "B2."

- *Uncovered (Active Down) Downtime—Nominally 78% of Downtime.* Uncovered (a.k.a., undetected, silent, sleeping) failures generally contribute the majority of service downtime because internal redundancy and high-availability mechanisms cannot mitigate downtime if they are not even activated, and if the system is unaware that it has failed, then a failover won't be initiated. As the primary system itself is unaware of the failure, it is possible that the primary system will continue to report that it is fully operational to the redundant system, so the redundant system will not promptly take any recovery action. Likewise, the human maintenance engineers are not likely to quickly become aware of the uncovered failure because the system itself does not raise a critical alarm (because it does not realize it has failed). Thus, neither system-driven nor manually controlled georedundant recovery are likely to dramatically reduce uncovered downtime. In contrast, clients attempting to access the service are likely to detect the failure promptly via either explicit failure responses (e.g., "503 Service Unavailable") or via expiration of protocol timers. Hence, client-initiated recovery should promptly recognize an uncovered down state and thus can rapidly initiate a recovery action, thereby somewhat mitigating uncovered downtime.
- *Covered Failure Downtime—Nominally 4% of Downtime.* Covered failures represent the downtime associated with successful operation of high-availability mechanisms: the failure was detected, diagnosed, and recovered automatically as designed. For system "B1" to reduce covered service downtime, service recovery onto redundant system "B2" must be faster than service recovery onto the internally operational redundant module in system "B1." In addition, the collateral service impact of switchover to "B2" and eventual switchback to "B1" must be no greater than for a local recovery and repair of "B1" alone. In most cases, covered failures are addressed with less overall service disruption by internal redundancy mechanisms than by georedundant recovery because the target system generally detects the failure before other systems or most clients, and internal service recovery in many cases is faster than having clients connect, reauthenticate, and retry a service request to a georedundant system.
- *Failed (Automatic, Internal) Failover Downtime—Nominally 8% of Downtime.* If an internal (to "B1") failover fails, then additional time and often manual effort is required to clear the failure(s) and recover service onto "B1." Since a failed automatic failover should raise a critical alarm, it is typically recovered via manual action of a human maintenance engineer; that human engineer theoretically has the option of either first continuing to attempt to recover service onto the failed primary system "B1," or focusing on recovering service onto georedundant system "B2" first and then debugging "B1" on a nonemergency basis after service has been restored onto "B2." Factors like typical overall service restoration latency and enterprise policy are likely to influence the decision of the

maintenance engineers on whether they immediately attempt manual georedundant recovery following failed automatic internal recovery, or if they try to manually recover service on "B1" instead. System-driven mechanisms may explicitly or eventually recognize failed automatic, internal recoveries, and thus it is theoretically possible that system-driven recovery can provide automatic recovery when internal recovery fails. Note that it is important to align policies for automatic system-driven recovery and manual recovery to avoid man and machine interfering with each other in service recovery. Client-initiated recovery mitigates time spent in this state because the client will autonomously attempt to recover to an alternate server after a period of server unavailability, regardless of the status of the service recovery of the primary system. Client-initiated recovery does not trigger recovery of the failed element, and thus does not interfere with its recovery.

- *Duplex Failure Downtime—Nominally 10% of Downtime.* Duplex failures can be directly mitigated via georedundancy, provided the georedundant switchover can be completed faster than a manual repair of a duplex (internal) failure. Since a manual repair of a duplex failure is inherently more complicated to troubleshoot and repair than a simplex failure, it is likely to take somewhat longer than a typical manual repair time to recover a standalone system that has experienced a duplex failure.

Table 6.1 summarizes the typical theoretical benefit of each category of georedundant recovery. Both manually controlled and system-driven recovery can nominally

TABLE 6.1. Mitigation of Service Downtime by Georedundancy Recovery Category

Service Downtime Category	Sample Percentage of Downtime	Addressable via Manually Controlled Georedundant Recovery	Addressable via System-Driven Georedundant Recovery	Addressable via Client-Initiated Georedundant Recovery
Uncovered downtime	78	No	Maybe	**Yes**
Failed automatic internal downtime	8	**Yes**	Yes	**Yes**
Covered downtime	4	No	No	No
Duplex (internal) failure downtime	10	**Yes**	Yes	**Yes**
Maximum feasible availability improvement compared to standalone sample system		18%	Between 18% and 96%	96%

mitigate approximately a fifth of internally redundant system downtime (i.e., failed failover and duplex failure downtime), and client-initiated recovery can nominally mitigate the vast majority of service downtime compared with standalone high-availability system deployments (i.e., uncovered failure as well as failed failover and duplex failure downtime).

Note that this example (i.e., the example from Section 3.2.2, "Modeling Active Standby Redundancy") assumes a failure coverage factor of 90%, which drove the uncovered downtime to be 78% of overall downtime. If the coverage factor were higher, then the predicted uncovered failure downtime would be lower; likewise, if the system had lower failure coverage factor (e.g., because it is new and/or has completed insufficient robustness testing), then the uncovered downtime prediction could be even higher.

The maximum feasible availability improvement for system-driven recovery will vary based largely on the effectiveness of the mechanism for the redundant system detecting uncovered failures of the primary system. These back-of-the-envelope upper bound estimates are refined by architecture-based Markov models of georedundant recovery presented later in this chapter.

6.3 GENERIC MARKOV AVAILABILITY MODEL OF GEOREDUNDANT RECOVERY

This section presents a continuous-time Markov model of the service availability of a georedundant system that considers four general recovery options:

1. Standalone internal high-availability recovery without georedundancy
2. Manually controlled georedundant recovery
3. System-driven georedundant recovery
4. Client-initiated georedundant recovery

6.3.1 Simplifying Assumptions

The georedundancy modeling in this chapter makes the following assumptions:

1. *Partial capacity loss outages are not considered* because simple all-or-nothing georedundant recovery is not necessarily the right option for partial capacity loss outages, since users not impacted by the primary failure may be impacted by the georedundancy failover and perhaps the eventual georedundant switch-back. In particular, standalone systems that support $N + K$ internal redundancy (e.g., using a load balancer to distribute load over a pool of processors in a single logical system) might have complex recovery strategies in which some partial capacity outages are mitigated by the standalone system itself, while other outages are addressed via georedundant recoveries. Thus, while

application-specific handling of partial outages can be modeled, for simplicity, this chapter ignores partial capacity outages.

2. *Partial functionality loss outages are not considered* because decisions to mitigate partial functionality loss events are inherently complex since those decisions must weigh the overall service impact on users of switching to a georedundant server, and eventually switching back, against the impact of the partial functionality loss.

3. *Service migrates from the georedundant server back to the original server* after the primary ("B1") server is repaired. While applications and systems can be configured so that georedundant servers can carry traffic indefinitely and thereby eliminate the need for a service migration state, many enterprises will designate primary servers for users and will migrate users back to those servers when feasible.

6.3.2 Standalone High-Availability Model

Real instances of critical enterprise systems often include some internal redundancy. From an external perspective, there is generally no practical difference between the different internal redundancy schemes. Thus, the generic georedundant model is built on the generic model of single (i.e., primary) system service availability shown in Figure 6.3. This simplified model can cover internally nonredundant systems (described in Section 3.1.1, "Simplex Configuration"), systems with internal active–active redundancy (described in Section 3.2.1, "Modeling Active–Active Redundancy"), systems with internal active–standby redundancy (described in Section 3.2.2, "Modeling Active Standby Redundancy"), or a combination of internal redundancy arrangements.

The simplified standalone high-availability downtime model of Figure 6.3 has five states:

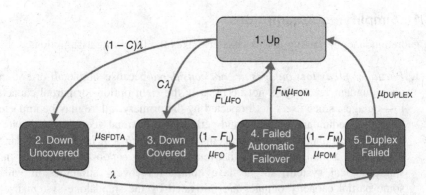

Figure 6.3. Simplified standalone high-availability downtime model.

- State 1 "Up" captures the time that the system is available for service. A critical system failure causes a transition to either state 2 "Down Uncovered" or to state 3 "Down Covered."
- State 2 "Down Uncovered" captures the time that service is unavailable, yet the failure has not been detected by the system itself, so internal high-availability mechanisms are not activated to initiate automatic recovery. The system typically leaves this state by eventually detecting the failure and transitioning to state 3 "Down Covered," but it is theoretically possible that a second critical system failure occurs, which causes a transition to state 5 "Duplex Failed."
- State 3 "Down Covered" captures the state after a critical failure is detected and the system activates high-availability mechanisms to recover service internally. The system typically leaves this state by a successful automatic recovery that transitions back to state 1 "Up." Unsuccessful automatic recoveries cause transition to state 4 "Failed Failover." While it is theoretically possible that a second critical failure occurs after the failure is detected (and hence state 3 is entered) and before the automatic failover time (μ_{FO}) elapses, this is so unlikely that the transition from state 3 to state 5 "Duplex Failed" is ignored.
- State 4 "Failed (Local) Failover" captures the dual failure situation of a critical failure followed by a failed internal automatic recovery action, like a failed internal (local) failover. Service can be restored by manual actions, thus returning the system to state 1 "Up." If, however, the initial manual recovery fails, then the system transitions to state 5 "Duplex Failed" from which more extensive and time consuming manual repair is required.
- State 5 "Duplex Failed" captures the complex failure scenario of at least two critical failures or a failed internal (local) failover followed by an initially unsuccessful manual recovery. Manual recovery will, of course, eventually be successful, but this state captures the extra time that is required to repair complex dual failures and restore service.

As explained in Section 6.3.1, "Simplifying Assumptions," this simplified model does not consider partial capacity loss or partial functionality loss downtime. If necessary, one might expand this simplified model to include a simplified partial outage state that is not mitigated by georedundant recovery. If any partial outages are mitigated by georedundancy, then an appropriate mitigateable partial outage state can be added alongside the unmitigateable partial outage state.

The transitions between the states in Figure 6.3 are mathematically modeled with the following parameters:

- λ—Failure Rate—gives the rate of service impacting failures on the standalone network element. This parameter explicitly includes both hardware and software attributed failures. Hardware failure rates are typically expressed as either mean time between failures (MTBF) or as failures per billion hours of operation (FIT). Software failure rates are often expressed as critical failures (e.g., crashes or failovers) per system per year. System failure rate aggregates both critical hardware and critical software failure rates.

- C—Failure Coverage Factor—gives the probability that a service impacting failure is automatically detected and isolated within a specified time (nominally $1/\mu_{FO}$). Note that "isolated" means that the system correctly diagnoses the failure to the active side, rather than reporting that the failure is on another element or on the standby side. Obviously, a diagnostic failure that indicts the wrong recoverable unit will prompt the system to activate automatic recovery of the wrong module, which will not restore service.

- μ_{FO}—Automatic Failover (or Takeover) Rate—characterizes how fast the system automatically detects failures and fails service over to an internally redundant unit to restore service. In this example, time is assumed to include failure detection and isolation latency, as well as failover latency. Since the rate is the mathematical reciprocal of the duration, $\mu_{FO} = 1/\text{typical\_automatic\_takeover\_duration} = 1/(\text{typical\_failure\_detection\_time} + \text{typical\_failover\_duration})$.

- μ_{FOM}—Manual Failover Rate. If automatic failover does not complete successfully, then manual intervention by a human operator is required; this parameter estimates the rate of a "typical" manual recovery. Since the rate is the mathematical reciprocal of the duration, $\mu_{FOM} = 1/\text{typical\_manual\_failover\_duration}$. The human operator will generally wait significantly longer than the typical automatic failover time to give the system sufficient opportunity to recover automatically. If the system does not automatically recover in a reasonable length of time, then the human operator will manually debug the failure(s), identify an appropriate recovery action, and manually initiate recovery action. Occasionally, the human operator will misdiagnose the problem, or other factors will complicate the manual recovery, so manual recoveries will sometimes take longer. Note that availability models generally use "typical" or median value estimates rather than worst-case values; assuming "median" values are used, half of the manual failovers will be faster (better) and half will be slower (worse). Failures that are "hard" and take significantly longer than typical manual failover duration are addressed by transitioning the system to state 6 "Duplex (Primary) Failed" which assumes that an additional $1/\mu_{DUPLEX}$ time is required to recover service.

- μ_{DUPLEX}—Duplex Failure Repair Rate. This parameter estimates the mathematical reciprocal of the typical time to recover from so-called "duplex failure" in which both active and standby units have failed (i.e., $\mu_{DUPLEX} = 1/\text{duplex\_failure\_repair\_time}$). While the time to repair a single field replaceable unit (FRU) is likely to be the same if one FRU or two FRUs have failed, the time to repair a duplex software failure or to repair the software portion of a hybrid hardware plus software failures is likely to be longer than the simplex repair rate for software.

- μ_{SFDTA}—Uncovered Silent Failure Detection Rate. This parameter estimates the mathematical reciprocal of the typical time to detect a service impacting uncovered failure. Operationally, if the system fails to automatically detect a failure, then eventually the failure will be manually detected by a human operator, alarmed by adjacent systems, or reported by end users.

- F_L—Automatic Local Failover Success Probability. Automatic internal failover is a complex operation, and occasionally service will not failover successfully; this parameter estimates the probability that automatic failover will succeed.

- F_M—Manual Local Failover Success Probability. Troubleshooting failures that were not properly recovered automatically by the system will take diligent effort by a maintenance engineer and will typically take the time estimated as the mathematical reciprocal of μ_{FOM} (manual failover rate). This parameter (F_M) estimates the probability that manual recovery actions will successfully restore service in approximately the typical manual recovery time ($1/\mu_{FOM}$). "Hard" problems may take significantly longer than this typical time. One minus manual failover success probability ($1 - F_M$) events will be "hard" and take substantially longer than the typical manual failover latency. For simplicity, the additional latency for "hard" problems is assumed to be the same as the duplex failure recovery time ($1/\mu_{DUPLEX}$).

6.3.3 Manually Controlled Georedundant Recovery

The simplified high-availability system downtime model of Figure 6.3 can be slightly expanded into Figure 6.4 to consider typical georedundant recovery by adding three additional states:

- State 6—"Up on Georedundant"—which represents the "up" state when service has been recovered onto the georedundant system via either manually driven, server-controlled or client-initiated georedundant recovery. Note that one assumes that after a period of $1/\mu_{GRECOVER}$, service is transitioned back to state 1 "Up on

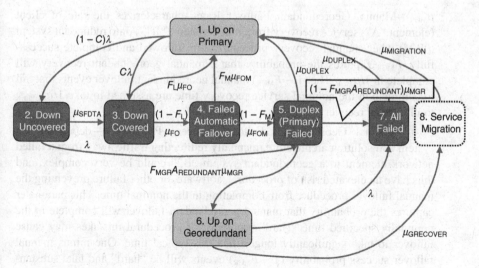

Figure 6.4. General georedundant manual recovery Markov transition diagram.

Primary." The model assumes that service reverts back to state 1 "Up on Primary" via state 8 "Service Migration" so that any service impact on migration can be properly estimated.

- State 7—"All Failed"—represents multiple failure scenarios in which both the primary "B1" is down and the recovery to the georedundant system "B2" has failed, and thus a significant repair time (assumed to be $1/\mu_{\text{DUPLEX}}$, the same time expected to bring service back up on primary system after a duplex failure of that system) is required to restore service on the primary system. In practice, maintenance engineers may find it more expedient to repair and restore service onto "B2" first rather than necessarily repairing "B1" first. Thus, logically, there is a potential transition from state 7 "All Failed" to state 6 "Up on Georedundant," but for simplicity, the model assumes that all manual recoveries of duplex failures transition directly to state 1 "Up on Primary."

- State 8—"Service Migration" represents the orderly service transition from one system "B2" (e.g., georedundant) to another system "B1" (e.g., primary). $1/\mu_{\text{MIGRATION}}$ represents the time that service is impacted on an orderly service migration. Systems that experience service disruption during migration will count time in this state as "down" (unavailable); systems that experience no service impact during migration will count time in this state as "up." Because the service migration state may count as either uptime or downtime, based on characteristics of the target system, the state is drawn differently from traditional "up" or "down" states in the following Figure 6.4 and other Markov transition diagrams.

Manually controlled georedundant recovery adds the following modeling parameters:

- μ_{MGR}—Manual Georedundant Failover Rate—characterizes the rate of client (element "A") service recovery from failed system ("B1") onto redundant system ("B2") when manual recovery procedures are followed and complete successfully. F_{MGR} captures the probability that a manual georedundant recovery will complete in $1/\mu_{\text{MGR}}$. The $(1 - F_{\text{MGR}})$ manual georedundant failover events that fail to complete in the nominal service recovery time are assumed to take $1/\mu_{\text{DUPLEX}}$ to ultimately recover service.

- F_{MGR}—Manual Georedundant Failover Success Probability—depending on system and solution architecture, manually redirecting traffic away from a failed network element to a georedundant system "B2" could be very complex, and thus have an elevated risk of procedural, software, or other failure preventing the manual failover procedure from completing in the nominal time. This parameter captures the probability that manual georedundant failover will complete in the nominally specified time "Hard" problems, or procedural mistakes may cause failover to take significantly longer than this typical time. One minus manual failover success probability $(1 - F_{\text{MGR}})$ events will be "hard" and take substantially longer than the typical manual failover latency. For simplicity, the additional latency for "hard" problems is assumed to be the same as the duplex failure recovery time $(1/\mu_{\text{DUPLEX}})$.

- $A_{\text{REDUNDANT}}$—Service Availability of Redundant External System—captures the probability that the external redundant system will be available to recover service when a failure of the primary system occurs. $A_{\text{REDUNDANT}}$ is typically the same as the standalone server availability when primary and redundant systems are similarly configured. $A_{\text{REDUNDANT}}$ could be higher than the availability of a standalone server if a pool of several active redundant servers is deployed.

Manually controlled switchback adds the following parameters:

- μ_{GRECOVER}—Planned Georedundant Recover Back Rate—characterizes the rate at which service is methodically recovered from the georedundant system "B2" to the (then repaired) primary system "B1." This value is the mathematical reciprocal of the typical time that the georedundant system carries traffic following a failure (rather than following a planned activity). μ_{GRECOVER} is typically much lower (meaning recovery time is longer) than μ_{DUPLEX}, μ_{GR}, μ_{MGR}, μ_{FOM}, or μ_{FO}.
- $\mu_{\text{MIGRATION}}$—Planned Georedundant Migration Disruption Rate—is the mathematical reciprocal of the time that service is disrupted due to an orderly migration of service from georedundant system "B2" to primary system "B1." If traffic migration is nonservice impacting, then this parameter should be set to a large value (e.g., 1/(1 second)), indicating little time is spent in the service migration state.

In manually controlled georedundant recovery (Fig. 6.4), transitions to state 6 "Up on Georedundant" are primarily from state 5 "Duplex (Primary) Failed"—when a human maintenance engineer recognizes that an internal failover on "B1" has failed, they attempt manual recovery of "B1" which fails, and then they initiate a manual georedundant recovery to "B2." The manual georedundant recovery nominally takes $1/\mu_{\text{MGR}}$, and the probability that the manual procedure is successful in that time is F_{MGR}.

Note that manually controlled recovery is NOT initiated from state 2 "Down Uncovered" because the human maintenance engineer is not yet aware that the primary is down and thus does not know to attempt manual recovery. The case in which the system fails to detect its own failure and manual recovery is performed is modeled as an implicit transition from state 2 "Down Uncovered" to state 4 "Failed Automatic Failover" from which manual recovery is attempted. Rather than creating an explicit transition from state 2 to state 4, this scenario is implicitly considered as the failure of automatic internal mechanisms and thus is captured in $(1 - F_{\text{L}})$.

Manually controlled recovery is not attempted from State 3 "Down Covered" because although the primary is down, it is presumed that automatic recovery of the primary will rapidly and automatically complete, and thus manual intervention is not appropriate. Manually controlled georedundant recovery is not modeled from state 4 "Failed Automatic Failover" because the maintenance engineer is likely to attempt manual recovery of the failed primary system before attempting to recover service to the georedundant system.

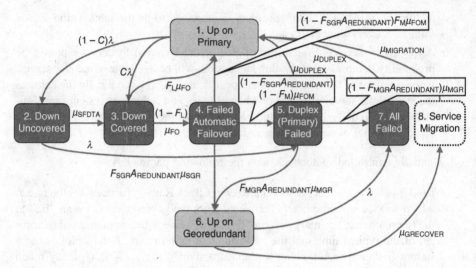

Figure 6.5. System-driven georedundant recovery Markov transition diagram.

6.3.4 System-Driven Georedundant Recovery

System-driven georedundant recovery is illustrated in Figure 6.5. System-driven geo-redundant recovery adds a transition between state 4 "Failed Automatic Failover" and "Up on Georedundant." State 4 "Failed Failover" to state 6 "Up on Georedundant" transitions at the, presumably faster, rate of μ_{SGR} for automatic recovery rather than the slower μ_{MGR} rate for manual recovery. Likewise, the probability of successful automatic georedundant recovery is given by F_{SGR} rather than by the manual recovery parameter F_{MGR}. While it is possible for manually controlled georedundancy to backup automatic system-driven recovery, human maintenance engineers are likely to wait longer—perhaps significantly longer—before initiating manual georedundant recovery than when automatic system-driven recovery is enabled to minimize the risk of outage prolonging complications caused by interference between simultaneous (and possibly conflicting) automatic system-driven and manually controlled georedundant recoveries. As system-driven recovery mechanisms rely on redundant systems periodically check-ing with the active system to determine if the active is operational, there is a clear risk that a failure of the primary system that is uncovered (i.e., undetected) by the primary system may not be obvious to the redundant system. For example, if the redundant system tests availability of the primary by verifying correct and timely response to a heartbeat message, then if the primary has experienced a critical failure that it is unaware of, then the primary is likely to respond to periodic heartbeat messages from the redundant server with "I'm OK" messages, and thus the redundant server will not be explicitly made aware of the uncovered failure of the primary system. System-driven recovery should be designed to give the primary system time to take automatic internal recovery actions before a failover to the alternate system is attempted, and thus system-driven recovery should not affect state 3 "Down Covered."

Note that this simplified model assumes that the primary server is more likely to detect its failures than the redundant server, and hence the model can ignore the possibility of system-driven recovery from state 2 "Down Uncovered" directly to state 6 "Up on Georedundant." If the redundant system is likely to automatically recover service directly from uncovered primary down situations (i.e., state 2), then a more elaborate model that carefully considers the interactions of imperfect local coverage by the primary system and better external coverage and recovery must be considered.

System-driven georedundancy adds the following modeling parameters:

- μ_{SGR}—Automatic System-Driven Georedundant Failover (or Takeover) Rate. $(1/\mu_{SGR})$ characterizes how fast client service (from "A") is recovered following system ("B1") failure onto the georedundant system ("B2") via system-driven recovery. This time is assumed to include failure detection and isolation latency, as well as failover latency.

- F_{SGR}—Automatic System-Driven Georedundant Failover Success Probability. Automatic georedundant failover can be a complex operation, and occasionally service will not failover to "B2" successfully; this parameter estimates the probability that automatic failover to "B2" will succeed.

6.3.5 Client-Initiated Georedundancy Recovery

Client-initiated georedundant recovery is illustrated in Figure 6.6. The key difference on the client-initiated diagram (Fig. 6.6) compared with the manually controlled

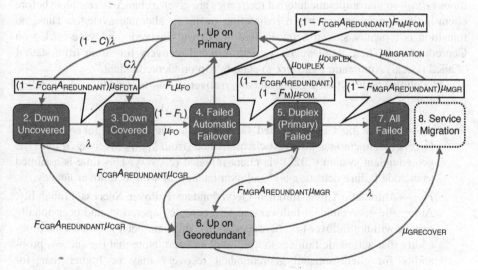

Figure 6.6. Client-initiated georedundant recovery Markov transition diagram.

diagram (Fig. 6.4) is the addition of a transition from state 2 "Down Uncovered" to state 6 "Up on Georedundant." Because the client system "A" interacts directly with the primary system "B1," it performs an operational test of "B1's" availability every time it attempts to interact with "B1." Fundamentally, if "B1" responds properly to client "A," then "B1" is effectively "up"; if "B1" does not respond to client "A" before the protocol timeout expires, then "B1" might be unavailable. If "B1" does not respond to one or more retransmitted requests, then "B1" is effectively unavailable to "A," presumably either because "B1" is down or because IP networking facilities or equipment linking "A" with "B1" are impacted. $1/\mu_{CGR}$ represents the time for client "A" to both detect unavailability of primary server "B1" and to complete the service recovery onto georedundant system "B2." Note that this model assumes georedundant system "B2" is fully operational (nominally "active") rather than in a standby state so that "B2" can rapidly process service requests from "A" for client-initiated recovery. F_{CGR} represents the probability that the client-initiated recovery will succeed.

Client-initiated recovery is best implemented when redundant servers are all active. This avoids the awkward uncovered failure situation in which some (or even all) clients detect the failure of the primary server "B1" and automatically attempt to recover to redundant server "B2" before "B2" has been promoted from standby to active. In this case, all of the clients will be denied service because "B2" hasn't yet been promoted to "active" since "B2" is unaware that "B1" has (silently) failed. This model assumes that the redundant server(s) is active, and thus the redundant server should be capable of accepting clients at any time, regardless of whether or not the failure of the primary server was detected/covered by "B1" or "B2," or not.

As the client may be unaware of the distinction between uncovered failures of "B1" and covered failures of "B1," there is logically a transition from state 3 "Down Covered" to state 6 "Up on Georedundant." To avoid excessive session churn, one typically sets client-driven recovery timeouts to be longer than typical internal recovery takeover times ($1/\mu_{FO}$) so that automatic internal recoveries are given a chance to complete before client-initiated mechanisms begin redirecting traffic to alternate systems. Thus, no transition is typically shown between state 3 "Down Covered" and state 6 "Up on Georedundant." There is, however, a client-initiated recovery transition from state 4 "Failed (Local) Automatic Failover" to state 6 "Up on Georedundant."

Modeling client-initiated georedundant recovery adds two additional modeling parameters:

- μ_{CGR}—Automatic Client-Initiated Georedundant Failover (or Takeover) Rate. ($1/\mu_{CGR}$) characterizes how fast client service (from "A") is recovered onto the georedundant system ("B2") via client-initiated recovery. This time is assumed to include failure detection and isolation latency, as well as failover latency.

- F_{CGR}—Automatic Client-Initiated Georedundant Failover Success Probability. Automatic georedundant failover can be a complex operation, and occasionally service will not failover to "B2" successfully; this parameter estimates the probability that automatic failover to "B2" will succeed. Note that the success probability for client-initiated georedundant recovery may be higher than for system-driven georedundant recovery because:

1. Client-initiated recovery may be similar—or even identical—to normal client logon to a server, and thus the probability of success for recovering to a redundant server "B2" may be comparable to the probability of successfully connecting to primary server "B1."

2. It is often simpler for a client to failover than for a server to direct and coordinate a failover of all the clients.

In the simplified model, F_{CGR} includes the case in which client recovery is not even attempted because the server masked the true nature of the failure from the client. Assume that when the primary server fails, it should return "server error" to the client to announce its unavailability; if the server experiences a secondary failure(s)—perhaps a residual defect in a leg of error code—and returns an incorrect error code, such as "format error" or "not implemented," then the client will be unaware of the true failure and not initiate recovery actions.

6.3.6 Complex Georedundant Recovery

Systems can be designed to support both client-initiated and system-driven georedundancy, both of which are backed up by manually controlled georedundant recovery. Assuming the redundant external system is active, this is modeled by augmenting the client-initiated recovery model of Figure 6.6 with a logical system-driven transition from state 4 "Failed Automatic Failover" to state 6 "Up on Georedundant," as shown in Figure 6.7. Note that this system-driven recovery applied only to the portion of traffic that was not successfully recovered via client-initiated mechanisms; mathematically

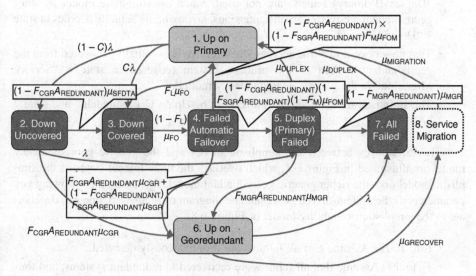

Figure 6.7. Client-initiated and system-driven georedundant recovery.

this is modeled by increasing the rate of state 4 "Automatic Failed Failover" to state 6 "Up on Georedundant" transitions by

$$(1 - F_{CGR} \times A_{REDUNDANT}) \times F_{SGR} \times A_{REDUNDANT} \times \mu_{SGR}.$$

If the redundant external system is normally in standby rather than active, then more complex modeling should be used to account for the situation in which clients attempt to recover to the redundant system before it has been promoted to active status. As configurations that support simultaneous automatic system-driven and client-initiated recovery to external systems are inherently complex, tailored modeling should be used to correctly capture the interactions between the various recovery mechanisms that are presumably operating both autonomously and nominally simultaneously.

6.3.7 Comparing the Generic Georedundancy Model to the Simplistic Model

Given the generic georedundancy model earlier in this section, it is easy to see how the simplistic model presented in Section 6.1 is unrealistic. The simplistic model assumes:

- That all failures are covered, and hence state 2 "Down Uncovered" is irrelevant; all failures transition to state 3 "Down Covered."
- That all of these covered failures are recovered onto the georedundant system; hence the new transition between state 3 "Down Covered" and state 6 "Up on Georedundant."
- That all failovers are successful, and hence state 4 "Failed Failover" and state 5 "Duplex (Primary) Failed" are not used. Since the simplistic model assumes georedundant recoveries are instantaneous, no downtime actually accrues in state 3 "Down Covered."
- That no service downtime accrues when service is eventually recovered from the georedundant system to the primary system (covered in state 8 "Service Migration" in the generic georedundancy model).
- The simplistic model does recognize state 6 "Up on Georedundant" and state 7 "All Failed."

The differences between the simplistic model and the generic georedundancy model are illustrated in Figure 6.8, which overlays the three logical states of the simplistic model onto the richer generic georedundant model. By setting the following key parameters of the system-driven georedundant diagram of Figure 6.5, one can degenerate to the simplistic availability model of Figure 6.8:

- C to 100%. Assume that all failures are instantaneously detected.
- F_L to 0%. Assume that all failures are recovered to redundant systems, and thus that no failures are recovered via internal redundancy mechanisms.

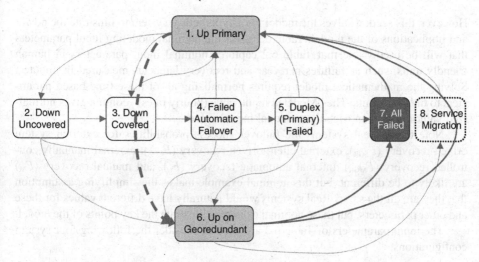

Figure 6.8. Overlaying generic georedundancy model onto simplistic model.

- $(1/\mu_{FO})$ to 0. Assume no time is required for automatic local recovery because automatic local recovery is not attempted (per $F_L = 0$ assumption).
- F_{SGR} to 100%. Assume that all system-driven georedundant recoveries are successful.
- $(1/\mu_{SGR})$ to 0. Assume system-driven georedundant recovery is instantaneous.
- Service migration is not service affecting and instantaneous, and thus state 8 "Service Migration" can be neglected.

Figure 6.8 makes it clear that the simplistic model is actually estimating only the smallest portion of service downtime that is likely to occur in actual georedundant system operation.

6.4 SOLVING THE GENERIC GEOREDUNDANCY MODEL

The generic georedundancy model can be mathematically solved via continuous-time Markov modeling. Interestingly, by setting F_{MGR}, F_{SGR} and F_{CGR} to 0, one can prevent the model from transitioning to state 6 "Up on Georedundant" or state 7 "All Failed" and indirectly preventing access to state 8 "Service Migration," and thus the model degenerates to the standard high availability model presented in Section 6.2, "Framing Service Availability of Standalone." Likewise, setting F_{CGR} to 0 disables client-initiated recovery; setting F_{SGR} to 0 disables system-driven recovery and setting F_{MGR} to 0 disables manual georedundant recovery.

All systems will have different critical failure rates, failure coverage factors, and other local and georedundancy-related recovery parameters, and thus it is infeasible to provide generic predictions of the service availability benefit of georedundancy.

However, this section solves the model for a hypothetical system to illustrate the power and implications of the model. Table 6.2 gives the nominal modeling input parameters that will be used. Note that Table 6.2 captures nominal input parameters in human friendly units, such as failures per year and recovery latencies measured in minutes. Solving the mathematical model requires normalizing all of these time-based parameters to the same units. The "Modeled input value (hourly rates)" column gives normalized values of human friendly "nominal input" values.

Note that in real systems the failover success probabilities for external system driven-recovery (F_{SGR}), external client driven recovery (F_{CGR}), external manually controlled recovery (F_{MGR}), internal automatic recovery (F_L), and manual recovery (F_M) are likely to be different, but this nominal example makes the simplifying assumption that they are all the same. Real systems would naturally have different values for these and other parameters, but these nominal examples illustrate the key points of the model.

The input parameters of Table 6.2 are used to consider the following four system configurations:

- *Standalone* for a single network element. This prediction is mathematically produced by setting F_{MGR}, F_{SGR}, and F_{CGR} to 0, thus preventing the model from transitioning to state 6 "Up on Georedundant" or state 7 "All Failed" and indirectly preventing access to state 8 "Service Migration."
- *Manual-controlled georedundant recovery* for a configuration with two systems ("B1" and "B2") in which the primary system "B1" is protected by manually controlled georedundant recovery to "B2." This prediction is mathematically produced by setting F_{SGR} and F_{CGR} to 0, thereby disabling access to georedundant states 6 "Up on Georedundant," state 7 "All Failed" and state 8 "Service Migration."
- *System-driven georedundant recovery* for a configuration with two elements in which the primary element "B1" is protected by automatic system-driven recovery to "B2." Both automatic local and system-driven georedundant recoveries are backed up by manually controlled georedundant recovery to "B2." This prediction is mathematically produced by setting F_{CGR} to 0, thereby excluding any client-initiated recovery.
- *Client-initiated georedundant recovery* for a configuration with two elements in which the primary element "B1" is protected by automatic client-initiated recovery to "B2." Both automatic local and client-initiated georedundant recoveries are backed up by manually controlled georedundant recovery to "B2." This prediction is mathematically produced by setting F_{SGR} to 0, thereby excluding any system-driven recovery.
- *Client plus server georedundant recovery* for a configuration in which client-initiated recover is backed up by both system-driven and manually controlled georedundant recovery.

Table 6.3 summarizes the predicted time spent in each of the down states, as well as the service availability and the predicted time that service will be up on the

TABLE 6.2. Nominal Modeling Parameters and Values

Description	Symbol	Nominal Unit	Nominal Input	Modeled Input Value (hourly rates)
Failure rate	λ	System fails per year	4	0.000456308
Failure coverage factor	C	Percentage successful	90%	90%
Availability of redundant element	$A_{\text{REDUNDANT}}$	Percentage service is available	99.997%	99.997%
Automatic failover (or takeover) rate	μ_{FO}	Median minutes to complete automatic local failover	0.17	360
Manual failover rate	μ_{FOM}	Median minutes to complete manual local failover	30.00	2
Duplex failure repair rate	μ_{DUPLEX}	Median hours to complete repair of duplex failure	4.00	0.25
Uncovered silent failure detection rate	μ_{SFDTA}	Median minutes to detect silent failure	30.00	2
Automatic local failover success probability	F_{L}	Percentage successful	99%	99%
Manual local failover success probability	F_{M}	Percentage successful	99%	99%
Manual georedundant failover rate	μ_{MGR}	Median minutes to complete manual GR failover	60.00	1.00
Manual georedundant failover success probability	F_{MGR}	Percentage successful	99%	99.0%
Planned georedundant recover back rate	μ_{GRECOVER}	Median hours to complete planned manual GR switchback	24.00	0.04
Planned georedundant migration disruption rate	$\mu_{\text{MIGRATION}}$	Median minutes of service disruption for orderly GR switchback	0.250	240
Automatic system-driven georedundant failover (or takeover) rate	μ_{SGR}	Median minutes to complete system-driven GR failover	5.00	12.00

(*Continued*)

TABLE 6.2. *Continued*

Description	Symbol	Nominal Unit	Nominal Input	Modeled Input Value (hourly rates)
Automatic system-driven georedundant failover success probability	F_{SGR}	Percentage successful	90%	90.0%
Automatic client-initiated georedundant failover (or takeover) rate	μ_{CGR}	Median minutes to complete client-initiated GR failover	1.00	60.00
Automatic client-initiated georedundant failover success probability	F_{CGR}	Percentage successful	98%	98.0%

georedundant system based on input parameters given in Table 6.2. These results are discussed in detail in the following sections.

6.4.1 Manually Controlled Georedundant Recovery Model

Table 6.3 shows that manually controlled georedundant recovery reduces the duplex (primary) downtime by more than an order of magnitude. However, since duplex (primary) downtime represented only about 1% of predicted downtime for the standalone system, *manually controlled georedundant recovery offers minimal improvement in predicted product attributed service downtime.* As a reminder, the reasons that manually controlled georedundant recovery is unlikely to mitigate other standalone system downtime are as follows:

- Uncovered downtime is not addressed by manual recovery because, by definition, uncovered downtime is unknown to both the system and the human maintenance engineer, and thus it is infeasible to initiate manual recovery from an event that is unknown to the maintenance engineer.
- Covered downtime represents the time spent by the standalone system to automatically detect, isolate, and recover from a failure. Since successful automatic detection, isolation and recovery is inherently faster than manually controlled recovery, there is no benefit to tampering with this category.
- Failed automatic failover downtime is typically mitigated by manually recovering service on the primary system itself, rather than executing a manual georedundant switchover because manual recovery of standalone is likely to be faster and less disruptive to the overall network, and there is no risk of eventual downtime when service is eventually migrated back to the primary system.

TABLE 6.3. Nominal Modeling Results Summary

Downtime	Standalone System		Manual Controlled Georedundant Recovery		System-Driven (plus Manually Controlled) Georedundant Recovery		Client-Initiated (plus Manually Controlled) Georedundant Recovery		Client plus System (plus Manually Controlled) Georedundant Recovery	
	Minutes	Percent	Minutes	Percent	Minutes	Percent	Minutes	Percent	Minutes	Percent
Down uncovered	11.997	85.81%	11.997	86.38%	11.996	92.29%	0.407	17.85%	0.407	17.85%
Down covered	0.667	4.77%	0.667	4.80%	0.667	5.13%	0.599	26.26%	0.599	26.26%
Failed automatic failover	1.200	8.58%	1.200	8.64%	0.218	1.68%	0.037	1.61%	0.037	1.60%
Duplex (primary) failed	0.118	0.84%	0.024	0.17%	0.005	0.04%	0.000	0.01%	0.000	0.01%
All failed	0.000	0.00%	0.002	0.01%	0.102	0.79%	1.131	49.57%	1.131	49.57%
Service migration	0.000	0.00%	0.000	0.00%	0.010	0.07%	0.108	4.71%	0.108	4.72%
Total annualized downtime	13.981	100.00%	13.889	100.00%	12.997	100.00%	2.283	100.00%	2.283	100.00%
Service availability	99.9973%		99.9974%		99.9975%		99.9996%		99.9996%	
Uptime on georedundant system	0.000		0.554		56.042		619.885		619.916	

6.4.2   System-Driven Georedundant Recovery Model

The prediction shows that system-driven georedundant recovery mitigates much of the failed automatic failover and duplex (primary) failure downtime of standalone deployment. However, since both of these categories combined represented less than 10% of the service downtime of the standalone configuration, system-driven georedundant recovery offered a maximum theoretical improvement of 10%. Imperfect and non-instantaneous recovery to a redundant server that is assumed to have essentially the same service availability as the primary server 99.997% service availability suggests that approximately 7% downtime reduction is likely with system-driven recovery relative to a standalone configuration.

6.4.3   Client-Initiated Georedundant Recovery Model

Client-initiated georedundant recovery provides a major improvement over both system-driven and manually controlled georedundancy and standalone deployment because clients are in a unique position to detect otherwise uncovered failures and promptly initiate recovery actions. While the failed system itself—and thus presumably both the human maintenance engineer and georedundant systems—may not be aware of a silent failure, clients will detect the server's unavailability as commands or keep-alive messages timeout without response or return error responses (e.g., 503 Service Unavailable). Thus, client-initiated recovery can directly address the majority of standalone system downtime that is consumed with uncovered downtime. While it is infeasible to drive uncovered downtime to 0% because some time is required for clients to detect a failure, initiate recovery, and successfully restore service onto a georedundant system, the bulk of uncovered downtime can be mitigated via client-initiated georedundant recovery.

Because client-initiated recovery is more likely to redirect service to the georedundant system rather than waiting for the local system to be recovered or for uncovered failures to be addressed, the georedundant system "B2" spends far more time delivering service to clients than in either manually controlled or system-driven scenarios. Because client-initiated georedundant recoveries are more likely, there are far more transitions through state 8 "Service Migration." The input parameters in Table 6.2 yield a prediction that more downtime will accrue for service migration than for covered failures of the primary system. Obviously, if the system supports nonservice impacting service migration, then "service migration" downtime drops to 0%. The practical importance of nonservice impacting service migration with client-initiated recovery is illustrated by noting that service migration is predicted to contribute about 5% of service downtime in this example.

Using the input parameters in Table 6.2, the model predicts when client-initiated georedundant recovery with nonservice impacting service migration (backed up with manually controlled georedundant recovery), service downtime is reduced by 84% compared with a standalone configuration. While some refinements are possible to further reduce the downtime predicted for client-initiated recovery scenarios, some practical considerations are likely to limit the service availability benefits of georedundancy for partial capacity loss and partial functionality loss outages.

6.4.4 Conclusion

To accrue maximum service availability benefit from georedundant configurations, client elements should explicitly be involved in automatic failure detection and recovery.

6.5 PRACTICAL MODELING OF GEOREDUNDANCY

While the generic georedundancy model enables one to compare and contrast idealized recovery behavior to characterize the maximum feasible availability benefit of manually controlled, system-driven and client-initiated recovery strategies relative to a stand-alone configuration, it is not ideal for estimating the likely service availability of a specific recovery strategy for a specific system. The generic model is unnecessarily complicated in most cases because the majority of systems that support external recovery will use either:

- Manually controlled recovery, only (i.e., primarily for disaster recovery)
- System-driven recovery, backed up with manually controlled recovery
- Client-initiated recovery, backed up with manually controlled recovery

The generic model is inherently suboptimal because the fundamental behaviors of the different recovery strategies have significant differences that are not reflected in the generic model, including:

- *It Does Not Consider Partial Capacity Outages.* Partial capacity outages were excluded from the generic model in part because client-initiated mechanisms inherently view partial capacity outages differently from system-driven and manually controlled recovery. Each individual client has a distinct perspective on whether or not they deem the system to be available, and each client can act individually based on their perceived state of system availability. In contrast, system-driven and manually controlled mechanisms operate at the coarser system level, so careful judgment must be applied to determine when outage extent is so great that system-driven or manually controlled recovery should be activated.

- *It Does Not Consider Partial Functionality Outages.* While it is unlikely that a partial functionality outage would be significant enough to warrant automatic system-driven or manually controlled recovery to an external system, it is easy to imagine a client deeming a failed response to a particular function to be critical and thus triggering client-initiated recovery.

Fortunately, one can degenerate the generic model for common georedundancy recovery strategies to address these limitations. The following sections consider practical modeling of service availability for manually controlled, system-driven and client-initiated georedundant configurations.

6.5.1   Practical Modeling of Manually Controlled External System Recovery

The service availability benefit of manually controlled external recovery is primarily determined by an enterprise's policy regarding when to use manually controlled external recovery. After all, manually controlled external recovery can not provide a benefit for service availability if it is not attempted, and enterprise policy will determine when it is attempted. An enterprise's policy regarding activation of georedundant recovery is generally driven by the following factors:

- *System Behavior.* Manually controlled external recovery is generally an all-or-nothing affair, with 100% of the traffic directed to either the primary system ("B1") or the secondary system ("B2"). Unless system "B1" is completely down, an external switchover will likely impact some users who aren't being impacted by the "B1" failure; thus manually controlled external recovery is not desirable for partial capacity loss or partial functionality loss operations. Eventually traffic is restored from an external system to the repaired primary system "B1," and the nature and duration of service impact when traffic is gracefully migrated back to a repair primary system is also likely to influence an enterprise's policy on use of manually controlled external recovery.

- *Operational Considerations.* Assuming that the primary system has reasonable diagnostics, maintenance engineers may generally find it simpler and faster to diagnose the failure of the primary system and repair it promptly to restore service rather than executing manual external recovery, then repairing the primary system, and finally redirecting service from the georedundant system back to the repaired primary system. If the redundant system is geographically remote, then engineers at the remote site may be required to participate in the recovery (especially if the system is "cold" and must be started up), further increasing operational complexity. In addition, the orderly external system switchback after repair of primary may add another service disruption; the customer impact of the second service disruption will vary based on the service itself.

- *Cost Tradeoffs.* Enterprise policy is likely to be fundamentally driven by business considerations that strive to deliver acceptable service at the lowest cost. Activating and manually switching service to a georedundant system and later switching service back to the repaired primary system obviously requires extra effort by the maintenance engineers—and thus presumably extra cost—compared with simply restoring the primary system.

The result is that enterprises often select a policy that manually controlled georedundant recovery is executed only following a total system outage in which service is not likely to be restored (either manually or automatically) on the primary system within several hours. Enterprises may establish formal or informal guidelines with expectations that if service isn't restored within a fixed time, then outage recovery activities must be escalated, such as to engage the next tier of support and perhaps notify the next level of enterprise management. For example, an enterprise might require local maintenance management to be notified of a total service outage of a critical system when outage duration reaches 15 minutes, and notify higher tiers of enterprise management if the service outage duration stretches to, say, 1 hour, 2 hours, etc. At some point in that escalation timeline, manually controlled georedundant recovery may be approved.

Thus, manually controlled external system recovery is likely to mitigate only total or major service outages that are not recovered fast enough on the primary system for the enterprise. Training and experience of the enterprise's maintenance engineers, as well as the enterprise's operational policies, will drive how long it takes to manually restore service; better run enterprises are likely to be significantly faster than poorly run enterprises. Combining the enterprise's policy on use of manually controlled external recovery with typical outage recovery times for primary systems, one can estimate the percentage of system outages that are candidates to be mitigated with external recovery. Practically, the enterprise's policy on external system recovery is likely to bound the duration of long duration outages by restoring service onto a redundant system.

Figure 6.9 illustrates the challenge of estimating the likely availability benefit of manually controlled external system recovery by considering actual durations of total outages of an internally redundant system operated by a sophisticated enterprise with well-trained staff and good operational policies. Almost half of the recorded outage events were recovered automatically by the system. Manually controlled recovery will not impact those events. Almost another 30% of the outages are recovered locally with some (obviously successful) manual intervention in 10 to 20 minutes. External system redundancy will not impact those events either. The remainder of the events take longer and longer to be recovered, presumably because of complicating factors, such as logistical issues (e.g., delays in assigning the appropriate expert to work the problem), incorrect or misleading diagnostics, failed recovery actions, or other factors. While manually

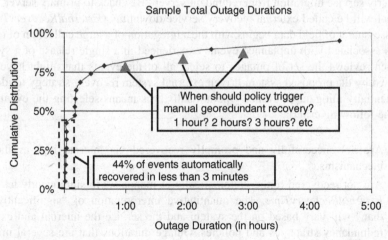

Figure 6.9. Outage durations for sample system with internal redundancy.

controlled external system recovery could theoretically recover service in a deterministic time rather than in the probabilistic outage duration that is typical when recovering from an unplanned outage, there is obviously a risk that given a few more minutes, the primary system might be recovered and thus make the incremental effort and expense of external system switchover and eventual switchback unnecessary.

The enterprises with experienced and well-trained staff and best-in-class policies and procedures are likely to be well equipped to efficiently execute manual external system recovery to address the root causes of long duration outages. Interestingly, these are also the enterprises that are likely to resolve outages requiring manual actions promptly and successfully, thus reducing the portion of outages with prolonged outage durations.

The net result is that manually controlled external system recovery is occasionally able to shorten the duration of a prolonged total or major service outage. It is relatively hard to accurately estimate either the rate of rare events that would qualify for manually controlled external recovery based on a particular enterprise's policies, or how long it would have taken those qualified outages to be repaired locally. Nevertheless, the overall service availability benefit of manually controlled external system recovery is likely to be very small, as suggested by the generic model in Section 6.4.

6.5.2 Practical Modeling of System-Driven Georedundant Recovery

System-driven external system recovery offers some availability improvement beyond manually controlled external system recovery because automatic recovery can replace at least some slow manual recoveries with faster system-driven recoveries, thereby reducing overall service downtime. The incremental availability benefit can be estimated heuristically from field outage data.

A key characteristic for system-driven recovery is the sum of the latency for system-driven recovery mechanism to activate plus the duration of service downtime for orderly service migration from redundant server "B2" back to primary server "B1"; this total will be called external recovery service downtime (*ExternalRecoveryTime*).

Assessment of field data begins with the aggregation of a large collection of outage records associated with unplanned events experienced in a single release of a system. One then reviews the set of outages to select all of the events that might have been addressed by the proposed system-driven external system recovery strategy to identify the potentially mitigatable events. Operationally, this means selecting the events that meet the following criteria:

1. Are not successfully and promptly recovered via internal high-availability mechanisms.
2. Are not recovered (either automatically or manually) in significantly less than *ExternalRecoveryTime*. The quantitative interpretation of "significantly less than" will vary based on the system and the service the internal and external redundancy strategies and policies. Outage durations that are several minutes longer than the time it takes the system to restart are probably candidates for

manual recovery. Ideally, internal high-availability mechanisms would detect all failures in no more than a few minutes with system restart usually being the most extreme automatic recovery action that can be taken by a standalone system. As a practical matter, this generally means selecting events that are longer than a few (perhaps 5) minutes, but the specific time criteria will vary based on system behavior, operational policies (e.g., timeouts, maximum retry counts, etc), and other factors.

3. Are of sufficient capacity loss that they should be mitigated via external recovery.

4. Are of sufficient functionality loss that they should be mitigated via external recovery.

A heuristic estimate of the incremental maximum feasible availability benefit of system-driven external system recovery is estimated by considering what portion of service downtime in the data set could potentially have been mitigated with system-driven georedundant recovery. Thus, one can estimate the upper bound of the percentage reduction of downtime for system-driven recovery with the following formula:

IncrementalBenefit <

$$\left[\frac{TotalDowntime - \sum_{MitigateableEvents} (EventDowntime - ExternalRecoveryTime) \times EventExtent}{TotalDowntime} \right]$$

Equation 6.2. Maximum Feasible Availability Benefit of System-Driven Recovery

Where TotalDowntime is the sum of prorated service downtime, EventDowntime is the actual duration of service disruption, and EventExtent is the capacity or functionality loss prorating of each event. The likely incremental benefit will be less—perhaps significantly less—than this upper bound because:

• Not all automatic system-driven recovery events will succeed.
• Failures that are uncovered (not detected) by the primary system are not necessarily more likely to be detected—and thus mitigated—by the external system.

One can refine the heuristic estimate by applying a success probability factor to the estimated downtime savings for mitigateable events. Presumably, well-designed system-driven recovery mechanisms should be effective in mitigating at least some service downtime for many or most mitigatable events.

6.5.3   Practical Modeling of Client-Initiated Recovery

Assuming first that system-driven recovery will be disabled or offer negligible availability improvement when client-initiated recovery is used, and, second, that the

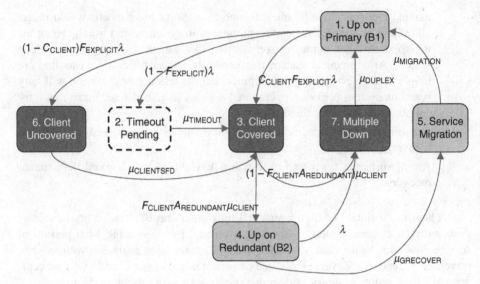

Figure 6.10. Simplified client-initiated recovery Markov model.

fallback option of manually controlled recovery offers negligible availability improvement, one can create the simplified, seven-state client-initiated recovery Markov diagram of Figure 6.10. While state 1 "Up on Primary ('B1')," state 4 "Up on Redundant ('B2')" and state 5 "Service Migration" are logically identical to the states of the same name in the generic recovery model of Figure 6.4, the following new states are created:

- *State 2 "Timeout Pending."* This state captures the time after the client sends a request to primary ("B1") following a critical failure of the primary system when the client hasn't yet decided that the primary system is unavailable. After deciding that the primary system is unavailable, the model transitions to state 3 "Client Covered." Note that the timeout pending state is special because although the primary server is not delivering service to the user, the length of time spent in this state should not exceed the maximum acceptable service disruption latency, and thus this time itself should not count as an outage. However, the sum of the time spent waiting for the request to timeout *plus* the time required for client-initiated recovery to complete may be long enough to be considered chargeable service downtime; for this reason, this state is illustrated differently in Figure 6.10.

- *State 3 "Client Covered."* This state captures the time between the client's determination that the primary server is unavailable and when service is recovered onto the redundant system. This state is reached either from state 1 "Up on Primary" via an explicit error message reporting unavailability, such as session initiation protocol's (SIP's) "503 Service Unavailable" return code, or from state 2 "Timeout Pending" via timeout expiration of retried requests.

- *State 6 "Client Uncovered."* This state captures the time during which the primary is down but the client mistakenly believes that the primary is up. This state is most likely to be reached because the primary system reports failure to the client with an improperly covered error or because of a failure in the client's recovery software. For example, if the primary system experiences a critical failure but maps it to a request failure (e.g., 400 Bad Request, 401 Unauthorized) rather than a service failure that activates client-initiated recovery (e.g., 503 Service Unavailable), then the client will not retry the request against an alternate server; thus the client must wait for the primary server to be recovered automatically or some manual recovery action.
- *State 7 "Multiple Down."* This state captures time when service is unavailable because both the primary ("B1") and redundant ("B2") systems are down.

Note that the simplified model of Figure 6.10 assumes that client-initiated recovery is the only automatic recovery mechanism supported and does not consider automatic, internal recovery of primary system "B1" (which significantly complicates the model). Systems with internal redundancy that operate in parallel with client-initiated recovery can use an enhanced client-initiated recovery model described in Section 6.5.3.1, "Modified Client-Initiated Recovery Model."

The simplified client-initiated recovery Markov model of Figure 6.10 introduces several new modeling parameters:

- F_{EXPLICIT}. This parameter captures the percentage of critical, service impacting failures that are explicitly reported to clients as errors via message responses, rather than being critical failures that result in protocol timeouts to expire in the client.
- C_{CLIENT}. This parameter captures the probability that an error message returned by the primary server following critical failure will cause the client to initiate recovery. For example, if only "500 Server Internal Error" and "503 Service Unavailable" trigger client-initiated recovery, then this parameter gives the probability that a critical failure results in the server sending an error response to the client that in turn causes the client to initiate service recovery to a redundant system. Note that F_{EXPLICIT} estimates the probability of a system experiencing critical failure returning *any* response to the client while C_{CLIENT} estimates the probability that a response returned to the client *triggers* client-initiated recovery actions. Service failure messages returned by primary server following critical failure that do not cause the client to initiate recovery actions are deemed explicitly reported but uncovered.
- $\mu_{\text{CLIENTSFD}}$. ($1/\mu_{\text{CLIENTSFD}}$) estimates the time that a client will take to determine that the primary server is unavailable when the failure is an uncovered failure. Note that the "uncovered" failure may actually be detected by the human user because service is unresponsive or otherwise of unacceptable quality. A user can often trigger a client-initiated recovery by restarting the client application.
- F_{CLIENT}. This parameter captures the probability that client-initiated recovery actions will be successful. Note that the probability of successful client-initiated

recovery is not likely to be as good as the probability that a typical initial server connection/session is established by the client because of:

1. *Increased Risk of Congestion and Overload.* Presumably all active clients will detect a server failure at roughly the same time via either message timeout or explicit failure response, and thus will all attempt client-initiated recovery at approximately the same time. The result is likely to be a spike in connection/session requests to redundant servers by all clients previously served by the failed system seconds after the primary system failure occurs. This traffic spike can cause congestion control mechanisms to activate, thus preventing some clients from immediately recovering service on the redundant system.

2. *Increased Complexity of Client Software Execution.* Software attempting client-initiated recovery must reestablish a session with an alternate system and resynchronize the client's state information with the alternate system. Defects in client software could prevent this from completing successfully, perhaps even requiring the client software to be restarted, reauthenticated and reregistered.

3. *Increased Risk of Server State/Consistency Errors.* The primary server may have exclusively held system resources on behalf of the client (e.g., held or "locked" exclusive access to the user's data or records), and software, architectural, or other defect may prevent a redundant system from promptly reacquiring these resources.

4. *Risk that Redundant Server Is Not Ready to Support Service.* In the case of a standby server taking over traffic for the active server; the client may attempt to recover to the redundant server before the standby has successfully taken over as the active server.

- μ_{CLIENT}. This parameter captures how quickly the typical (i.e., median or 50th percentile) client successfully restores service on a redundant server. The difficulty is that client-initiated recovery is likely to trigger a spike or surge in connection/session requests to alternate systems, which may activate congestion control mechanisms to shape the traffic, and thus the typical service restoration time when the service is under moderate or heavy load may be significantly longer than would be experienced when the system is under light load or when few clients are affected by a failure.

- $\mu_{TIMEOUT}$. This parameter captures how quickly the client times out due to a nonresponsive system, meaning the typical time for the initial request and all subsequent retries to timeout.

The simplified model reuses the following parameters from the generic external redundancy model of Figure 6.4:

- λ. Failure rate gives the rate of service impacting failures on the standalone network element. System failure rate aggregates both critical hardware and critical software failure rates.

- $A_{REDUNDANT}$. This parameter estimates the service availability of the redundant system, (or pool of systems), and hence the probability that a redundant system will be available to accept service when a client initiates a recovery. Typically, $A_{REDUNDANT}$ is the same as the predicted service availability of the primary system ("B1").

- $\mu_{GRECOVER}$—Planned Georedundant Recover Back Rate—characterizes the rate at which service is methodically recovered from the georedundant system "B2" to the (then repaired) primary system "B1." This value is the mathematical reciprocal of the typical time that the georedundant system carries traffic following a failure (rather than following a planned activity). Thus, if the georedundant system carries live traffic for an average of 4 hours following a failure event before traffic is migrated to the repaired primary system, and then $\mu_{GRECOVER}$ would be set to (1/4).

- $\mu_{MIGRATION}$—Planned Georedundant Migration Disruption Rate—is the mathematical reciprocal of the time that service is disrupted due to an orderly migration of service from georedundant system "B2" to primary system "B1"

Characteristics of the service, protocol, and client have major impacts on the likely availability benefit of client-initiated recovery. The Domain Name System (DNS) server and client implementations often leverage client-initiated recovery to maximize service availability and characteristics of the DNS protocol enable client-initiated recovery to offer a significant service availability boost. As DNS is often deployed across a pool of servers with no internal redundancy, the simplified client-initiated recovery model can be used; a complete case study and solution to the client-initiated recovery model for DNS is given in Chapter 8, "Case Study of Client-Initiated Recovery."

6.5.3.1 *Modified Client-Initiated Recovery Model.* A notable simplification of the client-initiated recovery Markov model of Figure 6.10 entails the omission of the automatic internal recovery of the primary server "B1," such as one would expect for a system deployed with internal redundancy. Often, clients will use protocol timeouts and maximum retry counts that permit lost IP packets and brief service disruptions to be overridden. These timeouts and maximum retry counts may be generous to permit systems with internal redundancy to recover internally, and thus not trigger client-initiated mechanisms too quickly. Adding internal automatic recovery of "B1" to the simplified model leads to the following changes:

1. A new state 8 "Primary Down" is added to capture the time that the client is simply waiting for primary "B1" to recover; this recovery rate is captured via the transition from state 8 to state 1 "Up on Primary ('B1')." While state 8 is logically similar to state 7 "Multiple Down," transitions from state 8 "Primary Down" to state 1 "Up on Primary ('B1')" are likely to be faster via automatic internal recovery mechanisms than would normally be expected from the more severe "multiple down" scenario captured by state 7.

2. The transition from state 3 "Client Covered" to state 7 "Multiple Down" in the simplified client-initiated model with rate $(1 - F_{CLIENT}A_{REDUNDANT})\,\mu_{CLIENT}$ is split into two transitions: one to state 7 "Multiple Down," another to state 8 "Primary

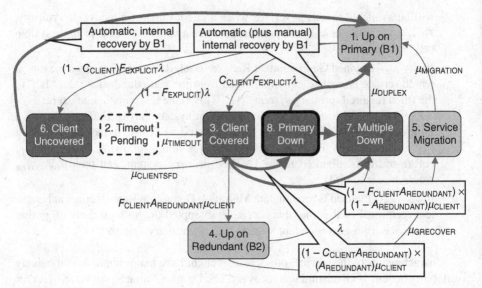

Figure 6.11. Modified client-initiated recovery model.

Down." The dominant transition will be from state 3 "Client Covered" to state 8 "Primary Down" at a rate of $(1 - F_{\text{CLIENT}}A_{\text{REDUNDANT}}) (A_{\text{REDUNDANT}})\mu_{\text{CLIENT}}$. The transition from state 3 "Client Covered" to state 7 "Multiple Down" now captures the much rarer event in which the external redundant system is down at the same time that the primary system is unavailable; this rate is $(1 - F_{\text{CLIENT}}A_{\text{REDUNDANT}}) (1 - A_{\text{REDUNDANT}})\mu_{\text{CLIENT}}$.

3. A transition is added from state 6 "Client Uncovered" to state 1 "Up on Primary ('B1')" to capture successful automatic internal recovery by "B1" before the client has explicitly recognized that the primary is unavailable.

The modified client-initiated recovery model is illustrated in Figure 6.11. Since automatic, internal recovery mechanisms have a variety of behaviors, and the relative timing and interactions of those mechanisms with client-initiated recovery logic will vary from system to system, the model of Figure 6.11 may be tailored or revised to reflect behaviors of specific systems.

6.6 ESTIMATING AVAILABILITY BENEFIT FOR PLANNED ACTIVITIES

Enterprise systems will routinely require planned maintenance actions to upgrade, update, patch, and/or retrofit platform or application software or firmware, grow hardware configurations, replace failed hardware modules, and so on. Some planned maintenance activities can be service impacting even with a robust internal redundancy infrastructure due to the nature of the change being introduced such as physically reconfiguring or relocating a network element or replacing a backplane. When considering leveraging geographic redundancy, one should take into account the expected service downtime and disruption (e.g., data loss or stable session loss) required for a successful maintenance activity, as well as the complexity of the activity and likelihood of success against the same characteristics of the geographic redundancy alternative. If a particular maintenance activity is low risk and entails zero or negligible downtime with no loss of stable sessions, leveraging geographic redundancy may not be useful or desired. However, if there is considerable downtime or risk involved with the maintenance activity, using standard procedures and executing a manually controlled geo-redundancy could be done with less downtime or risk it can provide a good alternative for managing the activity.

Planned maintenance activities are primarily manual activities, and as a result are prone to procedural errors, such as mistyping commands or entering incorrect data. Reducing procedural errors will have a positive impact on the success of the maintenance activity. By gracefully migrating traffic from primary systems to georedundant systems and performing the maintenance actions on an offline system some residual, benefits may be realized, such as:

- Reducing the risk of procedural error by eliminating the stress associated with executing maintenance actions on a "live" system.
- Mitigating the impact associated with any failure experienced during the maintenance action to the offline network element rather than the "live" system.
- Reducing the impact of other asynchronous activities (e.g., backups) negatively impacting the upgrade and the active system.
- Providing a safer environment offline to test and verify that the maintenance activity was successfully performed before activating it.

Thus, both the objective factors, as well as the more subjective ones, need to be taken into account when determining whether to leverage georedundancy for the maintenance activity.

6.7 ESTIMATING AVAILABILITY BENEFIT FOR DISASTERS

Predicting the rate of disasters or force majeure events is beyond the scope of this book. Likewise, this book does not consider the likely effectiveness of the risk reduction techniques that enterprises are likely to deploy to minimize the risk of a disaster event rendering a physical site temporarily inaccessible or unavailable, or even destroyed. Assuming georedundancy was properly engineered and client-initiated or system-driven recovery is used, the recovery time from a disaster should be the same as the recovery time from a critical server failure event.

If manual recovery is used, then the period of unavailability is estimated from the best estimates of recovery objectives described in 1.7 "Disaster Recovery Planning." Figure 6.12 is a simplified version of Figure 1.3 from Section 1.7, which illustrates the period of service unavailability or service impact which is the sum of:

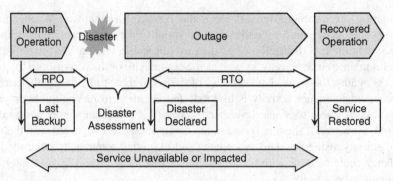

Figure 6.12. Estimating service unavailability during manual disaster recovery.

1. *RTO* to restore service after disaster has been declared and disaster recovery plan has been activated;
2. *Disaster assessment time* to determine the nature and magnitude of the disaster event and then formally activate a disaster recovery plan; and
3. *RPO* to account for the unavailability of business data which was damaged or lost due to the disaster event.

Even when service has been restored after the disaster assessment period and within the RTO period, a window of data changes is likely to have been lost. Thus, the period of service impact could include the RPO when estimating the expected window of data loss. Enterprises may elect a narrower definition of service unavailability and exclude RPO from consideration. Thus the duration of service impact caused by a disaster event can be estimated in minutes, hours, or days.

If georedundant recovery strategy "X" was expected to produce a 48-hour period of service unavailability after disaster and alternate strategy "Y" was expected to produce a 4 hour period of service unavailability after disaster, then one can estimate the incremental availability improvement of 44 hours per disaster event. It is presumably straightforward to estimate the incremental capital expense and operating expense of strategy "Y" compared with strategy "X." Enterprise leaders can decide which recovery option best balances the enterprise's service disruption tolerance following disaster with affordability to select the appropriate option.

7

UNDERSTANDING RECOVERY TIMING PARAMETERS

As explained in Chapter 6, "Modeling Service Availability with External System Redundancy," the following timing parameters are highly influential in various external redundancy recoveries:

1. μ_{TIMEOUT} (= $1/T_{\text{TIMEOUT}}$). This parameter captures how quickly the client times out due to a nonresponsive system, meaning the typical time for the initial request and all subsequent retries to timeout.

2. $\mu_{\text{KEEPALIVE}}$ (= $1/T_{\text{KEEPALIVE}}$): This parameter captures how frequently a client polls a server to verify that the server is still available.

3. μ_{CLIENT} (= $1/T_{\text{CLIENT}}$): This parameter captures how quickly the typical (i.e., median or 50th percentile) client successfully restores service on a redundant server.

This chapter begins by explaining the architectural and practical considerations that drive the timing parameters, shows how they relate to recovery time objectives (RTOs) for various recovery strategies, and then compares the strategies' expected real time objectives.

Beyond Redundancy: How Geographic Redundancy Can Improve Service Availability and Reliability of Computer-Based Systems, First Edition. Eric Bauer, Randee Adams, Daniel Eustace.
© 2012 Institute of Electrical and Electronics Engineers. Published 2012 by John Wiley & Sons, Inc.

7.1   DETECTING IMPLICIT FAILURES

While most functional failures are detected by explicit error responses, many critical failures prevent an explicit error response from reaching the client, and thus are detected implicitly based on lack of acknowledgment of a message, such as a command request or a keepalive. When the client sends a request, it should start a timer (called the response timer), and if the timer expires before a response is received from the server, it resends the request (called a retry) and restarts the response timer. If the timer expires again, the client continues to send retries until it reaches a maximum number of retries. Confirmation of the critical implicit failure, and hence initiation of any recovery action, is generally delayed by the initial response timeout plus the time to send the maximum number of unacknowledged retries.

It is important to support both a response timer and retries, because they are designed to detect different types of failures. The response timer detects server failures that prevent it from processing requests. Retries are needed to protect against network failures that can occasionally cause packets to be lost. Reliable transport protocols, such as transmission control protocol (TCP) and stream control transmission protocol (SCTP), support acknowledgments and retries. But even when one of these is used, it is still desirable to use a response timer at the application layer to protect against failures of the application process that might not impact the transport layer. For example, a TCP session might be up and properly sending packets and acknowledgments back and forth between the client and server, but the server-side TCP process might not be able to communicate with its application process. In this case, the client would not be aware of the problem unless there is a separate higher-level acknowledgment message between the client and server applications.

We need to be careful in setting the values of the response timer and maximum number of retries. It is desirable to use small values for these parameters to detect failures and failover to an alternate server as quickly as possible, minimizing downtime and failed requests. However, we also need to consider that failing over to an alternate server uses resources on that server to register the client and to retrieve the context information for that client. If too many clients failover simultaneously, a "registration storm" can be triggered, driving the alternate server into overload. Therefore, failovers for minor transient failures (such as blade failovers or temporarily slow processes due to a burst of traffic) should be avoided.

This section explores ways to set and adapt the timing parameters so that implicit failure detection is optimized.

7.1.1   Understanding and Optimizing $T_{TIMEOUT}$

One way to optimize the failure detection time is to collect data on response times and number of retries necessary for a successful response in order to adapt $T_{TIMEOUT}$ and the number of retries, to more rapidly detect faults and trigger a recovery than following the standard protocol timeout and retry strategy. Suppose, for example, the protocol used between a client and server has a standard timeout of 5 seconds with a maximum

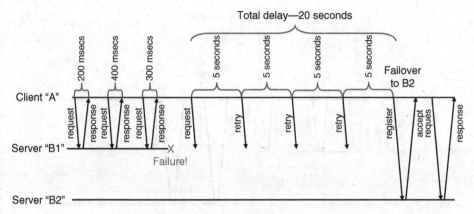

Figure 7.1. Standard protocol timeout.

of three retries. After the client sends a request to the server, it will wait 5 seconds for a response. If the server is down or unreachable and the timer expires, then the client will send a retry and wait another 5 seconds. After retrying two more times and waiting 5 seconds after each retry, the client will finally decide that the server is down after having spent a total of 20 seconds; the client can then attempt to send the request to another server, as shown in Figure 7.1.

However, the client can use historical information improve the failover time. In this example, the client can keep track of the response time of the server and measure the typical response time of the server to be between 200 and 400 ms. The client could decrease its timer value from 5 seconds to something like 2 seconds (five times the maximum observed response time), which has the benefit of contributing to a shorter recovery time using real observed behavior. Furthermore, the client could keep track of the number of retries it needs to send. If the server frequently does not respond until the second or third retry, then the client should continue to follow the protocol standard of three retries, or even increase the number of retries. But in this case, the server always responds on the first attempt, so there is little value in sending the second and third retries. If the client decides that it can use a 2-second timer with only one retry, then it has decreased the total failover time from 20 to 4 seconds as outlined in Figure 7.2.

After failing over to a new server, the client should go back to following the standard protocol values for the registration, and continue using the standard values for requests until it collects enough data on the new server to justify lower values.

Before lowering the protocol values too far, one needs to consider the processing time required to log on to the alternate server. If the client needs to establish a TCP session and get authenticated by the alternate server, then it becomes important to avoid bouncing back and forth between servers for minor interruptions (e.g., due to a simple blade failover, or due to a router failure that triggers an IP network reconfiguration). Therefore, a minimum timeout value should be set and at least one retry should always be attempted.

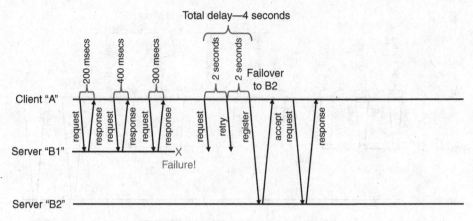

Figure 7.2. Adaptive protocol timeout.

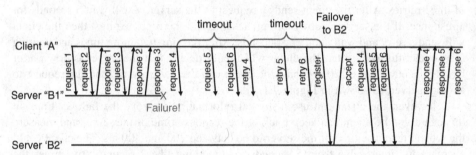

Figure 7.3. Timeout with multiple parallel requests.

Another mechanism would be to correlate failure messages to determine whether there is a trend indicating a critical failure of the server and the need to choose an alternate server. This applies if the client is sending many requests to the server simultaneously. If the server does not respond to one of the requests (or its retries), then it is no longer necessary to wait for a response on the other requests in progress, since those are likely to fail as well. The client could immediately failover and direct all the current requests to an alternate server, and should not send any more requests to the failed server until it gets an indication that it has recovered (e.g., with a heartbeat). For example, in Figure 7.3, the client can failover to the alternate server when the retry for request 4 fails, and then it can immediately retry requests 5 and 6 to the alternate server; it does not need to wait until the retries for 5 and 6 timeout.

For active–active configurations, particularly those which do not require a recovery of session context, clients should take immediate action upon detection of a failure of the server, or upon an explicit indication of the unavailability of the server via failure response or quarantine. For example, if a domain name system (DNS) server is down, the client shall go to another DNS server upon the first indication of a failure rather than waiting for that DNS server to recover. In this case, optimizing the failure detection time will reduce the client's service disruption time.

Optimizations are somewhat dependent on the redundancy type. For active–active configurations, optimizing the client's failure detection time will improve the RTO. However, for an active–standby configuration, if the client attempts to access the alternate server before it is prepared to accept service, the optimization may not reap any benefits. In addition, when working with active–standby servers, the client needs to be designed to give the standby time to take over service so that it doesn't start bouncing between the servers.

If the client is able to detect the server failure and attempts to log onto the alternate server, but the alternate server is still in the standby state and returns a not available response, the following techniques may be employed:

- Utilize the standard timeout/retry strategy to wait until the server is ready.
- Add backoff time to client before it reattempts to access the alternate server.
- Provide information to client (through heartbeating or another technique) that the alternate server is in the process of activating as opposed to being in a failure mode.

It is possible that although the primary server did not respond to a request, it recovered on its own before the alternate server took over. Therefore, if several attempts to log onto the alternate server have failed, the client should go to another alternate server if available; otherwise, it should go back to the primary server. In order to prevent the client from bouncing between servers, a maximum number of logon attempts on each side shall be set. Exceeding that number should result in alarms or some indication that manual intervention is required.

In the case of system-driven georedundancy, improvements can be made to the failure detection time through more explicit failure indications or messages. Similar to the adaptive timing for client-initiated recovery, the standby system can collect data on the number of heartbeats required to confirm the availability of the primary system. Suppose a heartbeat is sent every 60 seconds, and the standby system normally waits for three missed heartbeats before deciding that the active system has failed. If the standby keeps track of the number of missed heartbeats over time, and finds that the active almost never misses a heartbeat, then it can lower the heartbeat failure limit to 2, reducing the failure detection time by 60 seconds. As above, the failure detection time should not be lowered too far, since we do not want transient network failures (e.g., a reconfiguration due to a router failure) to cause unnecessary failovers of the application elements.

7.1.2 Understanding and Optimizing $T_{\text{KEEPALIVE}}$

In the previous section, the client did not recognize that the server was down until it failed to respond to a series of requests. This can negatively impact service:

- *Reverse Traffic Interruption.* Sometimes, a client/server relationship works in both directions (e.g., a cell phone can both initiate calls to a mobile switching center and receive calls from it). If a server is down, it will not process requests from the client, but it will also not send any requests to the client. If the client does not have a need to send any requests to the server for a while then during this interval, requests towards the client will fail.
- *End User Request Failures.* The request is delayed by $T_{\text{TIMEOUT}} \times$ (MaxRetryCount + 1), which in some cases is long enough to cause the end user's request to fail.

A solution to this problem is to send a heartbeat message periodically. The time between heartbeats is $T_{\text{KEEPALIVE}}$. If the client does not receive a response to a heartbeat from the server, then the client can use the same timeout/retry algorithm as it uses for normal requests to determine if the server has failed. The idea is that keepalives can detect server unavailability before an operational command would, so that service can automatically be recovered to an alternate server in time for "real" user requests to be promptly addressed by servers that are likely to be available. This is preferable to sending requests to servers when the client has no recent knowledge of the server's ability to serve clients. Note that heartbeats and keepalives are similar mechanisms, but heartbeats are used between redundant servers and keepalives are used between a client and server.

For example, in Figure 7.4, the client sends a periodic keepalive message to the primary server and expects to receive an acknowledgment. At the same time, the client is sending requests and receiving responses, but during periods of low traffic, there might not be any requests for a long time. If the primary server fails during this time, the client will detect the failure by a failed keepalive; if the primary server does not respond to a keepalive (or its retries), then the client should failover to the alternate server. Note that in this case, no requests are ever delayed.

An enhancement could be to restart the keepalive timer after every request/response, rather than after every keepalive. This will result in fewer keepalives during periods of higher traffic, while still ensuring that there are no long periods of inactivity with the server.

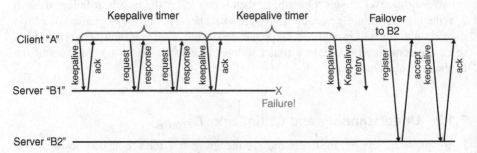

Figure 7.4. Client/server keepalive.

Another enhancement could be for the client to send keepalive messages periodically to alternate servers also, and keep track of their status. Then if the primary server fails, the client could avoid failing over to an alternate server that has also failed.

Servers can also monitor the keepalive messages to check if the clients are still operational. If a server detects that it is no longer receiving keepalive messages, or any other traffic, the server could send a message to the client in an attempt to wake it up, or at least report an alarm.

$T_{KEEPALIVE}$ should be set short enough to allow failures to be detected quickly enough to meet the availability requirements of the server, but not so short that the server is using an excessive amount of resources processing heartbeats from clients. The client can adapt the value of $T_{KEEPALIVE}$ based on the behavior of the server and IP network.

7.1.3 Understanding and Optimizing T_{CLIENT}

T_{CLIENT} is the time needed for a client to recover service on an alternate server. It includes the times for:

- Selecting an alternate server.
- Negotiating a protocol with the alternate server.
- Providing identification information.
- Exchanging authentication credentials (perhaps bilaterally).
- Checking authorization.
- Creating a session context on the server.
- Creating appropriate audit messages.

All of these things take time and consume some resource of the target server and perhaps other servers (e.g., AAA, user database servers, etc). Supporting user identification, authentication, authorization, and access control often requires T_{CLIENT} to be increased.

T_{CLIENT} can be reduced by having the clients maintain a "warm" session with a redundant server. That is, when registered and getting service from their primary server, they can also register with another server, so that if the primary server fails, they can immediately begin sending requests to the other server.

If many clients attempt to log onto a server at once (e.g., after failure of a server or networking facility), and significant resources are needed to support registration, then an overload situation may occur. This may be handled in several ways:

- Upon triggering the recovery to an alternate server, the clients can wait a configurable period of time based on the number of clients served or amount of traffic being handled to reduce incidence of a flood of messages redirected to backup system. The clients can wait a random amount of time before attempting to log onto the alternate server, but the mean time should be configurable, and set depending on the number of other clients that are likely to failover at the same time. If there are many other clients, then the mean time should be set to a higher value.

- The alternate server should handle the registration storm as normal overload, shedding traffic as needed until the situation clears. Some of the clients will be rejected when they attempt to log onto the server. They should wait a random period of time before reattempting.
- When rejecting a registration attempt, the alternate server can proactively indicate to the client how long it should back off (wait) before reattempting to log on to the server. This gives the server control to spread the registration traffic as much as necessary, and no more.
- In a load-sharing case where there are several servers, the servers can update the weights in their DNS SRV records depending on how overloaded they are. When one server fails, its clients will do a DNS query to determine an alternate server, so most of them will migrate to the least busy servers.

Note that any of these alternatives will increase the average T_{CLIENT}.

7.1.4   Timer Impact on Service Reliability

Ideally, failure detection and recovery mechanisms should be configured so that the service disruption period is shorter than the enterprise's maximum acceptable service disruption period, so failure events do not accrue chargeable service downtime and thus do not impact service availability metrics. However, activation of failure detection mechanisms and execution of recovery procedures may cause some individual service requests to fail. These service failures can either be outright failures (e.g., an unmitigated "503 Service Unavailable" message) or a latency-related failure because the request could not be completed via a redundant server quickly enough (e.g., before the user abandoned the service request or a higher level timeout expired). As explained in Section 2.1.2, "Service Reliability," those failures are captured in service reliability metrics and are often measured in defective operations per million attempts (DPM).

Service reliability can be different from service availability for a variety of reasons:

- For some client/server relationships, the RTO might be short enough that the client is able to failover in time to complete the user's request. In this case, the server is unavailable, but there is no impact on DPMs.
- For some client/server relationships, the server might only be down for a few seconds, but this is long enough to cause client requests to fail. In this case, the outage is too short to be considered downtime (e.g., less than 15 seconds as indicated in TL 9000—see Section 2.2.2, "Minimum Chargeable Disruption Duration," for details), but some request failures will increase the DPM count.
- Requests can fail due to software bugs or network problems (lost packets). Since the server does not fail completely, this does not count as downtime, but the failures will increase the DPM count.

Minimizing T_{TIMEOUT} and MaxRetryCount can reduce DPMs if they reduce the overall failover time sufficiently to allow user requests to survive. This time depends on the application. For telephone calls, if the calling user does not hear a ringing tone within 4 or 5 seconds after dialing a number, then they usually assume that the call has failed and hang up. To minimize DPMs, it is desirable for calls to complete even when a failover occurs, which requires that $T_{\text{TIMEOUT}} \times (\text{MaxRetryCount} + 1)$ be less than 4 or 5 seconds. In other applications, such as web browsing, users tend to be a little more patient, so it might be sufficient to keep the failover time below 15 seconds.

Also, as explained above, use of keepalives can reduce DPMs, since a client can detect server failures and failover before the next request needs to be processed.

Finally, T_{CLIENT} should be minimized, such as by maintaining redundant sessions with alternate servers, to avoid defects caused by failovers.

7.2 UNDERSTANDING AND OPTIMIZING RTO

A complete recovery requires the following generic failure detection and recovery steps:

- Failure detection (T_{Detect})
- Triggering recovery action (T_{Failover})
- Traffic redirection (T_{Redirect})
- Client failover (T_{Client})
- Service context preservation (T_{Context})

The overall recovery time is the sum of these times, so that in general, RTO that can be supported can be calculated as in Equation 7.1—General Equation for RTO.

$$\text{RTO} = T_{\text{Detect}} + T_{\text{Failover}} + T_{\text{Redirect}} + T_{\text{Client}} + T_{\text{Context}}$$

Equation 7.1. General Equation for RTO

This section describes the factors that affect these terms for manually controlled, system-driven, and client-initiated recoveries.

7.2.1 RTO for Manually Controlled Recovery

The recovery time for manually controlled recovery is illustrated in Figure 7.5. The recovery time for manually controlled recovery ($\text{RTO}_{\text{Manual}}$) is the sum of:

- T_{Detect}. Relying on customer complaints to determine when a component has failed will result in unsatisfied customers, as well as a long $\text{RTO}_{\text{Manual}}$. Therefore, it is recommended that all systems have robust failure detection, including:

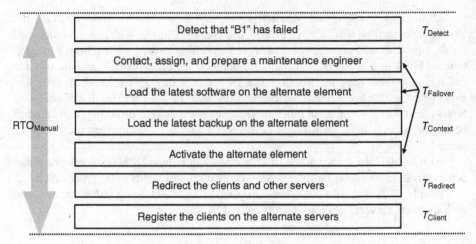

Figure 7.5. Manually controlled recovery timeline.

- Internal integrity checking (e.g., database audits, process monitors, defensive checks, etc.) that will report alarms (e.g., using SNMP) to a fault management system when inconsistencies are discovered.
- Monitoring by an external monitoring system that periodically checks if the server is still functional. This check might be a simple request, such as a request to return its current status. If the server fails to respond after a few retries, then the monitoring system should report an alarm.

   With sufficient monitoring, T_{Detect} should be less than a minute. However, if the failure is too subtle to be detected by the monitoring system, then the failure might not be detected until several users complain. It could take hours for the complaints to filter through to the maintenance engineers.

- T_{Failover} includes:
  - The time to assign and contact an engineer to perform the failover.
  - The time to validate that the target system has, in fact, failed and thus that manual failover of the target system is appropriate, rather than some other action (e.g., repairing networking equipment or facilities, etc).
  - The time for the engineer to prepare to perform the procedure, including time to travel to the site (if necessary), find the necessary procedure documents, and log on to the management system or standby element.
  - The time to load the software on the alternate element. This can be eliminated by always loading the current version of the software on backup elements.
  - The time to activate the alternate element. This can be minimized if the processes are always kept running on the standby element, so that only the state of the system needs to be updated to "active."

Note that the last two items on this list are not necessary if the servers run active–active instead of active–standby. With active–active, the maintenance engineer only needs to prepare the alternate server to accept the additional traffic from the failed server's clients.

$T_{Failover}$ depends on the complexity of the procedure, but is typically a few hours. It is recommended that alternate elements be periodically checked to ensure they are in working order so that no hardware problems need to be debugged during an emergency. This might consist of occasionally (e.g., every 6 months) doing a routine switchover to the alternate elements.

- $T_{Context}$. Restoring the service context is typically done as part of the failover procedure in manually controlled recovery. It consists of loading the failed server's latest backup. This might take 1 hour, or longer if larger datasets must be recovered. This step can be eliminated by always loading the backup onto the standby element whenever a new one is generated.

- $T_{Redirect}$ depends on the redirection method used (e.g., reprovision an IP address in the clients, provision a quarantine in the clients, and update a DNS record). Besides updating the clients (the A elements), it might also be necessary to update downstream servers (the C elements) to accept requests from the new server. This step might take up to about 1/2 hour. This time can be minimized by using client-initiated recovery techniques.

- T_{Client} is the time needed to register the clients on the alternate server. This could take several seconds.

7.2.2 RTO for System-Driven Recovery

The system-driven recovery timeline is illustrated in Figure 7.6.

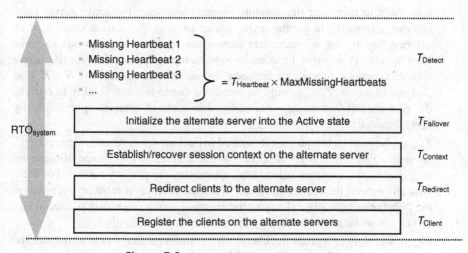

Figure 7.6. System-driven recovery timeline.

The recovery time for system-driven recovery (RTO_{System}) is the sum of:

- T_{Detect}. In a system-driven recovery scheme, heartbeats are sent from the primary server to either an alternate server or a monitoring system. The alternate server detects that the primary has failed when it fails to receive several consecutive heartbeats. Therefore, $T_{Detect} = T_{Heartbeat} \times$ MaxMissingHeartbeats, where $T_{Heartbeat}$ is the time between heartbeats, and MaxMissingHeartbeats is the missing heartbeat limit. These should be picked so that their product is low enough to meet the required RTO, but long enough that a failover is not triggered for transient failures. Typically, the $T_{Heartbeat}$ is a constant (e.g., 60 seconds), but the secondary server could adapt MaxMissingHeartbeats based on previous history. MaxMissingHeartbeats could be set to an initial value (e.g., 3), but then lowered (to 1 or 2) if the primary server is consistently sending heartbeats without missing any. If the primary server frequently fails to send a scheduled heartbeat, the secondary server might increase MaxMissingHeartbeats (to 4 or 5). $T_{Detect} = T_{Heartbeat} \times$ MaxMissingHeartbeats, so for example, if $T_{Heartbeat}$ is 60 seconds and MaxMissingHeartbeats is 3, T_{Detect} will be 3 minutes.
- $T_{Failover}$ is automatic and should be very fast if the standby is hot (i.e., processes are running and ready to take over at any time). The alternate server should verify that it has connectivity to the network (e.g., by pinging another network element), and then initialize itself into the proper state to support traffic. If the standby is warm, so that processes need to be initialized, then this could take a few minutes.
- $T_{Context}$. Under normal conditions, the active server can send session context information to the secondary server periodically (such as with the heartbeat) or whenever there is a major change to the state of a request. The secondary server should store this data in the same way as the active server, so that it is ready to take over the standing requests whenever the active server fails. Another alternative is for the active server to store the session context in an external registry so the secondary server can read it when it needs to make itself active. This might be done to save computing resources on the active server, to reduce bandwidth between the servers, or to support $N + K$ load sharing. However, $T_{Context}$ would be increased due to the time it takes to retrieve the context information for potentially thousands of sessions, potentially by several minutes.
- $T_{Redirect}$. Several techniques are described in Section 4.1.3, "Traffic Redirection," for redirecting traffic from the clients to the alternate server. Some of these are triggered by the alternate server (e.g., quarantine the primary server), but these typically extend the redirection time. With client-initiated recovery techniques, the clients can typically failover to the alternate server faster than the secondary server can make itself active. $T_{Redirect}$ should be a few seconds.
- T_{Client}. The time to register the clients on the alternate server (and to register the alternate server with its servers). This could take several seconds.

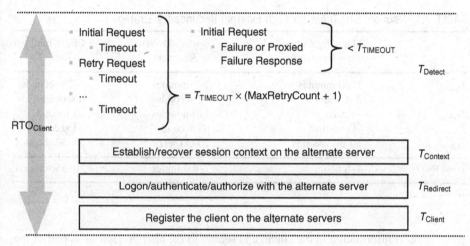

Figure 7.7. Client-initiated recovery timeline.

7.2.3 RTO for Client-Initiated Recovery

Client-initiated recovery timeline is illustrated in Figure 7.7. The recovery time for client-initiated recovery (RTO_{Client}) is the sum of:

- T_{Detect}. In a client-initiated recovery scheme, T_{Detect} is fundamentally different based on whether the recovery was triggered via an explicit failure response or implicitly via expiration of the maximum number of timeout periods with no response. In the first case, T_{Detect} is just the typical request response time. In the second case, T_{Detect} is $T_{TIMEOUT}$ * (MaxRetryCount + 1). The response timer and the maximum retry count limit should be picked so that their product is low enough to meet the required RTO, and ideally short enough that a failover does not cause the end user request to fail. However, they should be set long enough that a failover is not triggered for transient failures. Typically, the client/server protocol specifies the values that should be used, but the client could adapt these based on previous history. Some possibilities are described in Section 7.1.1, "RTO for System-driven Recovery." For most protocols, T_{Detect} is less than 30 seconds, and could be as low as a few seconds.

- $T_{Failover}$. Since the client does not depend on any other entity to failover, this is essentially 0 seconds.

- $T_{Context}$. If the servers use an active–active scheme, session context information can be shared the same as for an active–standby scheme with system-driven recovery. In a load-shared scheme with many servers, session context is usually not sent between servers. If it is necessary to preserve this information over failovers, it can be stored in a separate registry and read by the alternate server when the client goes through the logon procedure. It should only take a few seconds to retrieve this data for each client. A third option would be to store the

TABLE 7.1. Nominal RTO Times for Each External Redundancy Strategy

	Manually Controlled Recovery	System-Driven Recovery	Client-Initiated Recovery
T_{Detect}	1–30 minutes	2–3 minutes	5–20 seconds
$T_{Failover}$	2–4 hours	~3 seconds	0 seconds
$T_{Context}$	~1 hour	1–5 minutes	~3 seconds
$T_{Redirect}$	~½ hour	~3 seconds	~3 seconds
T_{Client}	10–30 seconds	10–30 seconds	10–30 seconds
Total RTO	4–6 hours	3–8 minutes	20–55 seconds

context information in the client, and send it to the alternate server as part of the logon procedure (HTTP cookies are an example of this technique).

- $T_{Redirect}$ is automatic and should be very fast. The IP address of the alternate server can be provisioned in the client, so that it can failover without any delay, but even if DNS is used, clients should cache the DNS records so that they already have the alternate server's address when it is needed. $T_{Failover}$ should not be more than a few seconds.

- T_{Client}. The time to register the client on the alternate server. This could take several seconds. If the registration time is significant, then we can consider having the clients always register simultaneously to an alternate server, so that when the primary server fails, they can immediately start using the alternate server. This will lower $T_{Redirect}$ to 0.

Note that the time needed to process an explicit failure time is much less than the time needed to timeout and retry multiple times for a profound failure.

7.2.4 Comparing External Redundancy Strategies

Table 7.1 shows nominal RTO times for each of the external redundancy strategies. Some of these times can vary widely depending on the application and implementation, but it is typical for RTO_{Manual} to take several hours, RTO_{System} to take several minutes, and RTO_{Client} to take several seconds.

CASE STUDY OF CLIENT-INITIATED RECOVERY

Domain name system (DNS) is a common service that typically leverages client-initiated recovery; this chapter estimates the service availability experienced by DNS clients across a pool of DNS servers as a case study. This section considers availability of the QUERY service offered by a hypothetical pool of DNS servers to a hypothetical DNS client in the context of the practical client-initiated recovery model presented in Section 6.5.3. This chapter begins with an overview of the DNS service, then explains how this service maps onto the practical client-initiated recovery model, estimates model input parameters, reviews the service availability prediction, and discusses the insights offered by the predicted results.

Note that this chapter models only the product-attributable service availability benefits of client-initiated recovery to external redundant systems. Georedundancy is also likely to offer significant availability benefits for nonproduct-attributable failures of networking gear (e.g., routers), transmission facilities, and site disasters.

8.1 OVERVIEW OF DNS

DNS is the ubiquitous service that translates domain names like http://www.google.com into IP addresses. DNS servers constantly resolve domain names entered by users or

Beyond Redundancy: How Geographic Redundancy Can Improve Service Availability and Reliability of Computer-Based Systems, First Edition. Eric Bauer, Randee Adams, Daniel Eustace.
© 2012 Institute of Electrical and Electronics Engineers. Published 2012 by John Wiley & Sons, Inc.

TABLE 8.1. DNS RCODE Return Code Values

RCODE	Description
0	No error condition—Successful execution
1	Format error—The name server was unable to interpret the query.
2	Server failure—The name server was unable to process this query due to a problem with the name server.
3	Name Error—Meaningful only for responses from an authoritative name server, this code signifies that the domain name referenced in the query does not exist.
4	Not Implemented—The name server does not support the requested kind of query.
5	Refused—The name server refuses to perform the specified operation for policy reasons. For example, a name server may not wish to provide the information to the particular requester, or a name server may not wish to perform a particular operation (e.g., zone transfer) for particular data.
6–15	Reserved for future use.

otherwise presented to applications into the IP addresses that are required for the networking infrastructure to route packets to the target system. DNS is specified in a series of IETF request for comments (RFCs), primarily RFC 1034, "Domain Names—Concepts and Facilities" (Internet Engineering Task Force, 1987a), and RFC 1035, "Domain Names—Implementation and Specification" (Internet Engineering Task Force, 1987b). DNS is typically configured as a stateless protocol running on connectionless UDP. Typically, multiple servers offer the same information, and clients are generally free to send their queries to any operational server. DNS server instances are often deployed without internal redundancy and leverage the ability of DNS clients to connect to alternate DNS server instances if one goes down. Thus, typical deployments of DNS leverage client-initiated recovery.

Table 8.1 shows the 4-bit "RCODE" response code values specified in RFC 1035 (Internet Engineering Task Force, 1987b) that are returned by DNS servers to DNS clients. Note that the DNS return codes for unsuccessful operations fall into two broad classes:

- *Request errors*, including format error, name error, not implemented and refused. Presumably, if a particular client request caused the DNS server to return one of these request errors, then there is no point in attempting the same request to a different DNS server instance.
- *Server failure*. Presumably, if the client retried the same request to a different DNS server instance, then they are likely to be successfully served.

8.2 MAPPING DNS ONTO PRACTICAL CLIENT-INITIATED RECOVERY MODEL

DNS RCODE values can be conveniently divided into those that indicate the server is operational (but, e.g., the client sent an invalid query) and those that indicate the server is unavailable, as shown in Table 8.2.

TABLE 8.2. Deducing Server Status from DNS RCODE

RCODE Indicating DNS Server is UP	RCODE Indicating DNS Server is DOWN
0—No error condition (i.e., Success) 1—Format error 3—Name error 4—Not implemented 5—Refused 5–15—Reserved	2—Server failure

Pool of DNS servers offering load shared service to DNS clients

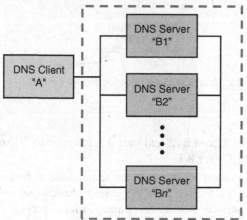

Figure 8.1. Generic model of DNS.

DNS clients implement message timers so that if a DNS server has not responded to a request before the timer expires, then the client typically retries the request to the same server up to a maximum number of retry attempts before contacting an alternate DNS server. DNS clients are generally free to implement somewhat different strategies, but all clients will include some timeout strategy to detect profound server failure and to recover service to an alternate DNS server.

In this chapter, we will consider the nominal DNS configuration of Figure 8.1, which includes a DNS client "A" that is assumed to typically work with DNS server "B1." The enterprise is assumed to have deployed additional DNS servers "B2" through "Bn." DNS servers "B1" through "Bn" are assumed to be equivalent in that any of them is capable of serving client "A" with acceptable quality. The case study in this chapter will predict availability of a simple two-server ("B1" and "B2") solution to enable direct comparison of this prediction with simpler mathematical models.

The practical client-initiated recovery model illustrated in Figure 6.10 and described in Section 6.5.3 is tailored for DNS in Figure 8.2 by making some refinements:

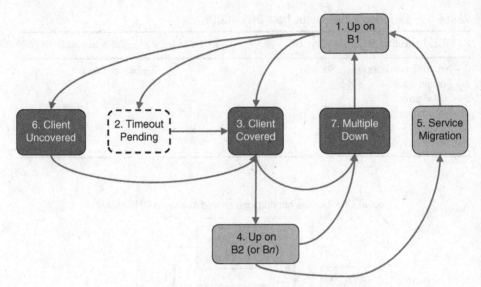

Figure 8.2. Practical client-initiated model for DNS.

- State 1 is renamed to "Up on B1," and state 4 is renamed to "Up on B2 (or Bn)" to be consistent with Figure 8.1.
- State 5 "Service Migration" is shown in the same shade as both state 1 "Up on B1" and state 4 "Up on B2 (or Bn)," because it also constitutes uptime. DNS supports planned service migrations during which service remains fully operational.

State 2 "Timeout Pending" retains a dotted border because arguments can both be made to count "Timeout Pending" as downtime (because "B1" actually is down) and to exclude it from downtime predictions, because a properly engineered timeout strategy should detect profound failure of "B1" rapidly enough so that there is time to resubmit the query to another DNS server without introducing unacceptable service latency to the end user. The predictions in Section 6.5.3 consider both cases: when "Timeout Pending" counts as service downtime and when it is excluded from downtime prediction.

8.2.1   Modeling Normal Operation

Normal DNS server operation consists of server "B1" correctly responding to requests from DNS clients (e.g., "A") with acceptable quality of service. Time spent in normal operation is represented in state 1 "Up on B1." Figure 8.3 illustrates this on the Markov model implicitly by showing that normal operation is nominally steady state; only failure events—by definition not normal operation—causes transitions out of state 1 "Up on B1."

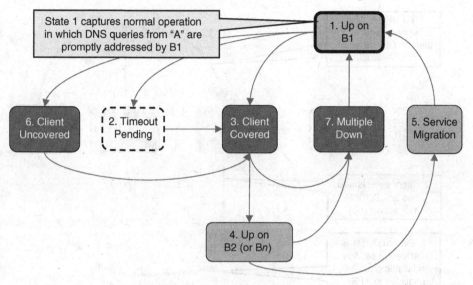

Figure 8.3. Modeling normal DNS operation.

8.2.2 Modeling Server Failure

Figure 8.4 illustrates the typical model for server failure when server "B1" explicitly reports failure to client "A" via the *2—Server Failure* RCODE value. Upon receipt of the *2—Server Failure*, the client recognizes that "B1" is unavailable and thus enters state 3 "Client Covered," in which the client attempts to identify an alternate DNS server and recover service onto that alternate server. Typically, the client will successfully select and reestablish service with an alternate DNS server, and thus transition to state 4 "Up on B2 (or B*n*)." Eventually, "B1" is repaired and returned to service. The nature of DNS service enables server instances to enter (or reenter) service and begin accepting new traffic without disrupting existing traffic. Since the service migration step is nonservice-impacting, there is little practical difference between the transitions from state 4 "Up on B2 (or B*n*)" to state 5 "Service Migration," and from state 5 "Service Migration" to state 1 "Up on B1." The bottom line is that the model returns to state 1 "Up on B1" with no service disruption or downtime.

8.2.3 Modeling Timeout Failure

Figure 8.5 illustrates the scenario of profound failure that renders "B1" completely nonresponsive. While this case study considers only product-attributable failures that render "B1" unavailable, this model also covers unavailability/inaccessibility caused by failure of networking equipment or facilities, site destruction, and so on. In this case, the client sends a query to "B1" without knowing that "B1" has failed and thus is incapable of responding to that query; thus the model transitions from state 1 "Up on B1" to state 2 "Timeout Pending." Eventually, the client's request timer expires, and

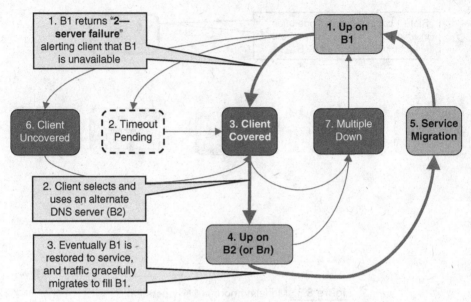

Figure 8.4. Modeling server failure.

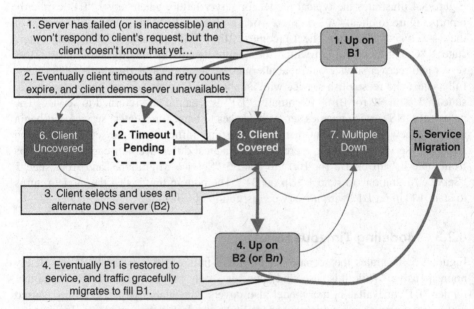

Figure 8.5. Modeling timeout failure.

the client resends the request; note that since DNS is typically implemented over the unreliable UDP datagram service, packet loss is routinely recovered via resending requests, so occasional retransmissions are not unusual. Since "B1" is unavailable, the resend request will fail, as will subsequent retries. Eventually, the client will timeout the maximum number of retries, and then deem "B1" to be unavailable, thus transitioning from state 2 "Timeout Pending" to state 3 "Client Covered." Having deemed "B1" to be unavailable, the client will now recover service onto "B2" (or B*n*) via the process described earlier in Section 8.2.2, "Modeling Server Failure."

8.2.4 Modeling Abnormal Server Failure

It is possible that multiple failures cause "B1" to return the wrong RCODE value, thereby misleading DNS client "A" to believe that it is available when it actually is not. For example, imagine a second defect in "B1's" software that causes it to return an RCODE other than *2—Server Error* after a critical error has occurred, such as an RCODE of *5—Refused*. In this case, the client will not immediately recognize that "B1" is unavailable and will not immediately attempt to locate an alternate DNS server. Thus, the client transitions from state 1 "Up on B1" to state 6 "Client Uncovered," in which "B1" is unavailable but responding to requests, and those responses do not cause client "A" to recognize that "B1" is unavailable. Eventually, it will be recognized that "B1" is not functioning properly, and the client will select an alternate DNS server and reestablish service with it, for example, when a user enters a well-known domain name like http://www.google.com and the DNS server returns an error (e.g., 3 Name Error). Note that recognizing "B1" has failed abnormally may be done automatically by client "A" (best case) or by a user who is frustrated by unacceptably slow or nonresponsive service and then attempts to manually recover service, such as by restarting the client application or rebooting the computer hosting client "A," or even the server "B1" itself.

Defects in DNS client software on "A" could also cause the transition from state 1 "Up on B1" to state 6 "Client Uncovered," such as if "B1" sent a response of *2—Server Error*, and the client "A" did not immediately identify and reestablish service with an alternate DNS server. Again, manual action on the client may be needed to recover service to an alternate DNS server.

Figure 8.6 illustrates this with the transition from state 1 "Up on B1" to State 6 "Client Uncovered" in which client uncovered represents the situation of "B1" being unavailable but the DNS client does not yet realize that. This model assumes that the DNS client offers some secondary failure detection logic so that eventually, the client will attempt to locate and reestablish service to an alternate server, thus transitioning to state 3 "Client Covered." From state 3 "Client Covered," the model typically transitions to state 4 "Up on B2 (or B*n*)," state 5 "Service Migration," and state 1 "Up on B1" as described in Section 8.2.2, "Modeling Server Failure."

In the event that the DNS client has no logic to detect and recover from abnormal server failures, then clients are likely to rely on manual failure detection and recovery. The simplest scenario is that end users eventually recognize unacceptable quality of service (often via poor performance of another application that uses DNS client) and

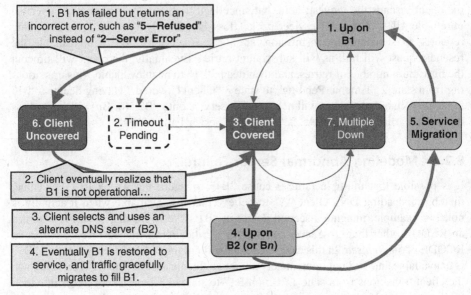

Figure 8.6. Modeling abnormal server failure.

the human user triggers a manual recovery action like restarting an application or rebooting the network element hosting the client application and/or DNS client.

8.2.5 Modeling Multiple Server Failure

Occasionally, a second DNS server (e.g., "B2") will fail before the first server is repaired. Two scenarios of interest are illustrated in Figure 8.7:

1. The alternate DNS server selected by the DNS client could be unavailable.
2. Server "B2" (or Bn) can fail before service is migrated back to the repaired "B1."

The simplest model of these multiple failure scenarios is to transition to state 7 "Multiple Down" and assume that manual recovery actions are required to restore service. Systems with more server redundancy (e.g., $N + 2$ system redundancy) may implement more sophisticated clients that may continue to look for alternate DNS servers, rather than giving up after attempting recovery to a single redundant server; richer models can be constructed to address that increased complexity.

8.3 ESTIMATING INPUT PARAMETERS

Figure 8.8 overlays mathematical formulas onto the client-initiated recovery model used for DNS; Table 8.3 describes each of the parameters. This section explains exactly how each part of the practical client-initiated recovery model applies to DNS service.

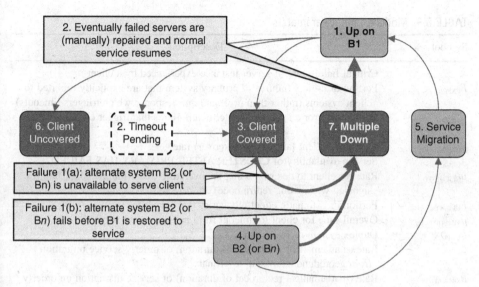

Figure 8.7. Modeling multiple server failures.

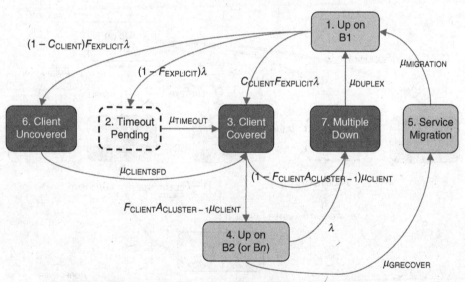

Figure 8.8. Simplified client-initiated recovery model with formulas.

8.3.1 Server Failure Rate

λ represents the failure rate of a single DNS server instance (e.g., "B1"). Figure 8.9 illustrates where λ is used in the model. Assuming that server instances (i.e., "B1," "B2," ..., "Bn") have no internal redundancy or high availability mechanisms to mitigate the affect of critical failures, the client-initiated recovery mechanism will be

TABLE 8.3. Modeling Input Parameters

Symbol	Description
λ	Critical failure rate of server instance experienced by a client
F_{EXPLICIT}	Portion of critical failures of primary system that are explicitly reported to client systems (rather than profound non-response which triggers timeouts)
C_{CLIENT}	Portion of error responses from critical failures that trigger client-initiated recovery
μ_{CLIENT}	Automatic client failover (or takeover) rate
$A_{\text{CLUSTER}-1}$	Service availability of CLUSTER AFTER PRIMARY HAS FAILED
$\mu_{\text{CLIENTSFD}}$	Rate for client to determine that uncovered-to-client failures (e.g., failures signaled with wrong return code) are detected
F_{CLIENT}	Portion of automatic client recoveries that succeed
μ_{TIMEOUT}	Overall time for client to timeout from nonresponsive server
μ_{DUPLEX}	Duplex system recovery rate
μ_{GRECOVER}	Rate (mathematical reciprocal of duration) of orderly service migration from georedundant system to primary
$\mu_{\text{MIGRATION}}$	Rate (mathematical reciprocal of duration) of service disruption on orderly service migration

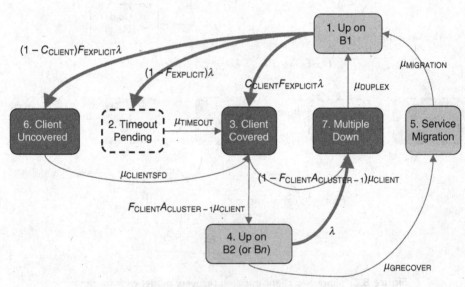

Figure 8.9. Critical failure rate parameter.

exposed to all critical hardware and software failures. Hardware failure rates are typically expressed as either FITs (failures per 10^9 hours) or MTBF (mean time between failures, often expressed in hours or years). Note that MTBF is the mathematical reciprocal of failure rate so a higher MTBF means a lower failure rate (and hence, higher reliability). Software failure rate captures the frequency of system crashes, process failures, and so on, and is typically expressed as failures (or crashes) per year. Thus, λ is the sum of the hardware failure rate and the software failure rate of a single servicer instance (e.g., "B1").

While hardware failure rates are commonly calculated by standard methods like MIL-STD 217F or Telcordia's SR-332 and quoted by suppliers, estimated software failure rates are not generally provided. Without a direct estimate of software failure rate, one must use an indirect technique to estimate overall system failure rate seen by client-initiated recovery mechanisms. The simplest technique is to crudely estimate that the software failure rate is roughly related to the hardware failure rate by some factor, perhaps between 2 and 5. Thus, if the hardware has a predicted failure rate of "X" fails per hour and it is assumed that there are approximately three software failures for every hardware failure, then the overall estimated system failure rate is "$(1 + 3) \times X$" or "$4X$" fails per hour.

If the system supplier quotes a service availability rating for each server instance, then this availability rating can be converted to an estimated system failure rate. Availability is mathematically related to MTBF and mean time to restore service (mean time to repair, MTTR) via the following formula:

$$\text{Availability} = \frac{\text{MTBF}}{\text{MTBF} + \text{MTTR}}$$

Equation 8.1. Availability as a Function of MTBF and MTTR

Solving for MTBF:

$$\text{MTBF} = \frac{\text{Availability}}{(1 - \text{Availability})} \times \text{MTTR} = \frac{1}{\lambda}$$

Equation 8.2. MTBF as a Function of Availability and MTTR

Solving for λ:

$$\lambda = \frac{(1 - \text{Availability})}{\text{Availability} \times \text{MTTR}}$$

Equation 8.3. Failure Rate as a Function of Availability and MTTR

Figure 8.10 illustrates the relationship of MTTR to failure rate as a function of service availability. In the real world, outages are a relatively rare occurrence, and there is often significant variation in the duration of events due to particulars of the failure itself, the policies of the enterprise, the timing and context of the failure event, and myriad other factors. The difficulty in estimating the MTTR compounds with the uncertainty in predicted service availability to make indirect failure rate estimates rather soft. Thus, one generally uses a conservative estimate of the likely rate of failures per year and then considers the downtime sensitivity across a plausible range of failure rates.

Assuming that a standalone DNS server instance has service availability of 99.97% and using an MTTR of 2 hours as is discussed in Section 8.3.6, "μ_{CLIENT} Parameter,"

Fails Per Year Against MTTR

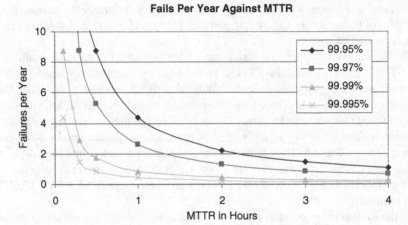

Figure 8.10. Failure rate as a function of MTTR. From "Sheet1" worksheet of "FPY v. MTTR.xls."

one computes a critical failure rate of 1.32 fails per year. This example will conservatively round this value up to 1.5 critical fails per year, which actually translates to 99.966% service availability.

8.3.2 $F_{EXPLICIT}$ Parameter

$F_{EXPLICIT}$ is the probability that after "B1" has experienced a critical failure, it will promptly respond to client requests with valid (but not necessarily correct) RCODE values. Figure 8.11 highlights how $F_{EXPLICIT}$ is used to differentiate state 2 "Timeout Pending" from state 3 "Client Covered" and state 6 "Client Uncovered":

- $F_{EXPLICIT}$ failures will permit "B1" to respond to client requests with either correct response (*2 Server Failure* triggering transition to state 3 "Client Covered") or incorrect response (e.g., *5 Refused* triggering transition to state 6 "Client Uncovered")
- $(1 - F_{EXPLICIT})$ failures will be so profound that the failed server will not respond to requests.

Since the case study assumes that each DNS server is deployed with no internal redundancy, many hardware and application failures will render the application incapable of returning any response to the client; thus, $F_{EXPLICIT}$ is assumed in this example to be 50%. Note that this parameter does not consider whether that response is correct (i.e., *2 Server Failure*) or incorrect (e.g., *1 Format Error*); correctness of responses is estimated with C_{CLIENT}.

8.3.3 C_{CLIENT} Parameter

As Figure 8.12 illustrates, C_{CLIENT} determines the portion of explicitly reported critical failures that are instantly determined by the client to be failures that trigger client-

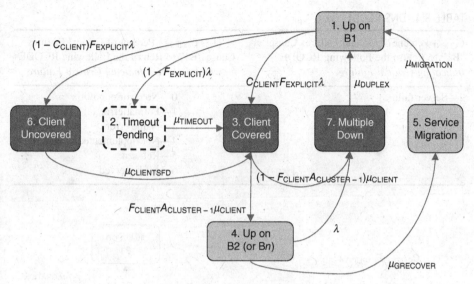

Figure 8.11. F_{EXPLICIT} parameter.

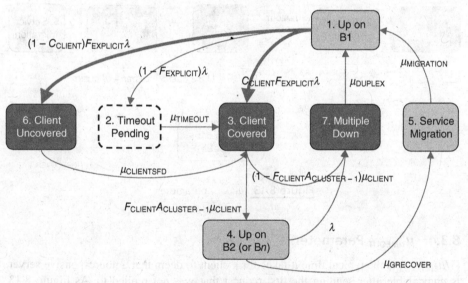

Figure 8.12. C_{CLIENT} parameter.

initiated recovery (state 3 "Client Covered") and what portion are not initially deemed by the client to be critical failures (state 6 "Client Uncovered"). C_{CLIENT} estimates the percentage of explicitly reported failures (logically the product of F_{EXPLICIT} and λ) that signal to the client that the server is unavailable. This concept can be clarified by reframing Table 8.2 by C_{CLIENT} to produce Table 8.4.

C_{CLIENT} is assumed in this example to be 99%.

TABLE 8.4. DNS RCODEs by C_{CLIENT}

C_{CLIENT} Percent of Critical Failures Cause "B1" to Return the Following RCODE *Indicating Critical Failure*	$(1 - C_{CLIENT})$ Percent of Critical Failures Cause "B1" to Return the Following RCODEs *which DO NOT Indicate Critical Failure*
2—Server failure	0—No error condition 1—Format error 3—Name error 4—Not implemented 5—Refused 6–15—Reserved

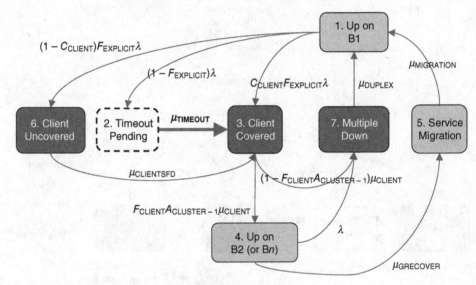

Figure 8.13. $\mu_{TIMEOUT}$ parameter.

8.3.4 $\mu_{TIMEOUT}$ Parameter

$(1/\mu_{TIMEOUT})$ is the typical time it takes for a client to deem that a nonresponsive server is unavailable after sending the first request that was not replied to. As Figure 8.13 shows, $\mu_{TIMEOUT}$ defines how quickly clients transition from State 2 "Timeout Pending" to State 3 "Client Covered" when client-initiated recovery is initiated. Timeout latency $(1/\mu_{TIMEOUT})$ is assumed to be 5 seconds in this example.

8.3.5 $\mu_{CLIENTSFD}$ Parameter

As shown in Figure 8.14, $\mu_{CLIENTSFD}$ estimates that rate at which initially unrecognized latent sever failures are recognized by the client, thereby transitioning from state 6

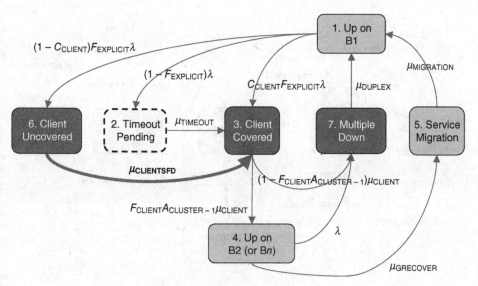

Figure 8.14. $\mu_{\text{CLIENTSFD}}$ parameter.

"Client Uncovered" to state 3 "Client Covered." Operationally, $(1/\mu_{\text{CLIENTSFD}})$ is how long it takes client software or the end user to recognize that although the server is responding to requests (and thus not unavailable) and not returning explicit failure messages, it is not returning correct results. For example, an uncovered database failure of an e-commerce website may cause the website to present correctly structured web pages to visitors, but without any inventory information displayed. Thus, the client browser will properly render pages to the end user, and it will be up to the end user to recognize that the service has somehow failed and take appropriate corrective actions, such as reconnecting to the website and hoping that they are connected to an operational server. The typical detection latency $(1/\mu_{\text{CLIENTSFD}})$ is assumed to be 5 minutes.

8.3.6 μ_{CLIENT} Parameter

As shown in Figure 8.15, μ_{CLIENT} estimates that rate at which the client "A" identifies an alternate server "B2" (or Bn), connects to that alternate server, reestablishes service with that alternate server, and resubmits the original request. Typically, this characterizes the rate at which a client transitions from state 3 "Client Covered" to state 4 "Up on B2 (or Bn)." Occasionally, this transition will fail because the alternate server is unavailable (see Section 8.3.7, "$A_{\text{CLUSTER-1}}$ Parameter") or because a failure in the client or alternate server prevents service from being properly restored onto the alternate server (see Section 8.3.8, "F_{CLIENT} Parameter"). Because of the stateless and connectionless nature of DNS, typical client recovery latency $(1/\mu_{\text{CLIENT}})$ for DNS is assumed to be only 10 milliseconds. Connection-oriented services that require clients to identify, authenticate, and authorize their session and then construct and maintain session state will have longer recovery latencies.

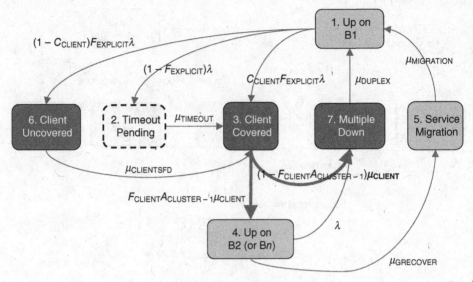

Figure 8.15. μ_{CLIENT} parameter.

8.3.7 $A_{CLUSTER-1}$ Parameter

$A_{CLUSTER-1}$ characterizes the likelihood that an alternate server (i.e., "B2" through "Bn" in this example) will be available when the client attempts to restore service following failure of "B1." As Figure 8.16 shows, $A_{CLUSTER-1}$ is crucial in determining a client-covered failure can be successfully recovered onto another server instance (e.g., "B2," . . . "Bn"), or if one transitions to state 7 "Multiple Down" because no redundant systems are available. If the cluster consists only of a pair of servers "B1" and "B2," then when "B1" is unavailable, $A_{CLUSTER-1}$ is the standalone availability of "B2" (which is presumably the same as the standalone availability of "B1"). If the service is provided by a load-shared pool of $N + K$ servers—as DNS generally is—then $A_{CLUSTER-1}$ is the availability of the $N + (K - 1)$ configuration of that pool of servers. Therefore, one typically estimates $A_{CLUSTER-1}$ via an $N + K$ load shared availability model with "N" servers to carry the engineered load and only $(K - 1)$ spare/redundant servers. For simplicity, we consider the simplest case of $1 + 1$ external redundancy so $A_{CLUSTER-1}$ equals $A_{STANDALONE}$; as Section 8.3.1, "Server Failure Rate," explained, $A_{STANDALONE}$ is assumed to be 99.97%, so $A_{CLUSTER-1}$ will also be assumed to be 99.97%.

8.3.8 F_{CLIENT} Parameter

F_{CLIENT} (Fig. 8.17) estimates the probability that the client-initiated recovery to an operational server "B2" (or "Bn") will be successful. Since DNS is a stateless, connectionless service, the probability of successfully establishing service to "B2" (or "Bn") is likely to be the same as the probability of successfully establishing service to "B1" was prior to the failure of "B1," which is conservatively assumed to be 99.99%.

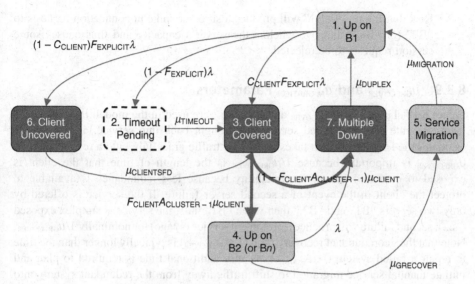

Figure 8.16. $A_{CLUSTER-1}$ parameter.

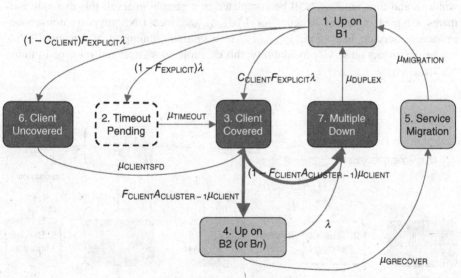

Figure 8.17. F_{CLIENT} parameter.

F_{CLIENT} may be lower for services that maintain session or service contexts and/or require identification, authentication, and authorization as the reliability of these operations may be impacted by:

- Risk that failure of "B1" compromised or locked some information or resources that are required to successfully reestablish service on "B2" (or "Bn").

- Risk that failure of "B1" will produce a surge or spike in connection requests to "B2" (or "Bn") that overwhelms the server's capacity and thus causes some session requests to be rejected.

8.3.9 $\mu_{GRECOVER}$ and $\mu_{MIGRATION}$ Parameters

Figure 8.18 shows how $\mu_{GRECOVER}$ and $\mu_{MIGRATION}$ are used in the model. $\mu_{GRECOVER}$ estimates the rate at which failed servers are brought back into service, and $\mu_{MIGRATION}$ estimates the length of time it takes to migrate traffic gracefully onto a restored server. $\mu_{GRECOVER}$ is important because $1/\mu_{GRECOVER}$ is the length of time that the client is exposed to increased risk of unavailability because less redundancy is available to protect the client in the event of a second server failure. If the service is offered by only two servers "B1" and "B2," then when "B1" fails, the service is simplex exposed (i.e., a second failure will produce a prolonged service outage) for nominally $1/\mu_{GRECOVER}$. Note that the georedundant recovery time ($1/\mu_{GRECOVER}$) is typically longer than the time to repair a failed system ($/1\mu_{PRIMARY}$) because additional time is required to plan and initiate manual service migration to shift traffic away from the redundant system onto the recovered system. Since DNS servers can be restored to service without impacting traffic, there is no reason to postpone server recovery to a low-traffic maintenance window, and thus recovery will be completed in a normal interval; this example estimates a typical value of 4 hours for $1/\mu_{GRECOVER}$. Since DNS supports nonservice-impacting service migration, $\mu_{MIGRATION}$ is essentially unimportant because it has negligible impact on service availability; this example uses a nominal value of 1 minute for $1/\mu_{MIGRATION}$.

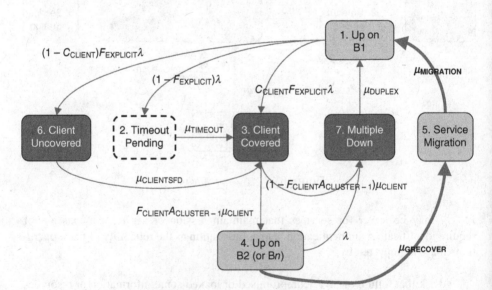

Figure 8.18. $\mu_{GRECOVER}$ and $\mu_{MIGRATION}$ parameters.

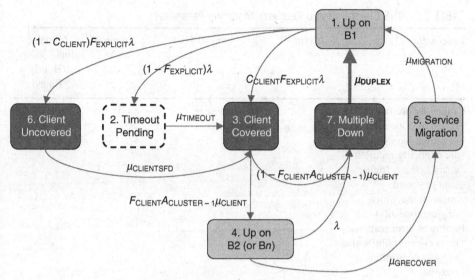

Figure 8.19. μ_{DUPLEX} parameter.

8.3.10 μ_{DUPLEX} **Parameter**

μ_{DUPLEX} (Fig. 8.19) estimates the rate at which service is restored following multiple failures. As μ_{DUPLEX} typically requires manual intervention, it is far slower than μ_{CLIENT}. While μ_{GRECOVER} is completed on a nonemergency basis because service is available, μ_{DUPLEX} is likely to be executed on an emergency basis because service is impacted. This example assumes that $1/\mu_{\text{DUPLEX}}$ is 2 hours.

8.3.11 Parameter Summary

The modeling parameters assumed for the DNS example are summarized in Table 8.5.

8.4 PREDICTED RESULTS

Table 8.6 gives the predicted time spent in each of the modeled states based on the input parameters of Table 8.5. Begin by considering the time predicted to be spent in each of the 7 modeled states:

- *State 1 "Up on B1."* About 99.93% of the time is estimated to be spent in this state, which is significantly less than the 99.966–99.97% that is assumed for the standalone service availability of "B1" itself. This is because while service is promptly recovered onto "B2" (or "B*n*") on failure of "B1," service is assumed to migrate back to "B1" on a nonemergency basis, so some time is spent in state 4 "Up on 'B2' (or 'B*n*')" even after "B1" has been restored to operational status.

TABLE 8.5. DNS Client-Initiated Recovery Modeling Parameters

Description	Symbol	Nominal Unit	Nominal Input	Modeled Input Value (Hourly Rates)
Critical failure rate	λ	Fails per year	1.5	0.00017112
Portion of critical failures of primary system that are explicitly reported to client systems (rather than profound nonresponse which triggers timeouts)	$F_{EXPLICIT}$	Percentage	50%	50%
Portion of error responses from critical failures that trigger client-initiated recovery	C_{CLIENT}	Percentage successful	99%	99%
Automatic client failover (or takeover) rate	μ_{CLIENT}	Median seconds for clients to recover service to redundant system following failure of primary	0.010	360,000
Service availability of cluster after primary has failed	$A_{CLUSTER-1}$	Percentage	99.970%	99.970%
Rate for client to determine that uncovered-to-client failures (e.g., failures signaled with wrong return code) are detected	$\mu_{CLIENTSFD}$	Median minutes for clients to recover service to redundant system following failure of primary	5.0	12
Portion of automatic client recoveries that succeed	F_{CLIENT}	Percentage	99.990%	99.990%
Overall time for client to timeout from profoundly nonresponsive server	$\mu_{TIMEOUT}$	Median seconds for clients to timeout failed primary system	5.0	720
Duplex system recovery rate	μ_{DUPLEX}	Hours to complete emergency repair of duplex failures	2.0	0.50
Planned georedundant recover back rate	$\mu_{GRECOVER}$	Median hours to complete planned manual GR switchback	4.00	0.25
Planned georedundant migration disruption rate	$\mu_{MIGRATION}$	Median minutes of service disruption for orderly GR switchback	1.0	60

TABLE 8.6. Predicted Service Availability for DNS

State	Name	Service Status	Annualized Minutes in State	Uptime (Excluding "Timeout Pending")	Uptime (Including "Timeout Pending")	% of Downtime
1	Up on B1	Up	525598.845	525598.845	525598.845	
2	Timeout pending	Dubious	0.062		0.062	21.2%
3	Client covered	Down	0.000			0.1%
4	Up on B2 (or Bn)	Up	359.363	359.363	359.363	
5	Service migration	Up (for DNS)	1.497	1.497	1.497	
6	Client uncovered	Down	0.037			12.7%
7	Multiple down	Down	0.195			66.1%
		Total uptime		525959.705	525959.767	
		Annualized system downtime		0.295	0.233	
		Availability		99.99994%	99.99996%	

- *State 2 "Timeout Pending."* About 21% of predicted downtime is spent waiting for timeouts to expire from critical server failures, largely because without internal redundancy, a significant portion of critical failures are likely to render the server incapable of responding to client requests. If timeout periods are set short enough, then clients may be able to detect implicit timeout failures and recover service to an alternate server within the maximum acceptable application service latency, and thus time in this state can be excluded from consideration as service downtime. If these timeout periods are very long relative to users' service latency expectations, then users might view time spent in timeout pending state as service downtime.

- *State 3 "Client Covered."* Less than 1% of predicted downtime is spent in covered downtime because this example assumes that the majority of critical failures are successfully recovered onto "B2" (or "Bn") in 10 milliseconds $(1/\mu_{CLIENT})$ per failure.

- *State 4 "Up on B2 (or Bn)."* About 6 hours per year is spent in this state because the majority of critical failures are recovered successfully onto "B2" (or "Bn"), and we assume that service is gracefully migrated back to "B1" (and hence transitions to State 1 "Up on B1") about 4 hours $(1/\mu_{GRECOVER})$ after the failure.

- *State 5 "Service Migration."* The small value of $(1/\mu_{MIGRATION})$ causes a small amount of time to be spent in this state, but the small time spent in this state is not materially different from time spent in either state 1 "Up on B1" or state 4 "Up on B2 (or Bn)."
- *State 6 "Client Uncovered."* About 13% of predicted downtime is spent in the client uncovered state. Both the absolute time and percentage of downtime spent in uncovered downtime is likely to be far less for client-initiated recovery strategies than in system-driven or manually controlled recovery schemes because clients are generally better positioned to detect failures (thus reducing the risk of uncovered, silent failures) than server-based mechanisms are likely to be.
- *State 7 "Multiple Down."* About 66% of predicted downtime is spent in the multiple down state. It should be noted that the client-initiated recovery model used did not account for the possibility of additional redundant servers being available (e.g., "Bn") and a second client-initiated recovery attempt if server "B2" (or Bn) fails before "B1" is repaired, returned to service, and traffic is migrated back to "B1."

When considering the availability predicted by the client-initiated recovery model for service across a pool of DNS server in Table 8.6, we assumed the availability of an individual standalone DNS server instance was 99.97% (more than 2.5 hours of annualized service downtime). Thus, this model predicts that client-initiated recovery improves DNS service availability by more than two orders of magnitude—or two "9's"—compared with a standalone DNS server with no internal redundancy.

8.4.1   Sensitivity Analysis

Mathematical modeling enables one to compute the sensitivity of a result to changes of individual input parameters. Operationally, one varies individual parameters over their feasible range of values to determine how influential each individual parameter is. By considering both the likely value of each input parameter and the effort required to drive the value of the parameter to a more optimal value, one can estimate the practical feasibility and resources required to drive a system to a particular service availability target.

It is convenient to visualize sensitivity analyses by plotting predicted results across the range of feasible input values. For example, consider Figure 8.20, which gives predicted downtime (on y-axis) as a function of critical failure rate (on x-axis). It is best to use the same predicted downtime scale on the y-axis for an entire family of sensitivity analyses so one can visually identify the most sensitive parameters by their steeper slope. For a detailed description of how to perform sensitivity analysis using commonly available spreadsheet programs, see Bauer et al. (2009).

8.4.1.1 Influential Modeling Parameters. Modeling of this sample DNS solution demonstrates that the following parameters are most influential:

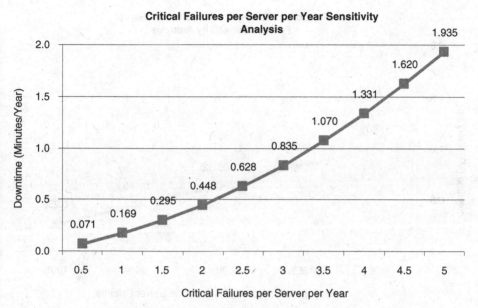

Figure 8.20. Sensitivity of critical failures per year.

- λ. Critical failures per year (see Fig. 8.20) are obviously highly influential; after all, if there were no critical failures, then availability of a standalone system would be 100%.

- C_{CLIENT}. Clients' ability to recognize failure indications from server (see Fig. 8.21)—obviously, if the client does not recognize or appropriately respond to an explicit critical failure indication from the server, or the server sends inappropriate responses, then the client would not promptly initiate recovery action, and thus service downtime will accrue.

- $\mu_{\text{GRECOVERY}}$. Nonredundant exposure time (see Fig. 8.22)—a service that is delivered by the redundant server without protection of the primary system is at higher risk of unavailability following critical failure. The longer the service remains simplex exposed (because the service has not been reverted to full redundant operation), the higher the risk of service downtime.

- μ_{DUPLEX}. Time to recover from duplex (multiple) failures (see Fig. 8.23). Duplex repair time is generally an influential parameter, but the simplified model overstates the influence of this parameter in DNS server deployments with pools of more than two server instances. This simplified model of client-initiated recovery does not consider the availability benefits of more than two deployed server instances. The model assumes that following failure of "B1," the client will select an alternate server "B2" (or "Bn"), and if the client cannot recover to that server because it is unavailable, then the client simply gives up and enters state 7 "multiple down." Robust real-world clients may be programmed to retry several times to different servers—thus increasing the likelihood of eventually transitioning to

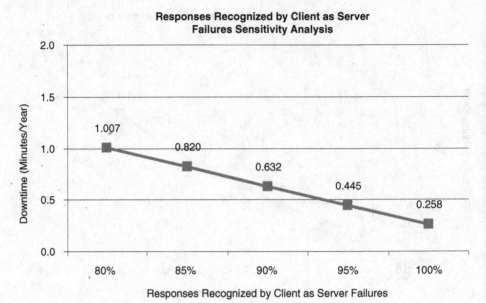

Figure 8.21. Sensitivity of C_{CLIENT}.

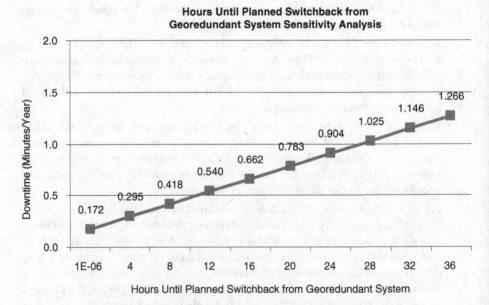

Figure 8.22. Sensitivity of $\mu_{GRECOVERY}$.

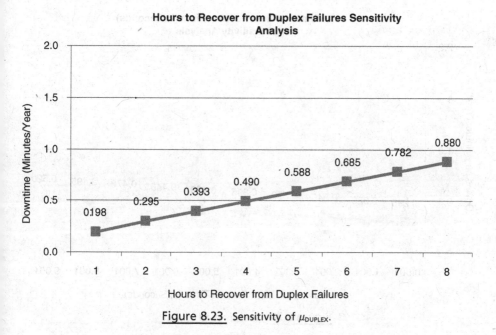

Figure 8.23. Sensitivity of μ_{DUPLEX}.

state 4 "up on B2 (or Bn)"—before eventually giving up and entering the "multiple down" state. As time spent in the "multiple down" state represents the bulk of predicted down time, more careful modeling of the recovery retry mechanism across a broader pool of servers could yield an even better result.

8.4.1.2 Less Influential Parameters. Given a set of assumed input values, modest changes of some parameters will cause significant changes to the predicted result, while modest changes to others will cause little or no change in the predicted result. For example, consider the sensitivity of the rate of client-initiated recovery, μ_{CLIENT}, as shown in Figure 8.24. As DNS is generally configured as a connectionless, stateless, and nonauthenticated service, clients can access service from alternate servers in milliseconds rather than minutes. The sensitivity chart in Figure 8.24 shows that there is little difference in the predicted result for a μ_{CLIENT} of 1 millisecond, 1 second (actually 1001 milliseconds) or 2 seconds (actually 2001 milliseconds); thus modest variations from the expected value of this parameter are not particularly influential on the predicted result.

Other parameters that are not particularly influential on predicted results when they vary across their expected range of values are:

- F_{CLIENT}. Portion of automatic client-initiated recoveries that succeed.
- $\mu_{\text{CLIENTSFD}}$. Rate for client to determine that uncovered (by client) failures are detected.
- $A_{\text{CLUSTER-1}}$. Service availability of cluster after primary server instance has failed.

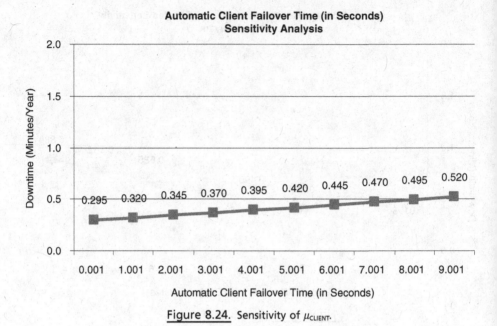

Figure 8.24. Sensitivity of μ_{CLIENT}.

- $F_{EXPLICIT}$. Portion of critical failures that are explicitly reported to client.
- $\mu_{TIMEOUT}$. Overall time for client to timeout from a nonresponsive server.

8.5 DISCUSSION OF PREDICTED RESULTS

As a connectionless and stateless service that typically operates with no identification, authentication, and authorization for query requests, DNS is the ideal demonstration of client-initiated recovery. The client-initiated recovery model for this sample DNS solution predicts that a pair of nominally 99.97% DNS servers can achieve approximately 99.99995% (six and a half 9's) product-attributable service availability, which is 1/574th the service downtime of a standalone 99.97% server.

The nominal upper bound for service availability of a pair of systems is defined as:

$$\text{TheoreticalAvailability}_{PAIR} \leq 2 \times A_{STANDALONE} - A_{STANDALONE}^2.$$

Solving this equation for $A_{STANDALONE}$ of 99.97% yields a theoretical upper bound of 99.999991% (seven 9's), which is 1/3333rd the service downtime of a standalone 99.97% server. Real-world considerations like noninstantaneous, imperfect failure detection and imperfect failure recovery will inevitably prevent real client-initiated recovery strategies from ever achieving the maximum TheoreticalAvailability$_{PAIR}$.

The 574 : 1 availability boost achieved in this example of client-initiated recovery is far greater than what is feasible for most other enterprise applications that can be engineered to support client-initiated recovery for the following reasons:

1. *Most Services Have Longer Client Recovery Latencies (μ_{CLIENT})*. Since DNS was modeled as an anonymous, connectionless, stateless service, negligible time was required for the client to reestablish service with "B2" after failure of "B1." Since most critical enterprise services require identification, authentication, and authorization before a session can be established, client recovery latencies are likely to contribute to service downtime.

2. *Lower Client-Initiated Recovery Success Probabilities (F_{CLIENT})*. Inevitably, it takes significant system resources to identify, authenticate, and authorize client users, and additional resources for servers to establish client sessions. A failure of the primary server will prompt literally all clients to quickly attempt to recover service onto a redundant server, and the processing load for completing the necessary identification, authentication, and authorization may saturate the server and cause congestion control mechanisms to activate. Successful engagement of congestion control mechanisms will cause at least some requests to reestablish service to be initially delayed or denied. While the clients should eventually reestablish service to the redundant server, some users may initially be unsuccessful at reestablishing service in the nominal ($1/\mu_{CLIENT}$) time.

3. *No Need to Recover, Resynchronize, and/or Reestablish Session Context*. Session-oriented services may maintain user-specific context information. For example, sessions with e-commerce websites maintain a shopping cart for each user throughout their shopping session which users expect to be maintained across failures and service disruptions. Recovering, resynchronizing, or rebuilding session context data will inevitably take some time (increasing $1/\mu_{CLIENT}$) and server resources (thus possibly triggering congestion controls and impacting $1/\mu_{CLIENT}$ and/or F_{CLIENT}).

4. *Less Aggressive Client Failover Criteria*. Since client-initiated failover may impact active sessions and service, session-oriented applications are likely to be less aggressive about switching to an alternate server, which guarantees a service disruption to the client. Thus, clients may want to be absolutely sure that the primary server is genuinely unavailable (and thus that service has been impacted) rather than quickly switching to an alternate server (which might unnecessarily impact service).

5. *Clients May Recover "Too Fast" for the Redundant Server*. If redundant servers must be promoted from standby to active or otherwise proactively changed to accept client service, there is the risk that clients will detect the failure and contact the redundant server before the redundant server is even aware that the primary server has failed. Thus, the client recovery will be delayed at least as long as it takes the redundant server to reconfigure itself to actively serve traffic.

9

SOLUTION AND CLUSTER RECOVERY

Many critical IT solutions require a suite of heterogeneous network elements to interwork in order to deliver service to users. Following site failure, it may be feasible to execute disaster recovery for each of the individual elements of a solution sequentially; however, disaster recovery times can often be shortened by recovering clusters of elements. This chapter explains solution and cluster recovery, compares cluster and element-level recovery, and considers modeling of cluster recovery.

9.1 UNDERSTANDING SOLUTIONS

Enterprises often rely on collections of individual elements integrated together to deliver complex and high-value services to users. These collections of systems are referred to as solutions. This section begins by reviewing typical entities that interact with solutions, followed by a model of a hypothetical solution that will be considered later in this chapter.

Beyond Redundancy: How Geographic Redundancy Can Improve Service Availability and Reliability of Computer-Based Systems, First Edition. Eric Bauer, Randee Adams, Daniel Eustace.
© 2012 Institute of Electrical and Electronics Engineers. Published 2012 by John Wiley & Sons, Inc.

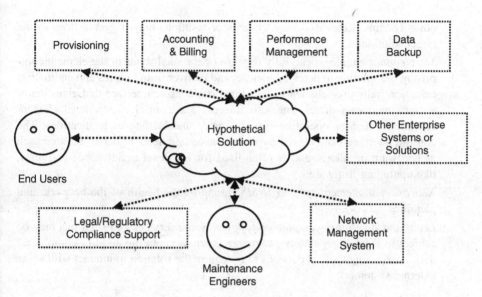

Figure 9.1. External interfaces to hypothetical solution.

9.1.1 Solution Users

Solutions typically expose a variety of distinct functions, services, or data to different users. The hypothetical enterprise solution exposes services, functionality, or data to the following users or entities, as shown in Figure 9.1.

- *End users* access the service via networked devices, such as a web browser on a PC or smartphone.
- *Provisioning* systems provide the tools and mechanisms for enterprise staff to add, modify, and delete user accounts, and to add and manipulate information about products and services offered by the solution.
- *Accounting and billing* systems support online and offline billing and general usage recording.
- *Performance management* systems record and analyze performance data (e.g., transaction volumes by time of day) for network and capacity planning.
- *Data backup* systems regularly backup key system configuration, user and other data to enable prompt recovery from data failures. Note that the backup data should be pushed into an off-site system or electronic vault, or written to physical media that is transported to another physical location to assure that a single site disaster does not impact both the element hosting the data and the backup copy.
- *Other enterprise systems or solutions.* Often user or other transactions trigger operations in other enterprise systems or solutions, such as order entry or e-commerce solutions triggering actions in enterprise resource planning and

other systems. Likewise, other systems or solutions may trigger actions in the target solution.

- *Maintenance engineers* carefully monitor operational status of the element comprising the solution to detect, diagnose, and recover from failures and anomalous behavior. Individual elements often support a console interface that gives maintenance engineers direct, interactive access and control of low-level element operations, such as operating system startup and loading of applications. The console interface can be used by maintenance engineers to debug failures such as hardware problems, and is often used for low-level maintenance activities, like upgrading firmware.
- *Network management systems (NMS)* monitors the health of the network, and identifies network issues.
- *Legal and regulatory compliance support.* Some services and solutions may be subject to legal or regulatory provisions, such as capturing audit or compliance data. Addressing these provisions may require the solution to interact with some external system(s).

9.1.2   Solution Architecture

Our hypothetical solution itself consists of a suite of network elements that are integrated together to offer the service to all consumers of the solution illustrated in Figure 9.1. Different network elements may directly support interfaces to different solution users and external support systems, and thus different solution users and external systems may require different suites of solution elements to be available and may use different client elements to access the solution. The hypothetical enterprise solution implements critical business processes that are constructed from the following systems:

- *Frontend server* that implements both user interface and application/business logic.
- *Authentication server* that controls access to the enterprise system and implements user authentication, authorization, and accounting.
- *Database server* that maintains the enterprise data.
- *Usage database* that records all user audit records for both compliance reporting and accounting (billing/chargeback).
- *Provisioning server* that adds, modifies, and deletes information held by the database server and user records held by the authentication server.
- *Element management system* that collects and analyzes data from the frontend, authentication and database servers; also monitors the alarms of all elements and supports other system management functions.
- *Backup system* that implements an electronic vault that captures backups from all elements in the solution.

Figure 9.2 shows a network diagram of how the elements of the hypothetical solution might connect.

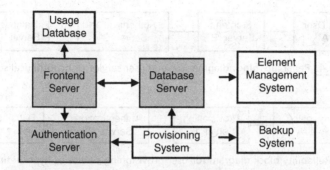

Figure 9.2. Network diagram of hypothetical solution.

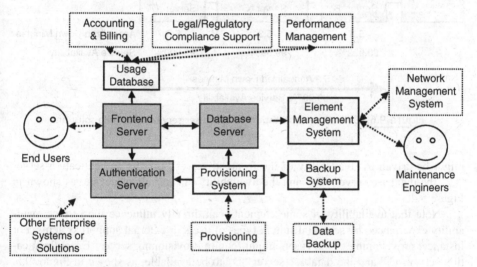

Figure 9.3. External interfaces to hypothetical solution.

Figure 9.3 overlays how the solution users of Section 9.1.1 access the hypothetical solution via interfaces to solution network elements.

9.2 ESTIMATING SOLUTION AVAILABILITY

Service availability experienced by different solution users would be driven by the aggregate service availability of different subsets of elements. Service availability experienced by a particular end user can be estimated by constructing a reliability block diagram (introduced in Section 3.1.3, "Single Point of Failure") with all of the elements that must be available for a particular type of service to be available arranged in series. For example, service availability experienced by end users of this hypothetical solution

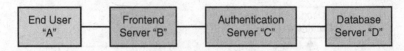

Figure 9.4. Reliability block diagram for end user service of hypothetical solution.

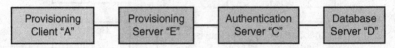

Figure 9.5. Reliability block diagram for user provisioning service of hypothetical solution.

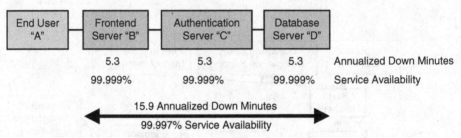

Figure 9.6. Downtime expectation for end user service of sample solution.

might be driven by availability of the frontend server "B," the authentication server "C," the database server "D," and the availability of their client device, as shown in Figure 9.4.

Note that availability of some elements can directly influence the service availability experienced by several different types of users or external support systems. For instance, provisioning of new users might require provisioning server "E," authentication server "C," and the database server "D" to be available, as shown in Figure 9.5. Thus, unavailability of either the authentication server "C" or the database server "D" would affect service availability experienced by both end users and provisioning engineers.

In a traditional nonredundant solution, service downtime is the sum of the downtime of the individual components that are required to be operational. Assuming frontend server "B," authentication server "C," and database server "D" are high-availability systems with five 9's availability expectations; one can overlay those downtime estimates onto the end user reliability block diagram of Figure 9.4 to produce Figure 9.6. From Figure 9.6, one sees that the overall unplanned service downtime for end users is expected to be about 16 minutes per year.

A solution service downtime estimate can be converted back to a service availability percentage via the following equation:

$$\text{Availability} = \frac{\text{MinutesPerYear} - \text{AnnualDownMinutes}}{\text{MinutesPerYear}}.$$

Counting leap years, the average year has 365.25 days; hence, the average MinutesPerYear is 365.25 days per average year times 24 hours per day times 60 minutes per hour, for a total of 525,960 minutes per average year. A 99.999% service availability means service is unavailable 0.001% of the time (100.000% − 99.999%). A 0.001% of 525,960 minutes per year is approximately 5.3 minutes of downtime per system per year. As shown in Figure 9.6, AnnualDownMinutes for end user service of the hypothetical solution (excluding user's client device "A" and networking gear and facilities) is estimated to be 5.3 down minutes for the frontend server plus 5.3 down minutes for the authentication server plus 5.3 down minutes for the database server, for a total of about 15.9 annualized down minutes. Thus:

$$\text{Availability}_{\text{SolutionEndUser}} = \frac{525960 - (3 \times 5.3)}{525960} = \frac{525960 - 15.9}{525960} = \frac{525944.1}{525960} = 99.997\%.$$

Pareto analysis of downtime contributions can often be helpful in planning solution availability improvements. Having estimated AnnualDownMinute, it is easy to compute the percentage of solution downtime expected to be contributed by each system element. In this example, we have assumed all three elements have the same availability—5.3 down minutes per year—and thus each element is estimated to contribute 33% of solution downtime (= 5.3 of 15.9 AnnualDownMinutes).

9.3   CLUSTER VERSUS ELEMENT RECOVERY

While recovery using external redundancy can often be executed sequentially by element type, one can potentially organize clusters of elements into recovery groups to enable faster or better recovery. Cluster-level recovery can be illustrated by generalizing the redundancy model of Figure 4.1, "Generic High Availability Model" into Figure 9.7, "Generic Redundant Cluster Model." While the reliability block diagram in Figure

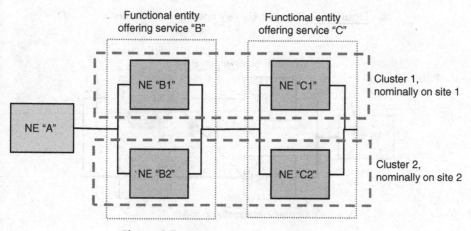

Figure 9.7. Generic redundant cluster model.

9.7 only adds redundant elements "C1" and "C2," one can add redundant "D1" and "D2," "E1" and "E2," and so on. All of the primary elements ("B1," "C1," etc) are assumed to be located at one site, and all of the redundant elements ("B2," "C2," etc) are assumed to be located on a second site.

Although there is only one recovery option from failure of an "edge" element of the cluster that directly interacts with the client (if "B1" fails, then client must recover to "B2"), there are two recovery options for failure of a cluster element inside the edge (C1):

1. *Element Recovery upon Element Failure* (Fig. 9.8). Failure of nonedge element "C1" can be recovered by "B1" switching to server "C2." Ideally, "B1" detects the failure fast enough and recovers sufficient session context with "C2" so that the recovery is transparent to the user of client "A."
2. *Cluster Recovery upon Element Failure* (Fig. 9.9). Failure of nonedge element "C1" can be recovered by switching the client away from cluster 1 to cluster 2. In this case, client "A" is explicitly involved in reestablishing service to "B2." Failure of element "C1" is explicitly communicated to client "A" via an error

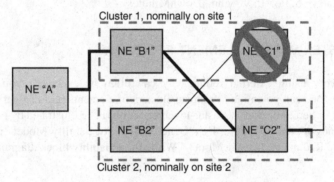

Figure 9.8. Element recovery upon element failure.

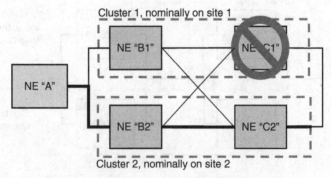

Figure 9.9. Cluster recovery upon element failure.

response (e.g., 503 Service Unavailable) that is returned by "B1" to "A" in response to failure of "C1," and the client is expected to initiate recovery to an alternate cluster. Note that in cluster recovery, the edge and/or other elements (e.g., "B1") explicitly proxy the failure response back to the client rather than attempting recovery. In addition, implicit failures (e.g., timeout expirations, loss of heartbeat) are translated by the edge element ("B1") into appropriate explicit failures, which are proxied back to the client and trigger it to failover to "B2."

Note that the distinction between element and cluster recovery can appear different to various elements in the solution. For example, while element "B1" executes element recovery from "C1" to "C2" in Figure 9.8, ideally, client "A" should be unaware any recovery action was taken. Likewise, cluster recovery from site 1 to site 2 in Figure 9.9 may appear to client "A" merely as element recovery to "B2" after an apparent failure of "B1." Disaster recovery plans generally try to make recovery from site disasters appear more like a cluster recovery than like a sequence of individual recoveries of each element in the solution, because fewer recovery actions are generally both faster and more likely to complete successfully.

Solutions with more than two elements (e.g., D1/D2, E1/E2, etc) may deploy hybrid recovery strategies in which some element failures are mitigated via element recovery and others are mitigated via cluster recovery. In addition, recovery clusters can be smaller than the suite of all solution elements on a site, thus a failure of one element on site 1 could cause some service to be recovered onto a small recovery cluster of elements on site 2 while other elements on site 1 continue delivering service.

One of the keys for implementing cluster recovery is to configure each element to send its service requests to local servers first, and to remote servers if none of the local servers are available. One way to accomplish this is with DNS SRV records, which allow a priority to be assigned to each server in a fully qualified domain name (FQDN) pool. With this configuration, when an element fails and service is switched to the remote site, that element will send its own requests to other elements in the same site. With most communication between elements occurring within the same site, latency is not increased as much as for single-element switchover.

In the example earlier, the FQDNs for the C1/C2 servers can be implemented this way. If the client fails over to "B2," then "B2" will automatically use local server "C2." However, if the client is using "B1" and "C1" fails, then "B1" will begin sending its requests to "C2." Since this traffic will flow between geographically remote sites, additional WAN bandwidth will be used and the latency of these requests will increase. In order to do a cluster failover in this case, "B1" must have special software logic to handle "C" server failures differently. After detecting the failure of "C1," "B1" needs to explicitly return an error code to the client that was defined to trigger it to initiate a recovery to an alternate server. For example, if the protocol between the client and "B1" is SIP, then "B1" server could return a "503 Service Unavailable" response to trigger the client to failover to the remote site.

9.4 ELEMENT FAILURE AND CLUSTER RECOVERY CASE STUDY

An interesting architectural question is whether cluster recovery is ever a better strategy for element failures than single element failover. The architectural considerations and tradeoffs are best illustrated via an example; consider the case of user service for the hypothetical solution described earlier in this chapter. As this sample solution implements a service critical to the enterprise, assume it is deployed with external redundancy on geographically separated sites. Figure 9.10 illustrates the reliability block diagram of georedundant configuration of the solution, with client "A" being served by the server cluster on site 1.

Consider the optimal recovery strategy from inevitable failure of one of the active elements in the solution:

- *Failure of Frontend Server "B1."* If the frontend server "B1" on site 1 fails, then service must be recovered onto the frontend server "B2." Given the high volume of data traffic between the frontend server and the database server, it is desirable for the frontend server to use a database server on the same site to minimize WAN traffic (by keeping frontend server and database traffic on the same LAN) and avoid service latency associated with long-haul data transport for transactions between frontend and database servers. Thus, the cluster recovery strategy shown in Figure 9.11 is best.
- *Failure of Authentication Server "C1."* The frontend server communicates with the authentication server when establishing sessions with clients and occasionally thereafter; there is negligible communication between the database server and the authentication server. Thus, element recovery of a failed authentication server will add only a small increment of load to the WAN traffic between site 1 and site 2, and the increased service latency to transit the increased physical distance

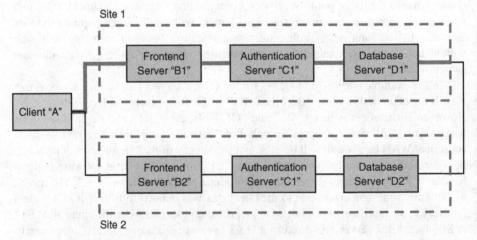

Figure 9.10. Reliability block diagram for georedundant redundant hypothetical solution.

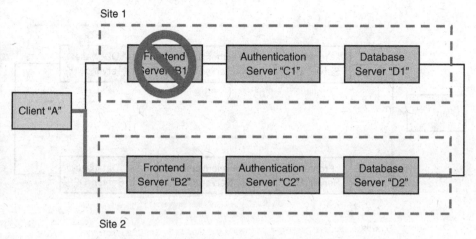

Figure 9.11. Client recovery for a frontend server failure.

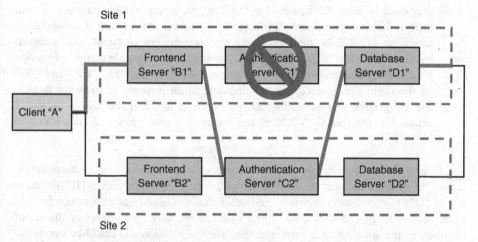

Figure 9.12. Element recovery of security server in sample solution.

between site 1 and site 2 for authentication transactions is likely to only slightly increase service latency seen by end users. Hence, element recovery of authentication server failure is likely to have negligible impact for the vast majority of normal end user operations. Cluster recovery of a failed authentication server is feasible, but that is likely to impact end user service when service is redirected from frontend server "B1" to frontend "B2." Therefore, element recovery for authentication server failures (illustrated in Fig. 9.12) is likely to have less overall service impact on users than cluster recovery would have.

- *Failure of Database Server "D1."* There is likely to be significant network traffic between the frontend server and database server backend; in fact, there

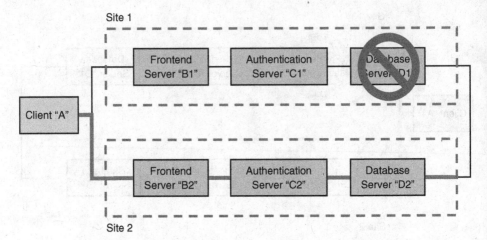

Figure 9.13. Cluster recovery of database server in sample solution.

may even be more traffic between the frontend server and database server than there is between the client and the frontend server. As a result if the database server on site 1 fails, then triggering cluster recovery so client "A" is served by frontend server "B2" is more likely to maintain acceptable quality of service for end users than an element-level recovery. With servers "B2," "C2," and "D2" on the same site, service is not vulnerable to an increase in transport latency and congestion due to routing all traffic from the frontend server on site 1 across the enterprise's WAN to the database server on site 2 (illustrated in Fig. 9.13).

Hybrid recovery strategies in which some element failures (e.g., authentication server "C") trigger element recovery while others (e.g., frontend server "B," database server "D") trigger cluster recovery may offer the best quality of experience for end users. Interestingly, the recovered cluster of elements may be a subset of the set of elements in the solution on a particular site. Thus, a solution site could be organized into one or more recovery clusters, and some number of elements could be recovered via individual element recovery. Recovery clusters can overlap. As explained in Section 9.1, solutions often include several different types of network elements that serve very different roles and may have very different operational and recovery characteristics. Some elements are directly involved in delivering service to the solution's primary users and thus have high-availability expectations while other elements may support less critical functions or users. Since an all-or-nothing cluster recovery of all solution elements located on a single site may have an unacceptable overall service impact for resolving typical service disruptions, two hybrid solution recovery strategies are often employed:

• *Recover some elements individually rather than via a multi element cluster.* If the service offered by a particular element can rapidly be restored with minimal

collateral service impact by recovering to a redundant instance of the failed element, then it is generally better to take this less impactful recovery option.
- *Factor the overall solution into two or more smaller recovery clusters.* While it may be impractical to individually recover each element that does not directly impact primary service to end users, it may be practical to organize a subset of elements that deliver that service into a recovery cluster to enable efficient recovery of that function with minimal overall service disruption of primary functionality to primary system users.

The result is that a large solution might have a hybrid recovery model comprised of one or more recovery clusters and several individually recoverable elements. The hypothetical solution of Section 9.1 might have the following recovery groups:

- user service recovery cluster: frontend server, authentication server, and database server; and
- element recovery for usage database, provisioning server, network management system, element management system, and backup vault.

Note that in the event of a WAN failure or site disaster that renders all or most of the solution elements on a single site unavailable or inaccessible, all solution service will be switched to the alternate site. The disaster recovery procedure will thus likely be different than sequential execution of the recovery procedures for individual elements.

Standalone high-availability systems often have several levels of automatic recovery such as:

1. abort and retry of failed transactions;
2. restart of failed processes; and
3. restarting operating system and application on a processor.

Thus, high-availability system architectures must assure that the multiple recovery options do not interfere with each other to prolong service disruptions. Typically, this is resolved by having more impactful recoveries (e.g., restarting a processor) triggered from an escalation after the failure of less impactful recoveries (e.g., retrying a transaction or restarting a process) and when called for superseded lower-level recoveries. Similarly, a cluster-level recovery will typically preempt element-level recovery by redirecting traffic earlier in the processing flow. Note that solutions must be carefully architected so that competing recoveries do not deadlock critical resources, such as exclusive access to user account records. Without careful design, an element-level recovery might seize and hold exclusive access to a user-related record that thus prevents the user from recovering service to a redundant cluster. Because georedundant recovery is fundamentally designed to recover from disasters that could leave some or all systems on the failed site in an unknown state, it is best to design georedundant cluster recovery to preempt network element-level recovery to avoid the risk of a compromised system on a disaster site blocking a georedundant recovery.

9.5 COMPARING ELEMENT AND CLUSTER RECOVERY

This chapter compares and contrasts cluster and element recovery across the external recovery actions of Section 4.1, "Generic External Redundancy Model," for element failure.

9.5.1 Failure Detection

External failure detection mechanisms such as protocol timeouts are more limited than inherently internal system failure mechanisms, like processor exceptions. For example, if element "B1" attempts to access an illegal memory location (e.g., dereferencing a null pointer), then the processor on "B1" can interrupt the software platform running on "B1" to explicitly report a processor exception. In contrast, both "B2" and "A" have a narrower set of failure detection mechanisms to determine if "B1" successfully detected and recovered from an internal failure. Viable failure detection mechanisms that could activate element-level client-initiated or system-driven recovery could be configured to activate cluster-level recovery. For example, upon detecting local failure (e.g., a processor exception), the server could potentially return an appropriate error to the client (e.g., 500 Server Internal Error). Note that prompt recovery action by the element immediately adjacent to the failure (e.g., "B1" if "C1" fails) may be important to prevent the client "A" from autonomously detecting the failure of "C1" and activating client-initiated recovery to "B2" (effectively a cluster recovery) even though element-level recovery is the preferred recovery strategy for failure of element "C1."

9.5.2 Triggering Recovery Action

Triggering recovery action for cluster recovery is likely to be somewhat more complex than simply activating element-level recovery because an appropriate error indication must be rapidly communicated to affected clients, and normal element-level recovery must be preempted. Care must be taken to assure that clients and elements within the cluster that support element-level recovery are carefully coordinated so that the clients and elements promptly and efficiently execute a coherent recovery strategy rather than experiencing a chaotic recovery in which not all elements execute consistent recovery actions, thus delaying service recovery and/or increasing service impact.

9.5.3 Traffic Redirection

Traffic redirection for cluster recovery is generally simpler than for element-level recovery because traffic redirection need only be supported between one pair of elements (nominally "A" redirecting traffic from "B1" to "B2") rather than between every pair of elements in the solution (e.g., "B1" recovering to "C2" on failure of "C1," "C1" recovering to "D2" on failure of "D1," etc). Logically, if a critical solution (excluding client "A") includes "N" elements, carefully designed, implemented, and tested element-level recovery should be supported for all "N" elements. Note that some elements may be shared by multiple solutions, such as the case of multiple-enterprise applications using a single-authenication server to efficiently support a single password for each user to all authorized applications. In those cases, the robustness testing of each solution should individually verify rapid and reliable automatic failure detection and recovery from likely failure modes of the shared element(s). In contrast, if strict cluster-level recovery is supported, then only one cluster-level recovery mechanism must be designed and tested.

9.5.4 Service Context Preservation

The extent of service context preservation is largely a function of how much dynamic context information the elements of the solution replicate to their mates (e.g., "B1" replication to "B2"), and the abilities of the communications protocols to rapidly and seamlessly resynchronize with the recovered element or cluster. Cluster recovery may simplify service context recovery because the client is explicitly involved in rebuilding service context by reconnecting to "B2," reauthenticating, and so on. Thus, cluster recovery may be slower while service context is rebuilt for each client, but it may be far simpler to accept the longer service recovery latency of cluster recovery rather than to implement and test service context preservation and recovery for each network element in the solution to support element-level recovery.

9.5.5 Graceful Migration

As with service context preservation, graceful service migration is primarily influenced by factors other than element or cluster recovery. For example, some application protocols are designed to support session timeouts with server disconnect due to inactivity. In that case, clients automatically reinitialize the session prior to re-interfacing with the server. Mechanisms for automatic server disconnection on inactivity can be used to gracefully drain traffic from the redundant server and then automatically reconnect clients to the recovered primary server when necessary.

9.6 MODELING CLUSTER RECOVERY

The generic redundant cluster model shown in Figure 9.7 can be simplified by treating each cluster as a logical "super element." For example, the cluster-level recovery shown in Figure 9.9 can be modeled as an element recovery of super element "BC," as shown in Figure 9.14. While the super element could include an arbitrary number of the elements (e.g., C1/C2, D1/D2, etc), this example refers to super elements generically as "BC1" and "BC2."

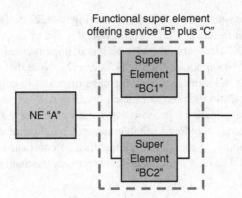

Figure 9.14. Modeling super element recovery.

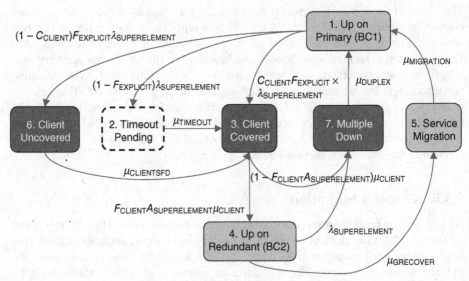

Figure 9.15. Client-initiated super element cluster recovery model.

Cluster recovery by element "A" from super element "BC1" to "BC2" can be modeled by applying the client-initiated recovery Markov model from Section 6.3.5, "Client-Initiated Georedundancy Recovery," to produce the model of Figure 9.15. Each of these states from Figure 9.15 is explained below:

- *State 1 "Up on Primary Cluster ('BC1').":* This is the normal state in which client "A" is served by their "normal" primary super element cluster ("BC1").
- *State 2 "Timeout Pending.":* This state captures the time after client "A" sends a request to primary super element cluster ("BC1") following a critical failure of some element within the primary cluster that is not explicitly reported to client

"A" and hence the client has not yet recognized that the primary cluster is unavailable. After client "A" decides that the primary cluster ("BC1") is unavailable, the model transitions to state 3 "client covered." Super element recovery is typically more complex than element recovery because multiple elements may be involved in failure detection and recovery decisions (e.g., "B1" detecting failure of "C1" and proxying back appropriate response to "A"). Thus, while time spent in the "timeout pending" state for client-initiated element recovery is generally designed to be less than the client's maximum acceptable service disruption time, typical timeout for super element recovery may be longer, especially if the solution and cluster are architected so that automatic internal recovery of cluster elements is given time to complete. Client-initiated super element recovery can be used to backup automatic element recovery that was not successful or that is taking longer than the super element timeout.

- *State 3 "Client Covered."* This state captures the time between the client's determination that the primary super element cluster "BC1" is unavailable and when service is recovered onto the redundant cluster "BC2." This state is reached either from state 1 "up on primary cluster ('BC1')" via an explicit error message reporting unavailability, such as SIP's "503 Service Unavailable" return code, or from state 2 "timeout pending" via timeout expiration of the maximum number of retried requests.

- *State 4 "Up on Redundant Cluster ('BC2')."* This state represents the time when client "A" is successfully served by redundant super element cluster "BC2."

- *State 5 "Service Migration."* This state captures orderly service migration of client "A" from redundant super element cluster "BC2" to recovered primary super element cluster "BC1." Depending on the architecture of the solution—such as the protocols, clients, and solution configuration—the actual migration procedure time in this state might not be considered service downtime.

- *State 6 "Client Uncovered."* This state captures the time during which the primary cluster "BC1" is down, but the client "A" mistakenly believes that the primary cluster is up. This state is most likely to be reached because the primary cluster reports failure to the client with an improperly covered error or because of a failure in the client's recovery software. For example, if the primary cluster experiences a critical failure but maps it to a request failure (e.g., 400 Bad Request, 401 Unauthorized) rather than a service failure that activates client-initiated recovery (e.g., 503 Service Unavailable), then the client will not retry the request against an alternate cluster and thus must wait for the primary cluster to be recovered automatically or through some manual recovery action.

- *State 7 "Multiple Down."* This state captures the time when service is unavailable because both the primary ("BC1") and redundant ("BC2") super element clusters are down.

If the cluster or solution is architected such that successful automatic internal recovery from some or all elements in the cluster are expected to occur before client-initiated super element recovery, then the super element recovery model will only "see" the fraction of critical element failures that were not successfully detected, isolated, and recovered faster than the client recovery timeout value. In this case, the individual availability models of standalone elements are logically considered first because super element recovery will only act on a fraction of the element failure events. This is detailed in Section 9.6.2, "Estimating $\lambda_{\text{SUPERELEMENT}}$."

9.6.1   Cluster Recovery Modeling Parameters

This section reviews the modeling parameters of the client-initiated super element recovery model of Figure 9.15, highlighting how these parameters differ between element and super element recovery. This comparison is summarized in Table 9.1; the implications of this comparison are discussed at the end of this section.

- **Failure Rate**—$\lambda_{\text{SUPERELEMENT}}$. The critical failure rate of a super element is nominally the sum of the chargeable critical failure rates of the elements that comprise the super element. Note that critical failures which are automatically recovered by elements within the super element and do not trigger cluster recovery are excluded from $\lambda_{\text{SUPERELEMENT}}$. For super elements built from individual network elements with internal redundancy, that often means that covered failures (failures which are successfully detected, isolated, and recovered) are excluded from this parameter. Whether covered element failures should be included or not is determined by how aggressive the client-initiated recovery is and the policy on minimum chargeable service outages. Estimation of $\lambda_{\text{SUPERELEMENT}}$ is detailed in Section 9.6.2.

- F_{EXPLICIT}. This parameter represents the probability that a critical failure of an element in the super element triggers a timely error response that the client recognizes as a signal to execute recovery to the redundant super element. While F_{EXPLICIT} for failures of "B1" in super element "BC1" are likely to be the same as F_{EXPLICIT} for standalone element "B1," the probability that failures of elements within the cluster (i.e., "C1," "D1," etc.) being correctly proxied to client "A" are likely to be somewhat lower. The overall F_{EXPLICIT} of the super element can be estimated as the average F_{EXPLICIT} of individual element failures within the cluster prorated by their relative critical failure rates. Mathematically, this is the average value of the product of each element's critical failure rate and its effective coverage factor (typically C_A) as described in Section 3.2, "Modeling Availability of Internal Redundancy." Note that if failures of a particular element are primarily expected to be recovered via automatic internal recovery rather than client-initiated super element recovery, then the successful internal recovery scenarios should be excluded from consideration when estimating this parameter.

- C_{CLIENT}. This parameter estimates the probability that the error explicitly returned from the cluster will cause the client to initiate recovery to the redundant cluster. Effectively, this parameter estimates the probability that a failure detected within the cluster will be properly reported to the client "A" (e.g., 503 Service

TABLE 9.1. Comparison of Client-Initiated Recovery Parameter Values

Client-Initiated Recovery Modeling Parameter	How Typical Value for Super Element Recovery Compares with Individual Element Recovery
λ	Worse. $\lambda_{\text{SUPERELEMENT}}$ is inherently larger than λ for an individual element because clients are exposed to at least some failures of additional elements (e.g., "C1," "D1," etc.) beyond a single element "B1." $\lambda_{\text{SUPERELEMENT}}$ is explained in detail in Section 9.6.2, "Estimating $\lambda_{\text{SUPERELEMENT}}$."
F_{EXPLICIT}	Similar to worse because of (somewhat) increased complexity of configuring various elements within the super element cluster to intelligently proxy critical failure indications to responses that trigger client-initiated recovery. As a practical matter, architecting cluster recovery generally prompts more careful consideration and methodical testing of rapid and automatic detection of both explicit and implicit failures of individual elements in the cluster.
C_{CLIENT}	Similar to worse because of the complexity of assuring that error codes from non-edge elements (i.e., "C1," "D1," etc) are properly mapped by "B1" to protocol errors that cause client "A" to initiate recovery to redundant super element "BC2."
μ_{CLIENT}	Worse because more elements in the solution are likely to have to recover or rebuild state/context information, and some of that rebuilding is likely to be serialized when many clients recover simultaneously following critical failure of an element in "BC1."
F_{CLIENT}	Better to similar. Client recovery to super element "BC2" is likely to have similar to identical reliability as service establishment to primary super element "BC1" because presumably super element recovery is essentially the same as normal service session establishment to the primary super element "BC1." In contrast, client-initiated recovery of an individual element is likely to be tested and executed far less, and thus may be somewhat less mature and reliable. Note that the reliability benefit of frequent client connection (and presumably reconnection) to a super element will be somewhat offset if large amounts of client context must be recovered onto numerous individual elements within the cluster.
μ_{TIMEOUT}	Same. Super element client timeout for "BC1" must abide by the same protocol restrictions that cover individual element "B1."
$\mu_{\text{CLIENTSFD}}$	Same to worse, depending on the specifics of the service, usage profiles, roles, and responsibilities of individual elements in the super element and other factors.
$A_{\text{SUPERELEMENT}}$	Worse, because more elements are required to be "up" for the super element to be available.
μ_{DUPLEX}	Same because the same operational policies are likely to be used by the enterprise for both element and cluster recovery.
$\mu_{\text{GRECOVERY}}$	Same because the same operational policies are likely to be used by the enterprise for both element and cluster recovery.
$\mu_{\text{MIGRATION}}$	Same because the same operational policies are likely to be used by the enterprise for both element and cluster recovery.

Unavailable) rather than as some error that does not trigger recovery by the client element (e.g., 400 Bad Request).

- μ_{CLIENT}. This value includes the time for:
  - the client to select and contact the redundant super element;
  - negotiate a protocol version;
  - complete any required identification, authentication and authorization to establish a session; and
  - recover or reestablish an appropriate session context to minimize user-visible service disruption.

    This parameter is the mathematical reciprocal of the time it takes the typical client (nominally 50th percentile latency) to recover service to the redundant cluster. The value of μ_{CLIENT} is assumed to be the same for failure of any element within the super element; thus μ_{CLIENT} should be the same for failure of "B1" as it is for failure of "C1," "D1," etc.

- F_{CLIENT}. Captures the probability that client-initiated recovery to the redundant cluster will succeed. Congestion and overload when many clients simultaneously attempt to recover to a redundant cluster can impact the probability of success, as can software bugs in both clients and elements within the redundant cluster. For example, if a critical element in the super element fails when the cluster is operating at full load, F_{CLIENT} considers the percentage of clients that will be successfully and automatically recovered onto redundant super element "BC2."

- μ_{TIMEOUT}. This is the mathematical reciprocal of the typical time it takes the client to detect nonresponse of element "B1." This value should be identical for element "B1" and for super element "BC1."

- $\mu_{\text{CLIENTSFD}}$. This is the mathematical reciprocal of the time it takes the client to detect a cluster failure that was not explicitly communicated and recognized. In the real world, this value is likely to vary with the usage profile of individual users. For example, users are much more likely to promptly recognize that their connection to the Internet has failed and that they need to take explicit corrective action (e.g., manually rebooting a cable modem or personal computer) when they are actively using the client device/system rather than when they are not actively using the service (e.g., while sleeping).

- $A_{\text{SUPERELEMENT}}$. $A_{\text{SUPERELEMENT}}$ of a super element is the product of the availability ratings of all elements in the cluster. For example, $A_{\text{SUPERELEMENT}}$ of super element "BC" (A_{BC}) is the product of service availability for element "B" (A_{B}) and service availability for element "C" (A_{C}), so $A_{\text{BC}} = A_{\text{B}} \times A_{\text{C}}$.

- μ_{DUPLEX}. Duplex failure repair time ($1/\mu_{\text{DUPLEX}}$) should be similar for cluster- and element-level recovery. Complex super element clusters may require more elaborate procedures to recover service from duplex failures than merely repairing one or more element failures. If more elaborate procedures are typically required, then longer ($1/\mu_{\text{DUPLEX}}$) values can be used.

- μ_{GRECOVER}. Enterprise operational policies govern how promptly service is migrated from a redundant server back to the repaired primary. For example,

many enterprises will gracefully migrate service during the first daily maintenance period following repair of the primary system. As the same operational
policy is likely to apply to both element and cluster recoveries, planned georedundant recovery time ($1/\mu_{GRECOVER}$) is likely to be the same for both element
and cluster recovery.

- $\mu_{MIGRATION}$. The service disruption time ($1/\mu_{MIGRATION}$) is likely to be the same for
  any cluster recovery but may be different for element recovery, depending on the
  element affected.

While modeling of super element recovery typically suggests the availability
benefit is likely to be lower than element-level client-initiated recovery because several
input parameters (λ, C_{CLIENT}, μ_{CLIENT}, $\mu_{CLIENTSFD}$) are likely to be somewhat worse and
only one parameter (F_{CLIENT}) is likely to be better, implementing and testing a single
client-initiated super element recovery architecture might be less complex than supporting client-initiated recovery of all individual elements in a solution.

9.6.2 Estimating $\lambda_{SUPERELEMENT}$

$\lambda_{SUPERELEMENT}$ is the rate of failures that confront the client-initiated recovery mechanism
for the super element; concretely, this is the sum of the critical failure rates of the
individual elements in the super element minus the failures that are recovered by internal redundancy fast enough that the super element recovery mechanism ignores them.
The rate of failures that are presented to the super element's client-initiated recovery
mechanism can be estimated from architecture-based Markov availability models for
each individual element in the super element.

Consider a hypothetical element with internal active–active redundancy that is
described in Section 3.2.1, "Modeling Active–Active Redundancy," and can be modeled
with Figure 3.9. Assume that state 4 "detected (covered) failure" downtime will be
addressed via automatic internal recovery (i.e., automatic failover ($1/\mu_{FO}$) is faster than
client timeout ($1/\mu_{TIMEOUT}$)) so that successful automatic internal recoveries will not
activate client-initiated recovery mechanisms. However, since the element's internal
silent failure detection time ($1/\mu_{SFDTA}$), manual recovery time ($1/\mu_{FOM}$), and duplex
repair time ($1/\mu_{DUPLEX}$) are much longer than ($1/\mu_{TIMEOUT}$), client-initiated super element
recovery can mitigate downtime in the three "slower" down states: state 3 "Undetected
(Uncovered) Failure," state 5 "Failed Failover," and state 6 "Duplex Failure." Figure
9.16 overlays comments onto the standard active–active redundancy model of Figure
3.9 to illustrate the downtime that can be mitigated by client-initiated recovery of failures that were not automatically recovered internally. Specifically:

- *State 3 "Undetected (Uncovered) Failure."* Client-initiated recovery should
  activate on failures that were uncovered by the failed system itself.
- *State 5 "Failed Failover."* Client-initiated recovery should activate on failed
  failover events that would otherwise require (slower) manual recovery
  actions.

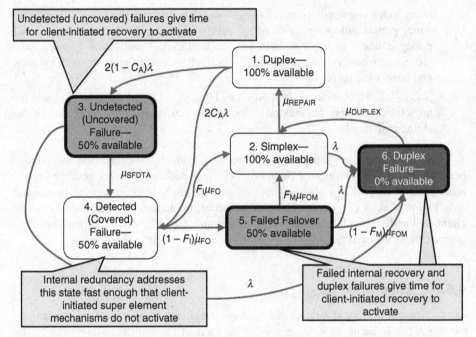

Figure 9.16. Active–active states that can be mitigated by client-initiated recovery.

- *State 6 "Duplex Failure."* Client-initiated recovery should activate on duplex failure events that require (slower) manual recovery actions to repair and restore service.

The rate of failure events that could activate client-initiated recovery mechanisms can be estimated by considering the three state transitions highlighted in Figure 9.17:

1. *State 1 "Duplex" to State 3 "Undetected (Uncovered) Failure."* This is the rate of undetected (uncovered) failures experienced by the system for which clients will experience some downtime until the failure is eventually detected and recovered, either internally or via a client-initiated recovery mechanism. The entry rate to this state is $2(1 - C_A)\lambda$ for an active–active system, but since only half of the clients will see the failure (the half that were served by the failed component), the effective failure contribution from this state is roughly estimated as $(1 - C_A)\lambda$.

2. *State 4 "Detected (Covered) Failure" to State 5 "Failed Failover."* Failed automatic internal recoveries can potentially be mitigated by client-initiated recovery mechanisms, and these events are captured in this transition. This rate is nominally $(1 - F_I)$ of the automatic recovery attempts, but to avoid double counting uncovered events (i.e., $(1 - C_A)\lambda$) considered in the previous point, we estimate this rate as only C_A (rather than (C_A plus $(1 - C_A)$, or 1). Thus, this particular transition rate is estimated as $C_A\lambda(1 - F_I)$.

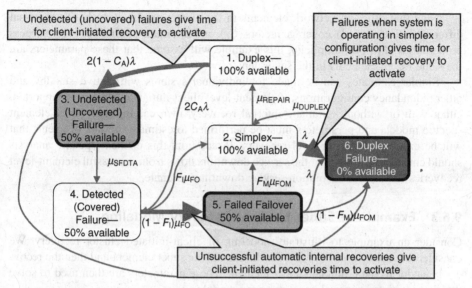

Figure 9.17. Active–active state transitions that can activate client-initiated recovery.

3. *State 2 "Simplex" to State 6 "Duplex Failure."* Well-run enterprises will promptly execute repairs to minimize the time redundant systems operate simplex exposed. For example, many enterprises will complete these repairs within hours (rather than days or weeks), and thus systems should spend very little of their operational time in the simplex state. This rate can be estimated by discounting the element failure rate λ by the fraction of time spent in state 2 "Simplex" (nominally $P_{SIMPLEX}$), or $P_{SIMPLEX}\lambda$. The actual time spent in state 2 "Simplex" will vary based on system characteristics and enterprise operational policies, but it is likely to be far less than 1% of the total operational period, and may easily be less than 0.01% of the total operational period.

Thus, the rate of failures that are visible to client-initiated recovery mechanisms of this system (λ_{CIR}) is estimated as follows:

$$\lambda_{CIR} \approx (1-C_A)\lambda + C_A\lambda(1-F_I) + P_{SIMPLEX}\lambda$$

$$\lambda_{CIR} \approx \lambda - C_A\lambda + C_A\lambda - C_A\lambda F_I + P_{SIMPLEX}\lambda$$

$$\lambda_{CIR} \approx \lambda - C_A\lambda F_I + P_{SIMPLEX}\lambda$$

$$\lambda_{CIR} \approx (1 - C_A F_I + P_{SIMPLEX})\lambda$$

The failure rates visible to the super element client-initiated recovery mechanism should sum across the individual elements of the super element, and thus:

$$\lambda_{SUPERELEMENT} \approx \sum_{ElementsInCluster} (1 - C_A F_I + P_{SIMPLEX})\lambda$$

Equation 9.1. Estimating $\lambda_{SUPERELEMENT}$

Note that different network elements in the cluster are likely to have somewhat different failure rates (λ), coverage factors (C_A), and automatic internal recovery success probabilities (F_I). For simplicity, this example will assume that these parameters are the same for all elements in the superelement.

Similar estimates can be made for individual systems with active–standby and other redundancy configurations. If element-level client-initiated recovery is supported, either with or without automatic internal recovery, then careful analysis of element specific models and parameters must be performed to estimate the rate of events that will be exposed to cluster-level recovery. In addition, this element specific analysis should consider how much of the service downtime flows from successful element-level recoveries to the overall solution service downtime estimate.

9.6.3 Example of Super Element Recovery Modeling

Consider an example to illustrate modeling of client-initiated cluster recovery. We consider the input parameters first for the standalone super element and then the recovery behavior of the redundant super element. These parameters are then used to solve the client-initiated super element recovery model.

9.6.3.1 Estimating Standalone Super Element Behavior. For simplicity, we shall assume that the super element is comprised of three elements ("B," "C," and "D"), all of which behave as the nominal active–active system described in Section 3.2.1, "Modeling Active–Active Redundancy." As a reminder, the assumed element input parameters are shown in Table 9.2 (repeated from Table 3.1), the time spent in each state is shown in Table 9.3 (repeated from Table 3.2), and the predicted service availability per element is 99.9972%.

As described in Section 9.6.2, "Estimating $\lambda_{\text{SUPERELEMENT}}$," $\lambda_{\text{SUPERELEMENT}}$ is estimated as $(1 - F_I C_A)\lambda$ for each individual system in the super element, or $3(1 - C_A F_I + P_{\text{SIMPLEX}})\lambda$ overall; note that P_{SIMPLEX} is predicted directly from the active–active Markov model to be 0.0456%. C_{CLIENT} is assumed to be 90%. Assuming B offers an authenticated session-oriented service to client "A," ($1/\mu_{\text{CLIENT}}$) is likely to require several seconds; example will assume 5 seconds. Since the super element contains three elements all of which are nominally 99.9972%, $A_{\text{SUPERELEMENT}}$ is $(99.9972\%)^3$, which is 99.9916%. Since the success probability of client recovery to the redundant super element is assumed to be the same as the success probability of service with the primary super element, F_{CLIENT} of 99.999% will be used. Other modeling parameters are assumed to be the same as were used in the DNS case study of Chapter 8, "Case Study of Client-Initiated Recovery." Table 9.4 enumerates the assumed input parameters for this example of client-initiated super element recovery. Results of the client-initiated super element recovery model with input parameters from Table 9.4 are shown in Table 9.5.

To compute the effective service availability seen by clients, one must combine the modeling results of standalone (i.e., internal) element availability for all three elements in the super element, and then deduct the downtime that is mitigated by client-initiated super element recovery, which is summarized in Table 9.6. The column *"Solution Downtime WITHOUT Client-Initiated Recovery"* captures the overall down-

TABLE 9.2. Input Parameters for Standalone Active–Active Model

Description	Symbol	Nominal Unit	Nominal Input	Modeled Input Value (Hourly Rates)
Failure rate	λ	System fails per year	4	0.000456308
Failure coverage factor of an active unit	C_A	Percentage successful	90%	90%
Automatic failover (or takeover) rate	μ_{FO}	Median minutes to complete automatic local failover	0.17	360
Manual failover rate	μ_{FOM}	Median minutes to complete manual local failover	30.00	2
Simplex failure repair rate	μ_{REPAIR}	Median minutes to complete manual repair	30.00	2
Duplex failure repair rate	μ_{DUPLEX}	Median hours to complete repair of simplex failure	4.00	0.25
Uncovered silent failure detection rate (active elements)	μ_{SFDTA}	Median minutes to detect silent failure of active elements	30.00	2
Automatic internal failover success probability	F_I	Percentage successful	99%	99%
Manual local failover success probability	F_M	Percentage successful	99%	99%

TABLE 9.3. Time Spent in Each Standalone Active–Active State

State	Annualized Minutes
1. Duplex	525,691.731
2. Simplex	239.878
3. Undetected (uncovered) failure	23.982
4. Detected (covered) failure	1.333
5. Failed failover	2.398
6. Duplex failure	0.678

time for the three individual elements in series, each of which is predicted to have about 15 minutes of downtime (99.997% service availability); note that the overall solution downtime is estimated at almost 44 minutes (99.9917% service availability). The column "*Solution Service Downtime WITH Client-Initiated Recovery*" replaces the downtime for the states, which can be mitigated by client-initiated super element

TABLE 9.4. Sample Cluster Client-Initiated Recovery Modeling Parameters

Description	Symbol	Nominal Unit	Nominal Input	Modeled Input Value (Hourly Rates)
Superelement failure rate	$\lambda_{\text{SUPERELEMENT}}$	Fails per year	$3(1 - F_t C_A + P_{\text{SIMPLEX}})\lambda$	0.0001498
Service availability of (redundant) super element	$A_{\text{SUPERELEMENT}}$	Percentage	$(99.9972\%)^3$	99.9910%
Portion of critical failures of primary system that are explicitly reported to client systems (rather than profound non-response which triggers timeouts)	F_{EXPLICIT}	Percentage	50%	50%
Portion of error responses from critical failures that trigger client-initiated recovery	C_{CLIENT}	Percentage successful	95%	95%
Automatic client failover (or takeover) rate	μ_{CLIENT}	Median seconds for clients to recover service to redundant system following failure of primary	20.0	180
Rate for client to determine that uncovered-to-client failures (e.g., failures signaled with wrong return code) are detected	$\mu_{\text{CLIENTSFD}}$	Median minutes for clients to recover service to redundant system following failure of primary	5.0	12
Portion of automatic client recoveries that succeed	F_{CLIENT}	Percentage	99.999%	99.999%

TABLE 9.4. *Continued*

Description	Symbol	Nominal Unit	Nominal Input	Modeled Input Value (Hourly Rates)
Overall time for client to timeout from non-responsive server	$\mu_{TIMEOUT}$	Median seconds for clients to timeout failed primary system	5.0	720
Duplex system recovery rate	μ_{DUPLEX}	Hours to complete emergency repair of duplex failures	4.0	0.25
Planned georedundant recover back rate	$\mu_{GRECOVER}$	Median hours to complete planned manual GR switchback	24.0	0.04
Planned georedundant migration disruption rate	$\mu_{MIGRATION}$	Median minutes of service disruption for orderly GR switchback	0.250	240

TABLE 9.5. Client-Initiated Recovery Prediction

State	Name	Annualized Minutes in State	Availability Status
1	Up on primary super element	524,080.163	UP
2	Timeout pending	0.055	dubious
3	Client covered	0.436	down
4	Up on redundant super element	1877.700	UP
5	Service migration	0.326	dubious
6	Client uncovered	0.164	down
7	Multiple down	1.157	down

recovery (undetected element failures, failed element failovers, and duplex failures of standalone elements) with the service downtime predicted by the client-initiated super element model from Table 9.6. The result is that client-initiated super element recovery can reduce estimated service downtime by more than an order of magnitude. The rightmost column *"Solution Service Downtime if Timeout and Service Migration Downtime are Excluded"* shows the solution downtime prediction if one assumes that time spent in both the "timeout pending" and "service migration" states is not counted as chargeable service downtime.

TABLE 9.6. Solution Downtime Prediction

Service State	Solution Downtime without Client-Initiated Recovery	Solution Service Downtime with Client-Initiated Recovery	Solution Service Downtime if Timeout and Service Migration Downtime Are Excluded
Detected (covered) element failures	1.999	1.999	1.999
Undetected (uncovered) element failures	35.973		
Failed element failovers	3.597		
Duplex failures	2.034		
Timeout pending		0.055	
Client covered		0.436	0.436
Service migration		0.326	
Client uncovered		0.164	0.164
Multiple down		1.157	1.157
Annualized service downtime	43.603	4.136	3.756
Service availability	99.9917%	99.9992%	99.9993%

Thus, client-initiated super element recovery can offer significant service availability improvements beyond those offered by internal redundancy and high-availability mechanisms alone. Client-initiated recovery to redundant instances of each element in the solution can also provide significant availability improvement beyond what is feasible from internal redundancy alone. The element-level client-initiated recovery model (illustrated in Chapter 8, "Case Study of Client-Initiated Recovery") and super element recovery model presented in this chapter can be solved to quantitatively assess the most appropriate external recovery strategy for specific solutions.

PART 3

RECOMMENDATIONS

10

GEOREDUNDANCY STRATEGY

Delivering acceptable service quality and availability to large user populations scattered across countries or continents for enterprise or commercial solutions often requires deploying equipment on multiple geographically distributed sites. This chapter reviews the practical considerations that drive enterprises to deploy critical solutions to more than one site, and the recovery strategies and architectures that can assure that those critical services are highly available with acceptable quality of service. The chapter concludes with a recommended analysis approach.

10.1 WHY SUPPORT MULTIPLE SITES?

Many critical systems and solutions support a variety of users who may be scattered across one or more regions, countries, or continents. Enterprises often opt to deploy such a system or solution across multiple locations for one or more of the following reasons:

- *Business Continuity and Disaster Recovery.* Building, local staff, power, communications facilities, and other critical infrastructure ingredients that support

Beyond Redundancy: How Geographic Redundancy Can Improve Service Availability and Reliability of Computer-Based Systems, First Edition. Eric Bauer, Randee Adams, Daniel Eustace.
© 2012 Institute of Electrical and Electronics Engineers. Published 2012 by John Wiley & Sons, Inc.

proper system operation are inherently vulnerable to a myriad of risks, as discussed in Section 1.3, "Catastrophic Failures and Geographic Redundancy." Geographic redundancy is a recognized best practice for mitigating the risk of service unavailability due to unavailability of a particular site.

- *Quality of Service.* Service latency, such as median (50th percentile) response latency for a transaction, is a key driver of quality of service; shorter service latency is better. Service latency can be shortened by locating servers physically close to customers to shorten propagation delays. This is particularly important for services with high bandwidth (e.g., viewing movies over the internet) or services that require short transmission latency (e.g., financial transactions and interactive/two-way communication).

- *Traffic Load.* As actual or expected traffic loads increase, additional hardware resources may become necessary. In some cases, modest traffic growth can be addressed by installing more hardware resources (e.g., memory, disks) on existing network elements, while in other cases, it is necessary to add new network element instances to serve the increased load. Hardware growth could occur on the same system and site or be implemented by the addition of another instance of the system. The new system instance could be deployed in the same site, but for additional protection against disasters, it might be better to deploy each new instance at a different site.

- *Legal or Regulatory Considerations.* Legal or regulatory considerations may impact what type of service can be provided (e.g., gambling, sales of particular a product), how user data must be protected (e.g., European data privacy laws), what regulatory and compliance reporting and business rules must be in place, or cover service-specific items (e.g., lawful interception of communications, more commonly known as "wiretapping"). Technical or legal factors could make it impractical to configure every site hosting the solution to comply with all legal and regulatory considerations for all countries in the world. Thus, business considerations could lead to configuring systems in particular sites to meet only the legal and regulatory requirements for the specific locales they are serving. For example, data privacy protections required in one locale may be too cumbersome or costly to deploy for global users.

- *Communications Considerations.* The cost and reliability of the communication links may dictate where the hardware elements should be located to best serve their users. For example, streaming high-definition movies to subscribers in one continent (e.g., North America) from servers in another continent (e.g., Asia) is likely to deliver a poor quality of experience to those subscribers.

10.2 RECOVERY REALMS

For the reasons enumerated in the previous section, it is often desirable to have several geographically distributed systems to support critical or popular applications to geographically distributed user communities. To support business continuity, one should explicitly consider which site(s) will be engineered to recover service following failure or unavailability of each individual site. For purposes of this discussion, the authors suggest the term "recovery realm" to refer to the logical set of sites that are engineered to handle service when another site is totally or partially unavailable. As an example of the use of a recovery realm, if users from European countries are subject to particularly restrictive data privacy regulations on their personal data that are costly to implement and overly restrictive for non-European users, then the enterprise might not want to coerce global users to abide by those policies. Instead, the enterprise may engineer several sites with appropriate hardware, software, procedures, and policies to conform to European data privacy rules and locate those systems on several sites across Europe. Those compliant sites would then constitute part of a recovery realm, meaning that any one of them can lawfully serve European users. Other global users could be served by sites that operated with more permissive policies and could be organized into one or more recovery realms of sites deployed in other countries and continents. As another example, recovery realms may be set up to ensure that the systems are located and configured with the necessary communications links (i.e., less jitter, packet loss and latency) in order to meet the specific standards or expectations for service quality required by different countries or markets. Note that there may be significant data communication between some sites within a recovery realm to replicate or backup critical data.

Thus, a recovery realm can define the geographic region which can lawfully serve users with acceptable service quality. Element and solution sites deployed in each recovery realm can then be configured to meet the specific legal, regulatory, and other constraints applicable when serving users in that particular recovery realm.

10.2.1 Choosing Site Locations

When deploying a georedundant solution, there are several issues that must be considered:

- The sites should not be located in particularly risky areas, such as in a flood zone, near an earthquake fault, or near the end of an airport runway. Section 1.3, "Catastrophic Failures and Geographic Redundancy," enumerates many potential risks to avoid. Many books on business continuity planning and disaster recovery give detailed guidance on selecting low risk locations.
- The sites should be sufficiently far apart from each other that it is unlikely that a disaster will affect more than one site. Separating sites by hundreds of miles or kilometers is usually sufficient.
- If two sites are very far apart, the messages between the sites can be significantly delayed. No two sites in the same recovery realm should be so far apart that the cross-site message delay materially increases service latency such that any site in the recovery realm would be unable to deliver acceptable quality of service to users of another site in the realm.
- For an international solution, it might be technically possible to deploy sites in different countries, but this creates more issues:

- The different countries might use different languages, different currencies, or different protocol variants (e.g., many countries create their own variant of ITU-T's ISUP protocol). Therefore, if service can fail over to a server in another country, the alternate server needs to support the language, currency, and protocols of the original country, as well as the language, currency, and protocols of its own country.

- Failing over to another country might violate local regulatory rules. For example, in telecommunications, most countries require that service providers support lawful interception of calls involving suspected criminals, so that law enforcement agencies can listen in on their calls. If the service is provided by an element in a foreign country, then the law enforcement agency would have to convince the foreign country's court that interception of the suspect's calls is justified. This is an added expense for the law enforcement agency, and the foreign court still might not agree. Therefore, countries typically require that calls involving intercept targets be processed within the local country.

10.3 RECOVERY STRATEGIES

Having factored the globe into recovery realms, one now considers what recovery strategy should be used when a site or system in each realm is totally or partially unavailable. There are three general recovery strategies to consider:

- *Unmitigated Failure Strategy.* This is the most basic strategy in which no special actions are taken following system or site failure to serve users while the failure is being repaired. Essentially, service becomes unavailable to some or all users when the system or site fails, and service remains unavailable until the failed system or site is repaired.

- *"Limp-Along" Strategy.* This strategy proactively attempts to mitigate the failure when traditional site redundancy is not deployed or available, typically by deliberately offering partial or degraded service to some or all users until the failure is repaired. For example, if site 1 fails and traffic is redirected to site 2, which has insufficient capacity to serve all users previously served by both site 1 and site 2, then site 2 might activate overload controls that restrict certain types of service, reject lower priority user sessions, or completely reject a percentage of requests based on the degree of overload. More sophisticated limp-along strategies might carefully balance the load of users previously served by the failed system to other sites in order to mitigate overload situations, but the system may also have to temporarily restrict either functionality offered (e.g., temporarily disabling or deferring some resource intensive services, such as system backups or performance management reports), reject lower priority requests, or decline service to users configured with a lower grade of service. By proactively monitoring, prioritizing, and reducing the service load on the remaining systems, a limp-along strategy can assure that at least high-priority users or requests are delivered acceptable quality service following failure. Limp-along service architectures are discussed in Section 10.4, "Limp-Along Architectures."

- *Traditional Georedundancy Strategy.* This strategy requires two or more systems in the recovery realm that can be engineered with sufficient capacity across the realm so that users can be served by a georedundant system with acceptable quality in the event that any one system becomes totally unavailable. Recovery strategies are implemented to meet defined recovery time and recovery point objectives for restoring user service to the specified quality of service. Engineering techniques for supporting this are described in Section 10.5, "Site Redundancy Options."

Since different products, markets, and regions may have different expectations for service availability, different recovery strategies may be appropriate for different recovery realms.

10.4 LIMP-ALONG ARCHITECTURES

As explained earlier in Section 10.3, "Recovery Strategies," the limp-along strategy is meant to provide an economical way for clients to recover to other servers or sites without the constraint that the other servers or sites be preengineered to serve the full-engineered load with normal quality of service. Fundamentally, site failure in a limp-along architecture means that there may be insufficient resources available to serve the engineered load with acceptable service quality, so the system proactively manages the load through overload controls to offer at least minimally acceptable service to selected (or all) users or requests until repairs can be completed and service returned to normal. In order for the operational site or system to provide some reasonable service to clients and mitigate critical failures on its part, the server could monitor client traffic, as well as internal resources, and determine the most efficient way of allotting those resources to clients.

In addition servers can determine that they are in overload based on resource usage, such as CPU, message buffers, or memory usage exceeding a certain threshold (e.g., 80%), and escalating if usage reaches a higher level (e.g., 90%). When a server is in overload, congestion control mechanisms can be used to prioritize traffic, determining which requests it should service and which it should deny or drop. The types and percentages of requests that are denied would increase with an increase in the level of overload. Prioritization could be based on qualifiers, such as user service class (e.g., platinum versus gold versus silver) or request type (e.g., service versus information). In addition, lower priority tasks (e.g., report generation, noncritical resource audits) can be deferred in order to preserve the critical resources for processing higher priority user requests.

When service is denied, the failure response can include an indication that the client that the server is in overload. When the client sees this indication, it should reduce the number of requests it sends to the server. The client could begin sending requests to alternate servers, but if too many clients do this, then the alternate servers could also be driven into overload. Therefore, if the client starts receiving overload indications from all the servers, it might need to begin rejecting service requests from its user.

Hysteresis should be used when activating and deactivating limp-along overload controls to minimize the risk of service oscillations. For example, if overload is triggered when CPU usage reaches 80%, then the system should not go back to normal behavior as soon as the CPU usage drops back below 80%, since it is likely that turning off the overload controls will cause the usage to go back above 80%. Overload should not be turned off until usage drops to a safe level (e.g., 70%). As more aggressive overload controls are activated (e.g., rejecting new session requests, rejecting selected traffic types, proactively disconnecting selected users), then longer hysteresis windows should be used to give all users a more stable and consistent experience. These techniques can also be used by servers during nonfailure modes when the systems are just experiencing intervals of overload due to unusually heavy traffic.

10.5 SITE REDUNDANCY OPTIONS

For business continuity reasons, enterprises should configure critical services on at least one site with excess (i.e., redundant) capacity so that service can be promptly recovered to that site if another site in the recovery realm becomes unavailable. As described in Section 1.4, "Geographically Separated Recovery Site," a georedundant site and elements on that site can be maintained at various levels of readiness, from cold standby to actively serving a share of the offered user traffic.

Architecturally, this site redundancy arrangement is referred to as $N + K$ where N sites are required to serve the engineered load and K redundant sites are configured. The "N" sites are nominally actively serving user traffic, and there are two general strategies for the "K" nominally redundant sites:

- *Standby Sites.* "K" spare sites are deployed to backup all of the "N" live sites. If any live site fails, a spare one is loaded with the configuration of the failed site and brought into service to replace it.
- N + K *Load Sharing.* $N + K$ live sites are deployed and the load is normally distributed evenly across all the sites that are nominally serving traffic. If any site fails, then its load must be evenly distributed across the remaining sites.

These options are described in more detail in the following sections.

10.5.1 Standby Sites

In a simple configuration, all the live sites, as well as the spare sites, are equipped with the same hardware configurations. Sometimes the various live sites have different hardware configurations and capacities due to different traffic loads and service mix needs. In this case, the spare site(s) must be able to handle the full engineered load of

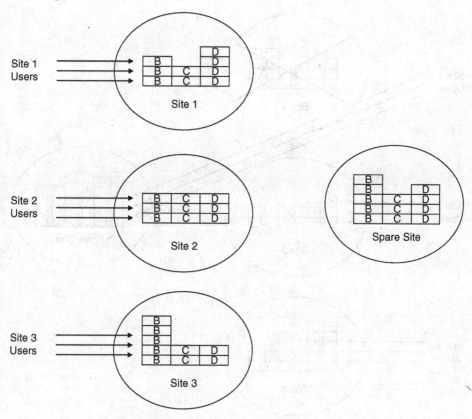

Figure 10.1. Georedundancy with a standby site.

the largest single live site with acceptable service quality so that it could assume the traffic for that large site in the event of a failure.

For example, Figure 10.1 shows a configuration with three live sites and one spare site. A separate set of users is served by each live site to balance the traffic load so service can be delivered with the desired service quality. The boxes in each site represent network elements that are needed in the solution; for the hypothetical solution discussed in Chapter 9, "Solution and Cluster Recovery," the "B" boxes might be web servers, the "C" boxes authentication servers, and the "D" boxes databases. Sites 1, 2, and 3 have different quantities of each element, so the spare site must have the maximum number of each to properly serve users following a site failure of either site 1, 2, or 3. This means that the spare site is nominally configured with 5 "B" elements (because site 3 has 5), 3 "C" elements (because site 2 has 3), and 4 "D" elements (because site 1 has 4).

If site 1 fails, then the spare site must be configured to match site 1 before its users are redirected to the spare site, as shown in Figure 10.2. Because the spare site is expected to be reconfigured to serve the traffic mix of the particular site it is recovering,

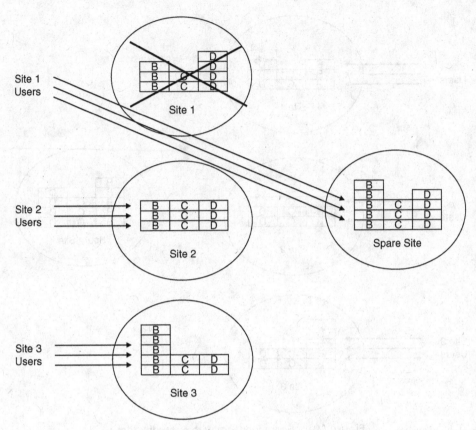

Figure 10.2. Spare site georedundancy after a failure.

the systems on the spare site may be "cold." If a live site fails, then a manual procedure is needed to activate the spare site to support its users. The basic steps in this activation procedure are:

1. The decision to activate standby site to recover service from a failed live site is made and announced.
2. The spare site is configured to match the configuration of the failed live site.
3. The spare site is loaded with the persistent and semi-persistent data of the failed site from a recent backup. Volatile data is typically not preserved due to the complexity of doing data replication for N sites with only K standbys.
4. The users of the failed site are redirected to the spare site (e.g., through DNS or client provisioning).
5. The failed site is repaired.
6. Service eventually migrates back to the repaired live site and the spare site reverts to standby status.

The key benefit of the standby site strategy is its relative simplicity. Since a manual procedure is used, no software is needed for automatic failure recovery, data replication, etc. The key disadvantage of this strategy is that it cannot meet very short RTO or RPO requirements. As explained in Chapter 7, "Understanding Recovery Timing Parameters," manual procedures to recover service to a standby site typically take several hours to execute. In this case, the additional time needed to configure the spare site to match the configuration of the failed site and restore all necessary data will extend the recovery time.

In the event of a single element failure (e.g., one of the "B" elements on site 1 fails), service to the users of that site might be degraded if the remaining elements at the site are driven into overload as they try to serve all the users. All elements of the solution should be designed to throttle some of the traffic when they are overloaded so that at least some users are served and the overloaded element does not itself suffer a critical failure. Thus, overload controls discussed in Section 10.4, "Limp-Along Architectures," are implemented and help maintain acceptable service quality.

10.5.2 $N + K$ Load Sharing

In $N + K$ load-sharing arrangements, all sites actively serve user traffic, and thus no sites are explicitly designated as "spare." The aggregate pool of $N + K$ sites are configured with sufficient excess capacity that the engineered load of the overall user load can be served with acceptable quality with up to "K" sites unavailable. Thus, $N + K$ load sharing means that each site is configured with an average of (K/N)th excess capacity so that users can be served with acceptable quality when one site is unavailable (e.g., due to planned maintenance, failure, or disaster).

Figure 10.3 shows an $N + K$ load-sharing solution with four sites ($N = 3$, $K = 1$). Each site is equipped with enough hardware to support its normal users, plus 1/3 (K/N) extra capacity that would be needed if one of the other sites fails, in this example 4 of the "B" elements, 2 of the "C" and 3 of the "D." Normally, 25% of the users get their service from each site. If one of the sites fails, its users must be redirected to the other sites, as shown in Figure 10.4: 1/3 of the failed site users must be redirected to each of the remaining three sites. Each site has enough hardware to support 1/3 of the users, so that if any one site fails, all the users can still be served.

The $N + K$ sites do not necessarily need to have the same engineered capacity (i.e., the same number of each type of element), but if the site capacities are different, then the mechanism that distributes the users among the sites would have to support a weighted distribution (e.g., by using the weight parameter of DNS SRV records). But deploying the same configuration in all sites can also be complex, because as the user traffic grows over time, the enterprise cannot just grow additional hardware in one site—all the sites must be grown equally.

$N + K$ georedundancy is best achieved when the network elements in the solution support a load-shared redundancy strategy. The load-shared elements simply need to be distributed across all the $N + K$ sites. A few more elements might need to be deployed to ensure that if one of the sites fails, the remaining sites have enough hardware capacity to support the entire load. For example, if six instances of the "C" element are

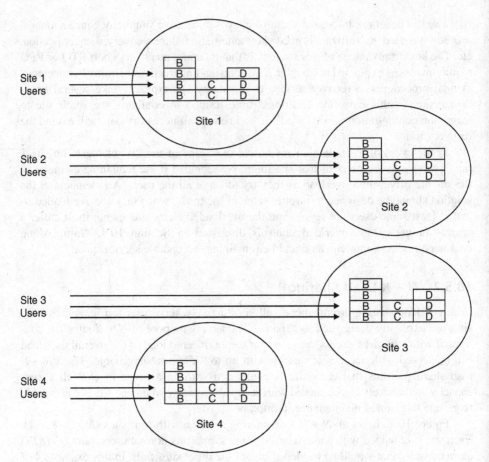

Figure 10.3. Georedundancy with *N* + *K* load sharing.

needed to handle the load, and the enterprise has four sites, then it can deploy two "C" elements in each site. There will be a total of eight "C" elements, but if any site is struck by a disaster, the remaining three sites will have a total of six "C" elements left to service the traffic.

There are a few options to recover from the failure of a single element. For example, if one "C" element fails, the design could support one of the following:

- Allow the clients to distribute their traffic among all seven operational elements in all four sites, but this could create significant intersite traffic.
- Make the clients served by the site hosting the failed element send as much traffic as possible to the remaining operational element at that site, but detect when it is in overload and then begin shedding traffic or diverting it to other sites. This alternative minimizes the intersite traffic, but adds complex flow control between the clients and servers.

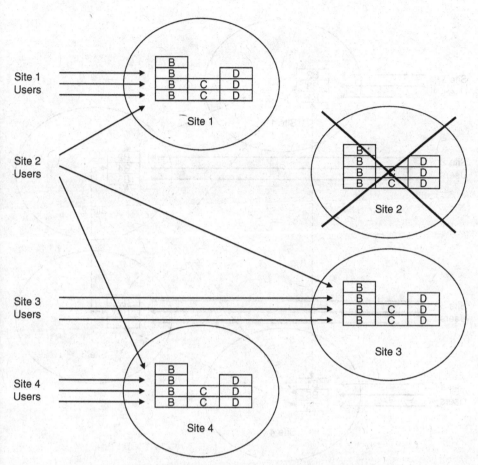

Figure 10.4. $N + K$ load sharing georedundancy after a failure.

$N + K$ site georedundancy does not work as well when there are $1 + 1$ (active–active or active–standby) network elements in the solution, because if one site fails, then all of the element's traffic is redirected to the other site. In order to meet the intent of $N + K$ georedundancy, we want an average of (K/N)th of the traffic to be redirected to each site. This can be achieved by deploying several pairs of elements with the pairs distributed over every combination of sites. For example, if there are four sites $(3 + 1)$, we can deploy six pairs of elements distributed as shown in Figure 10.5. The dashed lines represent interfaces between pairs of elements for heartbeating and data replication. In general, for $N + 1$ sites, $N \times (N + 1)/2$, pairs are required. If one of the sites fails, its users must be redirected to the other sites, as shown in Figure 10.6. In this case site 2 fails. The users who were getting service from "B2" in site 2 will fail over to its mate: "B2" in site 1. Similarly, users of "B4" and "B5" in site 2 will fail over to "B4" in site 3 and "B5" in site 4. The result is the same as in Figure 10.4—one-third of the failed site's users are redirected to each of the remaining three sites.

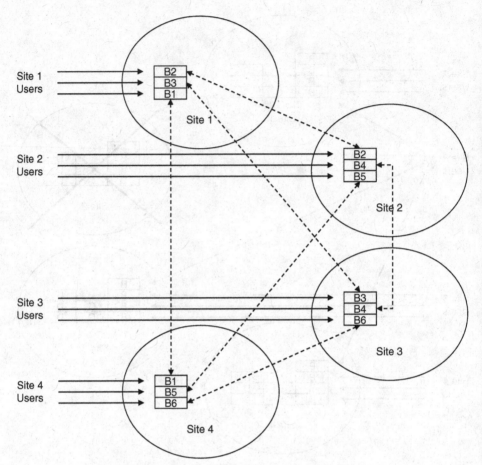

Figure 10.5. $N + K$ load sharing with $1 + 1$ redundant elements.

The primary problem with $1 + 1$ redundant elements is that deploying multiple pairs is not very scalable. The enterprise might not need six pairs of elements to support their traffic, but that is the minimum required for $3 + 1$ redundancy. If the element itself is scalable (e.g., it consists of a multi-slot chassis, and capacity can be increased by adding cards to the chassis), then the enterprise can deploy six pairs of minimally equipped elements. As their traffic grows, they can grow the hardware configuration of these elements, but this is rather complex because they would need to grow every element, rather than add new elements. If the six pairs are eventually fully equipped and the traffic continues to grow, then the next step would be to deploy six additional pairs of elements. Another problem with $1 + 1$ redundant elements is that since they need to be deployed in pairs, we cannot fully support $N + K$ sites, when $K > 1$. If more than one site fails, there is a possibility that both elements of one of the pairs will fail, and some users will lose service.

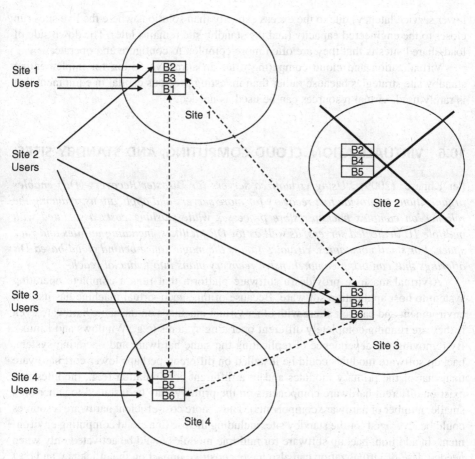

Figure 10.6. $N + K$ load sharing with $1 + 1$ redundancy after a failure.

10.5.3 Discussion

All elements and solution sites should be engineered with overload controls to properly manage periods of high traffic. Ideally, solutions will be engineered with sufficient excess capacity distributed across multiple sites so that traffic can be served with acceptable quality even following element or site failure, but overload controls can help here, as well when that was not done or when there is an anomaly in the traffic causing higher than expected loads.

While standby site arrangements are simpler than load-shared site arrangements, the equipment on the standby site is idle the vast majority of the time. There could be some sleeping issues detected with the equipment once it has been activated. In contrast, since all load-shared equipment actively serves customers, issues will more likely be detected and resolved during operation. Through proper solution engineering, it may be possible for all of the load-shared sites to deliver slightly better service quality (e.g., lower service latency) due to the excess capacity than solutions where the live sites run closer to the engineered capacity (and the standby site remains idle). The down side of load-shared sites is that they are often more complex to configure and operate.

Virtualization and cloud computing offer an attractive option for implementing standby site strategies because rather than investing precious capital in equipment that is rarely used, virtual resources can be used as needed.

10.6 VIRTUALIZATION, CLOUD COMPUTING, AND STANDBY SITES

Per Khnaser (2009), *"Using virtualized servers for Disaster Recovery (DR) enables organizations to provide fast recovery for more servers and applications, reducing the reliance on complex backup/restore processes while slashing costs associated with multiple 1U dedicated servers, as well as for DR facilities, including utilities and rack space. For small companies, virtualization is the magic sauce behind cloud-based DR offerings that can bring comprehensive recovery plans into financial reach."*

A virtual machine provides a software platform that runs a complete operating system to host application software. Because of this, each virtual machine has its own environment and can run along with other virtual machines on the same hardware even if they are running completely different operating systems (e.g., Windows and Linux). By removing the dependence of replicating the same hardware and operating system, backup software modules could be installed on different, perhaps lower cost hardware than that of the primary modules and in a different configuration (e.g., modules that exist on different hardware components on the primary may be installed together on a smaller number of hardware components). Thus, more cost-efficient hardware resources could be leveraged for the standby site, including the use of a cloud computing environment. In addition, backup software for multiple modules could be activated only when needed. Use of virtualization can also have a positive impact on the efficiency and cost effectiveness of a georedundant configuration and recovery.

Per the article "High Availability and Disaster Recovery for Virtual Environments," the benefits of virtualization include the following:

- *Server Consolidation.* Virtualization helps to consolidate multiple servers into one single physical server, thus offering improved operational performance.
- *Reduced Hardware Costs.* As the number of physical servers goes down, the cost of servers and associated costs like IT infrastructure, space, etc. will also decrease.
- *Improved Application Security.* By having a separate application in each virtual machine, any vulnerability is segregated and it does not affect other applications.
- *Reduced Maintenance.* Since virtual servers can be relocated and migrated, maintenance of hardware and software can be done with minimal downtime. However, there may be a penalty for operations, such as hardware maintenance, since they may impact all of the virtual machines that are installed on it.

- *Enhanced Scalability.* The ease with which virtual servers can be deployed will result in improved scalability of IT implementation.

Virtualization in itself does not compromise performance nor exempt the use of an automated recovery mechanism if the backup system is selected and configured to provide performance and capacity equivalency, but the greatest benefit from a geo-redundancy point of view is in virtualization's ability to provide a more cost effective backup.

Cloud computing may provide a cost-effective way to support disaster recovery since cloud computing reduces capital expenses by renting usage from a third-party vendor and paying only for resources that are actually used. Many of the companies supporting cloud computing provide backup as a service specializing in system or data recovery. Cloud computing combined with virtualization allows for flexibility in distributing and running the software and thus the possibility of reducing expenses usually associated with georedundancy and business continuity. Balaouras (2009) provides a good summary of the benefits of cloud computing as a way to affordably provide disaster recovery services.

Cloud computing for disaster recovery often works best for a system with active–standby external redundancy, since it provides services when the active system is not available. Since active–active external redundancy is the optimal form for high availability, cloud computing may provide a more cost-effective means of recovery, but it may not provide optimal recovery times. There may be a service latency penalty with cloud computing since available resources may be located at a great distance from its clients. In addition, a large part of the responsibility for an effective recovery is put in the hands of the cloud computing provider which adds a risk for the enterprise.

10.7 RECOMMENDED DESIGN METHODOLOGY

The strategy for a georedundant solution can be methodically developed by considering the following:

1. *Identify the practical, business, technical, and regulatory factors that constrain or prohibit any user from being served by any site following failure.* Consider recovering service to the most geographically distant site conceived, and assess the viability of recovering to that site. While recovering users in the United States to a site in China or recovering users in the European Union to a site in India might not be ideal, it is valuable to explicitly consider if it is lawful and feasible for these extreme recovery options to legally deliver acceptable service to users.

2. *Organize the regions served by the enterprise into recovery realms.* Use the practical, business, technical, and regulatory factors that constrain feasible recovery options, as well as the enterprise's organizational and practical considerations to map regions into recovery realms. Typically, recovery realms will align with national or continental boundaries. For example, the European Union

might be a single recovery realm; the United States or North America or all the Americas might be a single recovery realm; and so on.

3. *Define a service recovery strategy to each realm.* Recovery strategies may vary somewhat by service, but fundamentally they fall into three broad strategies following site or system failure:

   • Rapidly recover normal service for all users to redundant site(s);

   • Limp along with degraded functionality using overload controls to monitor and control critical resource usage and number of requests processed.

   • Service is unavailable to some users until failure is repaired.

4. *Set service recovery objectives for each realm.* Recovery time objectives (RTO) and recovery point objectives (RPO) should be specified for each recovery realm. Policies to shape or shed load should be specified for solutions that will limp along on failure. Typically, these service recovery policies will be captured in written requirements or an architecture document.

5. *Engineer and architect sites within each realm* to implement the assigned service recovery strategy and policy.

6. *Consider using virtualization or cloud computing* when applicable for meeting scalability needs and costs.

MAXIMIZING SERVICE AVAILABILITY VIA GEOREDUNDANCY

The earlier chapters provided technical details on several recovery options that could be implemented to maximize system availability. The purpose of this chapter is to draw from the information in the earlier chapters to provide recommendations for architecting a highly available system that can maximize the benefits of external system redundancy. The chapter will explain how client-initiated recovery can be further optimized to greatly improve the system availability of an externally redundant system over a standalone one.

11.1 THEORETICALLY OPTIMAL EXTERNAL REDUNDANCY

In Section 6.1, "The Simplistic Answer," we introduced the simplistic, theoretically optimal model of parallel availability:

$$\text{Availability}_{\text{Pair}} = 2 \times \text{Availability}_{\text{Element}} - \text{Availability}_{\text{Element}}^2.$$

Theoretically, this parallel availability could be approached by having client "A" send identical requests simultaneously to both "B1" and "B2" in order to maximize the

Beyond Redundancy: How Geographic Redundancy Can Improve Service Availability and Reliability of Computer-Based Systems, First Edition. Eric Bauer, Randee Adams, Daniel Eustace.
© 2012 Institute of Electrical and Electronics Engineers. Published 2012 by John Wiley & Sons, Inc.

probability of at least one successful response. Although this does increase the likelihood of a response, it also introduces increased complexity into the solution (e.g., how does the client handle a simultaneous response to the same request, how does the client determine which response is correct if the responses are different) and more traffic into the network (i.e., nominally twice the number of messages).

Parallel processing has the disadvantage of forcing clients and servers to properly manage the complexity of handling multiple identical and simultaneous requests or of dealing with nonidempotence, that is, choosing from different responses to the same request (based on even subtle differences between the systems). One can achieve nearly the same availability benefit by sending a single request at a time to a single server and focusing on immediately detecting failure of that server and quickly recovering service to an active redundant unit. Client-initiated recovery is a more reasonable approach to parallel processing, as the client can manage the requests based on the availability of "B1" and "B2," thus simplifying the message processing and lessening the traffic flow. This client-initiated recovery approach is not without some shortcomings, particularly if once the client chooses either "B1" or "B2," it must continue to send requests to "B1" or "B2" due to some affinity with it (e.g., due to registration or authentication). The following sections will offer some recommendations on mitigating the shortcomings and providing a more practical means of nearing optimal availability.

11.2 PRACTICALLY OPTIMAL RECOVERY STRATEGIES

This section presents general strategies for optimizing service availability by leveraging external redundancy. We begin by comparing and contrasting internal and external redundancy, and then review the following topics:

- Why client-initiated recovery maximizes the service availability benefit of external redundancy
- Active–active operation
- Optimizing timeout and retry parameters
- Rapid session (re)establishment
- Rapid context restoration
- Overload control

11.2.1 Internal versus External Redundancy

Internal redundancy supported by a high-availability infrastructure is generally an effective way of providing a high level of service availability if it is built with robust capabilities of fault detection, isolation, reporting and recovery. Most of the unplanned service downtime of well-designed systems with internal redundancy comes from undetected (uncovered) failures. As explained in Chapter 6, "Modeling Service Availability with External System Redundancy," neither system-driven nor manually controlled recovery onto redundant systems is likely to mitigate the bulk of uncovered downtime, which represents the majority of standalone system unavailability. Fortunately, the risk of unsuccessful automatic failure detection, isolation, and recovery of internal system redundancy can be significantly mitigated by client-initiated recovery onto a redundant system.

Many products have both internal as well as external redundancy mechanisms. Depending on the nature of the failure and its impact, the appropriate mechanism may be executed. The option of internal versus external recovery is dependent upon the fail over latency, impact to stable sessions, and failover success probability using internal recovery mechanisms against the same characteristics using an external recovery mechanism. Internal mechanisms generally have shorter latencies because everything is coordinated and managed by a single high-availability control mechanism, and incur less service impact because it is generally easier and faster to recover context information within a system than via interworking with another system. External redundancy provides an additional layer of robustness to internal redundancy when the primary site or network element has failed, is undergoing a maintenance activity, or is experiencing a high level of overload.

For several reasons, it is desirable to give internal redundancy some time to restore service before initiating an external failover:

- *Extension of Partial Outages to All Users.* A partial outage might affect only a subset of the users, for example, those using a particular service, or those attached to a particular process or blade. An external failover would possibly cause a brief service disruption for all subscribers rather than simply those who were previously impacted.
- *Out-of-Date Databases.* Many redundant elements do data replication between the active and standby sites, so that the standby element can immediately take over service if the active one fails. However, in the case of georedundancy, the distance between the sites is typically hundreds of kilometers, and due to the bandwidth constraints and latency of the communications channel, it might not be possible to keep the standby element's database fully synchronized with current real time data; instead, data updates may be replicated every few minutes or hours. After a georedundant failover, all changes after the most recent data replication or backup will be lost.
- *Registration Problems.* When a session-oriented service does an external failover, it might be necessary for users to reregister to the alternate site. This can cause a registration storm that will trigger overload in the redundant server. The server or even the network may delay (e.g., via traffic shaping) or drop some registrations to keep the traffic at a supportable level, thereby extending the period of service unavailability for some users.
- *Increase in Service Latency.* For time critical services, users will typically be configured to use the physically closest operational server to minimize latency required to physically transport IP traffic between the client and server systems. If service is switched away from the closest server to a more remote system, then service latency will increase, perhaps by several milliseconds for each IP packet passed to and from the georedundant system.

- *Increasing Traffic Load in Remote Sites Might Affect Operations.* Each site should be engineered to support the alternate site's traffic if it fails, but since disasters that require georedundant failovers are rare, it is difficult to be sure that each site really has sufficient capacity. Therefore, there is a risk that the increased traffic might trigger overload, network management controls, alarms, etc. in the remote site.

- *Operational Cost of the External Switchback Procedure.* Generally, the initial external failover procedure is fairly simple, since it is important to restore service quickly. However, after the failed network element is repaired and restored, if it is necessary to return service to the restored element, it must be done manually and according to a detailed procedure to minimize any service impact. The procedure might involve synchronizing databases to ensure service is not lost during the failback. This synchronization might take several hours, and in some cases, provisioning updates have to be locked out during this time to ensure everything is copied accurately. Also, registering clients must be migrated gradually back to the restored system to avoid causing a registration storm. Since georedundant systems are inherently in different physical locations, it may be necessary for maintenance engineers in two locations to execute the switchback procedure.

11.2.2 Client-Initiated Recovery as Optimal External Recovery Strategy

Based on the comparison of system-driven and client-initiated recovery strategies detailed in earlier chapters, it is clear that the client-initiated recovery strategy has many advantages over the system-driven recovery strategy, particularly when volatile data, such as state and registration status, do not have to be maintained. An uncovered system failure may not be detected any better by its external system-driven mechanism than by the primary system's internal mechanism. A client, however, as an independent entity, can often quickly identify and react to a failure of a network element that might not be as easily detected and recovered by the system itself. An uncovered failure on the part of the system may be a covered (i.e., detected) failure from the client's point of view through an explicit error return or a timeout. This can result in a great improvement on the service availability. There is no need to also do system-driven recovery since client-initiated can provide more complete failure detection and recovery. In the DNS example in Section 8.2, "Mapping DNS onto Practical Client-Initiated Recovery Model," a pool of standalone systems with an availability in the range of 99.97% can potentially reach six 9's with a client-initiated external redundancy scheme if the service is optimized for client-initiated recovery.

An optimal strategy for a client-initiated recovery mechanism is one in which the client can quickly detect and recover from the failure of a component it is attempting to communicate with. As pointed out in Section 6.4.3, "Client-Initiated Georedundant Recovery Model," if client-initiated recovery of explicitly reported failures is fast enough to avoid accruing service downtime, then the portion of client-initiated recoveries that were explicitly detected (rather than having to timeout) does not count against service availability measurements. DNS records and quarantine lists are two ways to support the rapid identification and assignment of available network elements. (See Section 4.1.3, "Traffic Redirection" for more details on traffic redirection via DNS or quarantine.) Specific error messages or timeouts support the client's ability to quickly and clearly learn of or detect a failure of the component and serve as triggers for a recovery action.

If client timeout mechanisms (i.e., timeout interval and number of retries) are further optimized through heuristics as prescribed in Section 11.2.5, "Optimizing Timeout and Retry Parameters," so that neither system failures detected via timeout expiration nor covered failures explicitly detected accrue service downtime, then service availability can improve even more. The requirements specified in Section 12.4.2, "Client-Initiated Recovery," provide further guidance in designing the optimal strategy.

11.2.3 Multi-Site Strategy

As explained in Section 10.7, "Recommended Design Methodology," it is important to consider setting up recovery realms based on practical, business, technical, and regulatory factors that provide necessary constraints on the recovery strategy. The constraints can include which sites are preferred or feasible to take over for a failed site at the risk of issues, such as performance degradation or regulatory restrictions. Within each recovery realm, RPO and RTO requirements can be defined and provide the basis for the most appropriate recovery architecture. The most aggressive RPO and RTO requirements are generally best served by active–active sites that can quickly assume traffic from a failed site. The following sections will provide recommendations on various contributors to the recovery strategy that affords optimal availability characteristics.

11.2.4 Active–Active Server Operation

Active–active redundancy can provide faster failover times than active–standby since by definition the element is already initialized and running and does not have to spend time in setup. Active–active redundancy mitigates the risk of clients detecting failure of the primary server and attempting to recover to the redundant system before the standby is even aware of the failure, and thus service recovery is delayed while the standby recognizes the failure of the primary and promotes itself to active status. Client "A" can thus make use of optimizations in fault detection and recovery time, since it does not have to wait for "B2" to be active.

Per the modeling comparisons in Section 3.2.3, "Service Availability Comparison," active–active redundancy offers a small availability benefit over active–standby redundancy even for system-driven recovery due to the capacity loss prorating of outages in active–active configurations. Active–active configurations have twice as many elements carrying user traffic as active–standby configurations, and thus one of the two active elements in active–active is twice as likely to fail as the single active element in an active–standby configuration. However, because each unit in an active–active configuration is nominally carrying 50% of the user traffic, the doubled failure rate is discounted by the 50% capacity loss associated with the failure of one active unit in active–active configuration. Thus, the doubled failure rate and 50% capacity loss per failure essentially cancel out to become approximately equivalent to the service impact of active–standby configurations. Although the availability benefits are not much better between active–active and active–standby redundancy, the ability to mitigate the shortcomings of the client-initiated recovery strategy reinforce active–active as the preferred redundancy strategy.

Active–active can also be expanded to include a cluster of active elements all sharing the load. An example of this is the DNS configuration explained in the Case Study in Chapter 8. The client has the choice of several elements it may interface with in the event of a failure of one of the elements. A load-shared configuration is particularly beneficial in cases like DNS that do not have to maintain volatile information about the client–server interface, such as registration or session state. The client can choose any available element that offers the requested information. If the server must maintain information about its interaction with the client, such as registration or login information, then the client can only choose from those elements that have maintained the information. This stresses the importance of meeting the recovery point objective, keeping needed data, such as registration or session state data, synchronized between multiple elements so that if one fails, another can assume the traffic without a loss of functionality for the client.

11.2.5 Optimizing Timeout and Retry Parameters

When clear explicit error indications are not sent, the client must have other ways to determine when an element has failed or cannot provide the service being requested. Two mechanisms to facilitate that failure detection and possible recovery are timers and retries. These are captured in the model with the parameters:

1. μ_{TIMEOUT} $(=1/T_{\text{TIMEOUT}})$. This parameter captures how quickly the client times out due to a nonresponsive system, meaning the typical time for the initial request and all subsequent retries to timeout.
2. $\mu_{\text{KEEPALIVE}}$ $(=1/T_{\text{KEEPALIVE}})$. This parameter captures how frequently a client polls a server to verify that the server is still available.

If the requested service has not been provided by a server within a designated period of time (marked by a timer), the client may retry (a designated maximum number of times) the request to that element. A way to optimize the failure detection and recovery times is to lower the timeout and number of retries as much as possible without incurring the adverse effect of false positive failure detection to a transient failure. There is often a fine balance between waiting too long for a system to recover itself versus switching too quickly to an alternate system. This is particularly an issue if there is a penalty to re-direct traffic to an alternate system, such as the need to re-register with the other system. Optimization strategies should take this balance into account, as well as understanding about the historic behavior of the system in different scenarios (including high and low traffic periods). Optimization strategies are discussed in detail in Chapter 7. Optimizing the timeout values and number of retries will have a positive impact on the failure detection and recovery times.

11.2.6 Rapid Relogon

Client logon or relogon is often a complex process involving protocol exchanges to negotiate a protocol version to use; exchange identification data, encryption keys, and cryptographic credentials, which are then authenticated; perform authorization and access control checks; record security audit and usage information; and create and initialize session context information. All of these actions both consume real time— thereby delaying service recovery for client users—and put a processing load on the server—thus increasing the risk of system overload if multiple clients logon immediately following failure of the primary system.

A remediation for this would be for the client to register/logon to both "B1" and "B2." If both "B1" and "B2" have the registration/login information, client "A" can send requests to either "B1" or "B2" without paying the penalty of a reregistration/ relogon as part of its recovery. This does have the disadvantage of having to keep this information in synch, but it will save relogon time in the case of a server failure and recovery to a redundant server.

11.2.7 Rapid Context Restoration

Similarly to the mitigation of the reregistration/relogin issue, the loss of session data can be addressed through real-time (or near real-time) synchronization of state/session data, so that the client "A" does not drop its stable sessions (previously established with "B1") and thus does not need to reestablish them on "B2" as part of its recovery to "B2" from a failed "B1." Note that to facilitate this synchronization, sufficient bandwidth should be provided between the elements so that data can be exchanged in real time with low latency. Again, the session data can be sent to or replicated to both "B1" and "B2" or maintained in a common data store.

This seamlessness driven by replication of session and registration/authentication data is critical to reduce defects or failures in service due to dropped or failed sessions (sometimes referred to as defects per million or DPM) realized due to the transition of traffic from one element to another. For example, if data concerning the status of a session such as instant message (IM) initiated on "B1" is not replicated on a redundant element "B2," those sessions maintained by "B1" may not be supported on "B2," and therefore could be prematurely dropped from the point of view of the client. This would be counted as a defect. Systems with active–active, synchronized elements are more likely to meet strict service reliability requirements. For certain systems, this is worth the added resource cost and complexity of keeping the data in synch.

One way context data is maintained is through the use of cookies. A cookie per Wikipedia "is a piece of text stored on a user's computer by their web browser. A cookie can be used for authentication, storing site preferences, shopping cart contents, the identifier for a server-based session, or anything else that can be accomplished through storing text data." By the use of cookies, if there is a failure of a web server, user service is easily restored to another server without loss of functionality (e.g., shopping cart contents).

11.2.8   Automatic Switchback

The benefit of active–active, load-shared redundancy is that traffic can be rerouted from a failed component to the element(s) that are already sharing the traffic load. A robust load-shared system should be configured to meet traffic needs even in the event of a failure of one (or more) of its elements. Although the system should be able to run with fewer elements, service is at higher risk because another failure could cause an outage; service may also be delivered at lower quality/performance (e.g., longer service latency) than users are accustomed to. As a result, once the failed element(s) have recovered, the load should be rebalanced. If a switchback is required, then it needs to be as seamless as possible to the client so as not to provide any further disruption to service. In a load-shared system, mechanisms that support adding the recovered network element back to the list of available elements and directing new traffic to the recovered network element can avoid the need for a procedural switchback of traffic and thus avoid any potential downtime or data loss possibilities.

11.2.9   Overload Control

Automatic client-initiated recovery mechanisms are likely to detect failure of a server at essentially the same time, and thus initiate recovery to a redundant server at roughly the same time. Thus, a failure event during a busy period can trigger a large number of clients to simultaneously attempt to logon to a redundant server. As described in Section 11.2.6, "Rapid Relogon," logon is a resource-intensive operation, so this abnormal volume of logon requests are unlikely to be successfully served in real time. Thus, appropriate overload control mechanisms must be deployed to assure that slow responses from the redundant server to logon requests do not prompt clients to resend logon requests, thereby exacerbating the overload condition. Overload situations can also occur when the system is not properly engineered to support capacity loads when one or more of the network elements has failed. In either case, overload controls are needed. See Section 10.4, "Limp along Architectures," for details on overload strategies.

11.2.10   Network Element versus Cluster-Level Recovery

As summarized in Section 9.3, "Cluster versus Element Recovery," client-initiated cluster recovery can offer significant service availability improvements beyond those offered by internal redundancy and high-availability mechanisms. This is also true of client-initiated network element recovery; however, the question of whether to use cluster versus network element-level recovery depends on characteristics and requirements for the specific solution. In some cases, cluster-level recovery provides a faster recovery mechanism with better performance characteristics than network element-level recovery. For other solutions, network element-level recovery may be less impactful to its clients. While a catastrophic site failure should trigger a cluster-like failover in which client service switches from the impacted site to the alternate site, the recovery strategy for failure of an individual element in the solution is not obvious because the solution might be able to use a potentially less impactful element failover rather than a cluster failover.

Element recovery is generally preferable over cluster recovery for systems not directly interacting with clients because it:

- *Minimizes Visible Service Impact on End Users.* Elements in the solution not directly interfacing with the end users can failover themselves rather than instructing (usually via a proxy) the end user to failover.
- *Minimizes Complexity of Software.* Standard DNS SRV records can be used instead of adding special processing to handle failures of some internal elements.

However, the following factors can make element recovery less practical than cluster recovery:

- *Large Volume of Network Traffic between Elements in the Cluster.* When an element in another site is used, requests/responses need to be sent back and forth between the sites.
- *Increased Service Latency.* The time to process requests is increased due to the extra time needed to transport messages between sites.

As discussed in Section 4.2, "Technical Distinctions between Georedundancy and Co-Located Redundancy," if there is a failure of a single Network element within a Cluster, the failing over of only that Network element may result in increased communication latency and bandwidth usage between the Network elements due to the increase in distance to the alternate Network element at the remote site. Solving the bandwidth and latency problems by failing over the entire cluster may address that problem yet introduce the problem of complexity, additional downtime, or session loss stemming from the failover of the other Network elements in the cluster.

Some of the issues around cluster-level recovery are:

- A sequencing of the failover of the Network elements within the cluster may be needed to lessen disruption. A robust cluster architecture should impose no such sequencing requirement since it does add complexity to the recovery procedure, particularly if there are any failures during the execution of the procedure.
- Some of the remote network elements may not be prepared to take over the traffic due to hardware problems, overload conditions, etc.
- RTO and maintenance interval may be more difficult to achieve with a cluster-level recovery.
- RPO may be more difficult to achieve with a cluster-level recovery.
- An independent controller may be needed to manage cluster-level failovers.

When determining whether to do a cluster-level recovery when only a network element-level recovery is required will involve taking into account objective factors, such as downtime and session/data loss compared against decrease in performance and increase in communication latency, as well as more subjective factors, such as procedure complexity and success probability.

11.3 OTHER CONSIDERATIONS

11.3.1 Architecting to Facilitate Planned Maintenance Activities

Maintenance activities, such as software upgrade, are often performed by splitting the redundant system, upgrading the standby modules, switching them over to active, and then upgrading the once-active modules. This ensures minimal impact to a live system for most upgrades, as well as for other maintenance activities, such as hardware replacement and growth. The system can keep running on the active modules while the standby modules are being upgraded or replaced, minimizing the downtime impact for the customer. However, that mechanism does result in a certain amount of simplex time while the upgrade is being performed. Some other activities, such as backplane replacement for a single chassis component that impacts the redundant modules at the same time, may not be effectively managed with this split system-type mechanism and may result in extended outages. Since maintenance activities are planned, manually controlled georedundancy may be a good alternative for this type of a situation.

In order to direct traffic to the backup site while performing the maintenance operations, the following steps are typically followed:

- Verifying health of the backup system
- Draining of traffic from the active module to minimize impact on stable sessions
- Synchronizing data before switching to georedundant site
- Manually redirecting traffic

If manually controlled georedundancy is being used, the *manual georedundant failover rate* (μ_{MGR}) must be less than the maintenance activity downtime without georedundancy. The *manual georedundant failover success probability* (F_{MGR}) must be very high, thus the solution must be able to effectively manually redirect traffic away from the network element undergoing maintenance with a high confidence rate. That entails a lot of automation or easy to follow procedures and a well-trained staff to lessen the probability of procedural errors. Manually controlled switchback must also be considered with an equally high-success probability and short disruption time. As explained in the associated model for manually controlled georedundancy on most systems, there is assumed to be no service disruption on orderly and successful service migrations.

11.3.2 Procedural Considerations

As indicated in Section 1.8, "Human Factors," human factors plays a large part in the successful execution of a disaster recovery or geographical redundancy plan—particularly one that is manually controlled. As a result, the following considerations must be taken into account:

- Ensure that the staff that will be executing the plan is well trained in the procedures, how to interpret results, and how to recover from any failures arising during execution of these procedures.
- Ensure that the staff executes the plan using the official documentation, that the documentation is clear and accurate, and that the system detects, isolates, and reports problems clearly.
- Keep the number of steps as small as possible. Keep it simple.
- Automate as many of the steps as possible to reduce the incidence of manual error.
- The complexity of the solution must be taken into account as it will require more staff, and thus more coordination among the staff to perform the recovery. Operational testing should include the actual team performing the recovery as a way to ensure that each person understands their role in the procedure.
- Ensure that error scenarios are well documented along with their associated recovery techniques. Documentation and training should include descriptions of error reports (e.g., alarms) and recommendations on how to trouble shoot and recover from errors. These trouble shooting activities should be practiced by the staff to ensure that the documentation is well understood and effective.

12

GEOREDUNDANCY REQUIREMENTS

Complete and verifiable requirements are essential to assure the optimal mechanisms are properly implemented by developers and verified by testers. This chapter frames the availability-related requirements that should be considered for any element, cluster, or solution that supports external redundancy, especially georedundancy. This chapter first describes requirements for a standalone element with internal redundancy, then gives additional requirements needed to make the solution externally redundant solution with manual procedures, and finally covers additional requirements needed to support automatic external redundancy.

12.1 INTERNAL REDUNDANCY REQUIREMENTS

A complex solution might be expected to support multiple related services, such as:

- Several user services, including authenticating users, providing media or information, taking orders for products/services, etc.
- Multiple classes of quality of service (QoS) based on the quality expected by each user (e.g., silver, gold, and platinum).

Beyond Redundancy: How Geographic Redundancy Can Improve Service Availability and Reliability of Computer-Based Systems, First Edition. Eric Bauer, Randee Adams, Daniel Eustace.
© 2012 Institute of Electrical and Electronics Engineers. Published 2012 by John Wiley & Sons, Inc.

- Operational functions, such as recording usage, generating alarms, provisioning users and service, and generating performance reports.

The availability expectations might be different for each of these services. For example, the primary function of mission control applications are usually required to be available 99.999% of the time, but enterprises will often accept lower service availability for less critical functionality. While some operational functions like usage recording may be required to have the same service availability expectation to meet regulatory compliance or enterprise policy requirements, other less critical functions like generating and emitting performance data may have significantly lower availability expectations.

12.1.1 Standalone Network Element Redundancy Requirements

Complex solutions usually require multiple network elements to support different functions. Requirements, such as the following, are appropriate for each individual network element in the solution:

- *REQ STANDALONE-01.* The prorated, product-attributable, service availability of the <Name of Network Element> shall be at least <Availability>%.

    In the initial release, the service availability shall be predicted based on modeling (FIT rates, MTTR, coverage factor validated by testing, etc.). After field deployment, the service availability shall be calculated using actual field data.

    In this requirement, availability is a percentage, typically between 99.9% and 99.999%, depending on the criticality of the element. Since service availability tends to improve over time due to improvements in fault-detection capabilities, the required service availability might be low in the initial release, but increase in the first few releases until it reaches the expected availability. The term "prorated" refers to the loss of partial capacity or functionality—see Section 2.2.1, "Total and Partial Outages." The term "product-attributable" means that failures due to *force majeure* events (floods, earthquakes, etc.) or errors in following manual procedures should not be included in the measurement of the service availability.

- *REQ STANDALONE-02.* It shall be possible to replace any field replaceable unit (e.g., a single blade in a chassis) without unacceptable service disruption.

    It should be possible to remove a failed blade from a chassis without powering down the entire chassis, and to insert a new blade while the chassis is still powered up, without damaging the new blade.

- *REQ STANDALONE-03.* It shall be possible to apply and activate software patches, updates, and upgrades without causing an interruption of service that exceeds that supported by the enterprise.

    For example, TL9000 allows a downtime of 15 seconds. See Section 2.2.2, "Minimum Chargeable Disruption Duration," for details. Some enterprises allow interruptions but only during a specified maintenance interval.

- *REQ STANDALONE-04.* It shall be possible to grow the capacity or functionality of the element without impacting service.

  "Growing" an element means adding a new blade to a chassis or a new chassis to the solution, usually to increase capacity or support new functionality.

- *REQ STANDALONE-05.* Degrowing an element shall not impact service.

  As application usage and traffic patterns change, it often becomes necessary to adjust capacity of different applications and elements. As usage drops on individual servers, system resources (e.g., compute blades or rack mounted servers) may be removed from one element and redeployed to another element with higher traffic and/or utilization. The removal of an element is referred to as degrowing the element. This element reconfiguration should generally not cause an interruption of service unless it is the last element in the configuration.

More comprehensive reliability and availability requirements are typically specified for high-availability elements with internal redundancy; see Bauer (2010) for a more complete suite of internal reliability requirements.

12.1.2 Basic Solution Redundancy Requirements

End-to-end solution requirements are also needed to specify the overall availability and reliability for services delivered by a suite of elements. The following requirements are needed for each primary service supported by the solution (user services, provisioning, usage reporting, etc.):

- *REQ SOLUTION-01.* The end-to-end, prorated, product-attributable, service availability of the <Name of Service> service shall be <Availability>%.

  The end-to-end service availability shall be predicted based on the expected service availabilities of the network elements needed to provide the service. In a nonexternally redundant system, the end-to-end service availability is the product of the availabilities of each of the network elements. For example, if five elements are required to provide the service, and each has a service availability of 99.999%, then the end-to-end service availability should be approximately 99.995%. The term "prorated" refers to the loss of partial capacity or functionality—see Section 2.2.1, "Total and Partial Outages." The term "product-attributable" means that failures due to *force majeure* events (floods, earthquakes, etc.) or errors in following manual procedures should not be included in the measurement of the service availability. This does not include any downtime due to failures of the IP network used for communications between the elements.

- *REQ SOLUTION-02.* When the solution is operating at advertised capacity, valid service requests shall fail at a rate of less than <MaxFailureRate> defects per million attempts (DPMs). If a request is satisfied, but takes longer than <MaxTime> seconds, then it shall be counted as a defect.

DPMs are defects per million, so for example, if MaxFailureRate is 100 DPMs, then the solution is meeting this requirement if it fails less than 100 out of every 1,000,000 service requests (or 1 per 10,000). MaxTime should be set to the maximum time that the end user is willing to wait for the request to complete. Requests that take longer than this time are counted as defects, since the user is likely to give up and retry the request before it completes.

12.2 EXTERNAL REDUNDANCY REQUIREMENTS

Using the techniques described earlier in this book, external redundancy can improve the service availability and reliability of a critical system or solution. The first requirement is needed to support external recovery (either co-located or geographically distributed):

- *REQ REDUNDANT-01.* The solution shall support redundant instances of each network element. If an element fails, it shall be possible to transfer its workload to a redundant element.

  Details on how the workload is transferred are in subsequent requirements.

Geographical redundancy can also be deployed to support continuity of service in the event of a disaster. The following requirements specify that geographical redundancy should be supported.

- *REQ REDUNDANT-02.* The solution shall allow its network elements to be distributed among multiple sites in a realm. If any single site fails, the elements in the rest of the sites in the same realm shall have sufficient capacity to serve the full engineered traffic load with acceptable service quality.
- *REQ REDUNDANT-03.* Communications links between sites in the same realm shall have sufficient bandwidth to support replicating/synchronizing data between georedundant elements when operating at full engineered capacity with all elements operational.
- *REQ REDUNDANT-04.* The solution shall operate properly if the message latency through the communication network between sites in the same realm is less than <Latency> milliseconds.

  The latency depends on the distance between sites and the technology and topology of the network. This must be taken into account when setting values for T_{TIMEOUT}, T_{CLIENT}, etc.

The services provided by the solution could have different recovery time objective (RTO) requirements. Provisioning elements might have an RTO of several hours, since the only people impacted by an outage are some of the enterprise's internal employees. User services might have an RTO of only a few minutes, because the enterprise's customers are impacted.

Similarly, the services might also have different recovery point objective (RPO) requirements. If the enterprise wants session-oriented requests to be preserved over a georedundant failover, then the RPO would need to be less than a minute. However, if the enterprise allows these sessions to be lost, then the RPO would be longer than the length of a typical session (presumably, the cost of a solution with an RPO of a few minutes will be less than the cost of one with an RPO < 1 minute). The RPO for a provisioning element might be several hours, but it should be low enough that the lost data can be reprovisioned after the failover.

Therefore, we expect the enterprise to be able to specify the following requirements for every service performed by the solution:

- *REQ SERVICE-01.* In the event of a failure of any single element in the solution, a failure of an entire site, or a partial IP network failure, service shall be restored within <RTO> minutes by a failover to an externally redundant element.

  A realistic RTO value for the entire solution should be at least a few minutes, although some of the elements might support an RTO less than this (e.g., if they use active–active redundancy with automatic client-initiated recovery). The RTO for a noncritical service could be a few hours, permitting a manual georedundancy recovery strategy. If the solution requires the clients to register/logon to a different site, then the capacity of the solution must be sufficient to process the registration storm within the RTO value. The required RTO value should not be lower than necessary to minimize the cost of the solution.

- *REQ SERVICE-02.* In the event of an external network element failover, the newly active element's persistent data should not be out-of-date by more than <PersistentRPO> minutes. In addition, session-oriented requests that have been active for more than <VolatileRPO> minutes shall be preserved. This applies to failover of a single element, an entire site, or a partial IP network failure.

  Persistent data is data that is provisioned and changes infrequently. If this data is provisioned on both elements roughly simultaneously, PersistentRPO can be only a few seconds. If it is not necessary to preserve session request data over a failover, the VolatileRPO will be undefined, implying that data replication is not necessary. If only long-term sessions need to be preserved, the VolatileRPO might be a minute. The required RPO values should not be lower than necessary to minimize the cost of the solution.

Surviving elements must be able to continue to handle the traffic with quality until the failed element(s) have fully recovered. This may be an extended period of time particularly in the case of a real disaster.

- *REQ SERVICE-03.* In the event of a failure of any single element in the solution, a failure of an entire site, or a partial IP network failure, the surviving elements must be able to provide required services with quality until the failed element(s) have fully recovered.

12.3 MANUALLY CONTROLLED REDUNDANCY REQUIREMENTS

If external redundancy is required (requirement REDUNDANT-01 has been specified), then manual procedures are needed for emergency switchover, graceful switchover, and switchback.

12.3.1 Manual Failover Requirements

Requirements are needed to support a manual failover procedure to an alternate element when a primary element fails. These requirements are needed even if automatic recovery will be supported to provide a backup option in case the automatic failover is not successful, or if georedundancy is being used to support planned maintenance activities.

- *REQ MANUAL-01.* A snapshot of the database on the primary element shall be saved periodically so that the redundant element can be recovered in the event of a failure of the primary. The recovery data shall be stored in a different location than the primary element.

    This is needed so that the recovery data can be loaded onto the redundant element if a failure occurs. The recovery data must never be out of date by more than the persistent RPO requirement.
- *REQ MANUAL-02.* Appropriate alarms shall be generated within <MaxAlarmDelay> minutes after the active element fails.

    This could be implemented by having some external monitoring element periodically check if the active element is still operational.
- *REQ MANUAL-03.* A procedure for restoring the database on a redundant element from the recovery data shall be provided and documented.
- *REQ MANUAL-04.* A procedure for providing a manual failover to a redundant element shall be provided and documented.
- *REQ MANUAL-05.* The documented procedures shall precisely detail all of the operations that must be performed, as well as a clarification on errors that might be reported and how to resolve them.
- *REQ MANUAL-06.* Tools shall be provided to verify that the redundant element is healthy.

    Executing this health check increases the probability that the manual switchover will succeed. The health check should include activities, such as ensuring the hardware is functional and the file systems have sufficient free space.
- *REQ MANUAL-07.* The redundancy failover mechanism shall be supported between elements whose version number is the same or differs by 1 (release N works with release $N - 1$).

    Typically failover is only supported if both the primary and alternate elements are running on the same software version number. But if the software upgrade procedures are too complex to support upgrading both elements at the same time, or if geographical redundancy will be used to perform software upgrade, then a requirement is needed to support different releases. However, loading the alternate element with recovery data that was generated from the primary element when it was running in a different release will require some software to convert the data. If many release combinations need to be supported, then this conversion software can get very complex and slow. Therefore, this requirement should be avoided if possible. If the required RTO is long enough to load the latest version of software into the alternate server, then this requirement is not needed.

Note that whenever possible, the procedures shall be automated. Automating the steps simplifies the procedure and minimizes the risk of human error.

12.3.2 Graceful Switchover Requirements

The enterprise might require that a manual switchover procedure be supported so that they can take an active element out of service for maintenance activities (such as hardware growth/repair or software update). This procedure should have minimal impact on service. Typical requirements are:

- *REQ SWITCHOVER-01.* A procedure to synchronize the database in the alternate element with the primary element shall be documented.

    If a normal data replication mechanism exists, then that might be sufficient, but to reduce the RPO, it might need to be triggered immediately before the graceful switchover.
- *REQ SWITCHOVER-02.* The solution shall allow multiple servers to be operational simultaneously.

    This is needed so that new traffic can be directed towards one element while the other one finishes processing existing sessions.
- *REQ SWITCHOVER-03.* A procedure for gracefully shedding traffic from the primary component shall be provided and documented.

    This requires that there be a way to redirect traffic for new requests to the alternate element while the primary element finishes processing the existing requests (e.g., by updating a DNS entry). Also, the primary element must have a mechanism to report how many requests are in progress, so that it can be determined when it is idle.
- *REQ SWITCHOVER-04.* A procedure to take the primary element out of service shall be provided and documented.

12.3.3 Switchback Requirements

After a primary element has recovered, it needs to be put back into service. It should be possible to do this in a controlled manner so that there is minimal impact on service. Typical requirements are:

- *REQ SWITCHBACK-01.* A procedure to synchronize the database in the recovering element with the active element shall be provided and documented.

  The synchronization mechanism is usually the same as the normal data replication mechanism between the active and standby elements. So if backup/restore is normally used to update the standby element, then it can also be used to synchronize the recovering element. And if a data replication interface is available to update the standby element, then it can also be used for synchronizing the recovering element.

- *REQ SWITCHBACK-02.* A procedure to activate the recovering element and put the alternate element back into the standby state shall be provided and documented.

  If the elements run active–active or load shared, then the second part of this requirement is not necessary; the other element can remain active.

- *REQ SWITCHBACK-03.* When the recovering element is activated, the service unavailability during the switchback shall be less than <MaxSwitchbackTime> minutes.

12.4 AUTOMATIC EXTERNAL RECOVERY REQUIREMENTS

If the required RTO (in requirement SERVICE-01) is too short to be supported by manual recovery, then automatic failover support will be needed, using either a system-driven or client-initiated strategy, or both. The following requirement should be specified for every client/server interface in the solution:

- *REQ AUTOMATIC-01.* The interface between <Client> and <Server> shall utilize an automatic [System-driven | Client-Initiated | both client-initiated and system-driven] recovery strategy.

  If a system-driven recovery strategy (or both) is required, then the requirements in Section 12.4.1, "System-Driven Recovery," must be implemented. If a client-initiated recovery strategy (or both) is required, then the requirements in Section 12.4.2, "Client-Initiated Recovery," must be implemented.

12.4.1 System-Driven Recovery

The following requirements apply to systems supporting automatic system-driven recovery.

- *REQ SYSTEM-01.* A mechanism shall be provided to ensure that the same service configuration is applied to both the primary and redundant elements. Any provisioning updates shall be applied to both elements.

  The elements should be provisioned with the same data within the Persistent RPO requirement.

- *REQ SYSTEM-02.* An automatic data replication mechanism shall be provided for the primary element to periodically send its state data to the redundant element (less than <VolatileRPO> minutes between updates).

    Alternatively, the data could be backed up in a separate registry.

- *REQ SYSTEM-03.* The primary and redundant element shall exchange heartbeats every <HeartbeatInterval> seconds. After <MaxMissingHeartbeats> consecutive failed heartbeats, the redundant element shall check that it still has connectivity to the network. If this check passes, it shall be assumed that the primary element is down/unavailable. The HeartbeatInterval and MaxMissingHeartbeats parameters shall be configurable.

    If the primary element heartbeats every HeartbeatInterval seconds and MaxMissingHeartbeats failures are needed before a failover is triggered, then HeartbeatInterval times MaxMissingHeartbeats, plus the time needed for the alternate element to become active, must be less than the required RTO. It is recommended that these values be configurable in case it is discovered after deployment that the communications channel is slow or frequently loses heartbeats. The requirement should specify whether the heartbeats are sent directly to an alternate element or another element that monitors the availability of the primary element.

- *REQ SYSTEM-04.* The redundant element shall acknowledge the heartbeats it receives from the primary element. If the primary element does not receive <MaxMissingHeartbeats> consecutive acknowledgments, it shall be assumed that the redundant element is down/unavailable and generate an alarm.

    The primary element should report an alarm if it detects that the redundant element has failed to trigger maintenance personnel to fix the element so that it is ready to take over service when needed.

- *REQ SYSTEM-05.* When a primary element has failed, the redundant element shall wait <StandaloneRecoveryWaitTime> minutes before activating the alternate element. StandaloneRecoveryWaitTime shall be configurable.

    Recall that it is preferable to give the primary element some time to recover on its own before failing over to avoid the operational costs of failing over and switching back. StandaloneRecoveryWaitTime should be set to give the primary element a reasonable amount of time to recover on its own. If there are no significant costs for the failover, then StandaloneRecoveryWaitTime could be zero. It is recommended that StandaloneRecoveryWaitTime be configurable since it might be necessary to change it after more is known from field experience about the typical time needed to recover the primary element.

- *REQ SYSTEM-06.* A mechanism shall be provided to disable automatic system-driven recovery.

    This could be used if it appears that the failed element is in the process of recovering successfully or if geographical redundancy is being used for a planned activity, such as software upgrade.

- *REQ SYSTEM-07.* Automatic system-driven failover shall be successful on at least <ServerDrivenSuccessRate>% of the failover attempts.

ServerDrivenSuccessRate should be in the range of 90–99%. This requirement applies to all types of failures (total site failures due to disaster, failures of just the active element, communications network failures, etc.). A "successful" failover is one in which:

- The primary element is removed from service.
- The redundant element takes over service.
- The clients are redirected to the redundant server.
- The entire failover completes in less than the RTO requirement (requirement SERVICE-01).
- Service context is restored and is out-of-date by less than the RPO requirement (requirement SERVICE-02).

12.4.2   Client-Initiated Recovery

For client-initiated recovery to work properly, requirements are needed on both the client and the server. The following requirements apply to the server.

- *REQ CLIENT-01.* When a server receives an invalid request from a client, it shall return explicit failure code for $<F_{CLIENT}>\%$ of the failed requests.

    When possible, the server shall send an explicit failure code rather than ignoring an invalid request, so that the client can take immediate action without waiting for a response timer to expire and attempting retries.

- *REQ CLIENT-02.* If a server cannot satisfy requests for a client, then it shall reject requests with failure code(s) <XXXX>.

    An example would be if there is an internal problem in the server (e.g., a corrupt database) or a subsequent server that is required to satisfy requests for the client is not available. This failure code would trigger the client to reregister with another server, which might not have the same problem. XXXX could be a list of failure codes. C_{CLIENT} (defined in Chapter 6) is the percentage of the total failure responses that have an XXXX failure code.

The requirements on the client depend on whether the client will be using network element recovery or cluster recovery. With network element recovery, if the client detects that a server has failed, it should attempt to recovery to an alternate server. The following requirements apply to clients that use network element recovery.

- *REQ CLIENT-03.* Clients shall support a mechanism to load share their requests among multiple servers.

    Generally, DNS is the most flexible mechanism—when a new server is added to the solution, only a new DNS record is needed, and the clients are not impacted. Alternately, a list of IP addresses can be provisioned in the client.

- *REQ CLIENT-04.* The load-sharing mechanism shall support a means of optimally selecting servers (e.g., choosing co-located servers before remote servers).

If DNS was required in requirement CLIENT-01, then this would require the use of separate FQDNs for local and remote servers (using A or AAAA records), or SRV records (with different priorities for local and remote servers). If a list of addresses is acceptable, then this would require separate lists for local and remote servers.

- *REQ CLIENT-05.* The clients shall support registering with a redundant server so that they do not have to go through the registration process during a failover. They should send periodic keepalive messages to the redundant server to ensure that the session is operational.

  This is an optional requirement that can be added to reduce failover time.

- *REQ CLIENT-06.* When a server does not respond to requests, the client shall detect the failure, and resend its request to one of the redundant servers that it registered with for requirement CLIENT-05. The clients shall initially use the standard response timer values (T_{TIMEOUT}) and retry counts (MaxRetryCount). The clients shall keep track of the typical response time of their server and the maximum number of retries required. The clients can lower T_{TIMEOUT} from the standard value to $<X>$ times the typical response time (whichever is lower), and reduce MaxRetryCount to the maximum number previously sent, plus one (whichever is lower). $<X>$ shall be provisionable.

  If CLIENT-05 was not implemented, the client should resend its request to any of the available servers identified through requirement CLIENT-03. The response timer and retry adaptations in this requirement are useful if the server is using active–active or load-shared redundancy. They are not as useful for active–standby servers, since it is likely that the servers will take longer to failover than the clients. The adaptations can reduce the timer value and retry counts from the standard, but they should not be increased above the standard values. The value of X depends on how aggressively the enterprise is willing to lower T_{TIMEOUT}. A typical value of X would be 5. μ_{TIMEOUT} (defined in Chapter 6) is $1/[(1 + \text{MaxRetryCount}) \times T_{\text{TIMEOUT}}]$.

- *REQ CLIENT-07.* When a server responds to a request with failure code(s) $<XXXX>$, the client shall initiate recovery to the redundant server it registered with for REQ CLIENT-05. The client shall failover within $<1/\mu_{\text{CLIENT}}>$ seconds, and failovers shall be successful on $<F_{\text{CLIENT}}>\%$ of the attempts. When a server responds with any other failure code, the client shall map the failure code to an appropriate failure code for the end user.

  The XXXX failure code(s) indicates that the server cannot satisfy the request, but another server might. Other failure codes indicate that the request is invalid or cannot be satisfied by any server.

- *REQ CLIENT-08.* While the server is in the failed state, the load-sharing mechanism indicated in REQ CLIENT-03 shall mark the server as unavailable for service until it has fully recovered.

- *REQ CLIENT-09.* Clients shall periodically check if a failed server has recovered, and automatically resume using a recovered server when practical.

- *REQ CLIENT-10.* When the client determines that it should failover to alternate server, it shall be successful on at least <ClientInitiatedSuccessRate>% of the failover attempts.

  ClientInitiatedSuccessRate should be in the range of 95% to 99%. This requirement applies to all types of failures (timer expiry, failure response, etc.). A "successful" failover is one in which:

  - The client recognizes that it should fail over.
  - The client chooses a valid alternate server.
  - The client successfully registers with the new server.

With cluster recovery, the client should always send its requests to the local server. If it detects that the local server has failed, it should return a failure to its client (which we'll assume is the end user) that is expected to trigger the end user to failover to an alternate site. The following requirements apply to clients that use cluster recovery.

- *REQ CLIENT-11.* Clients shall always send requests to a local server.
- *REQ CLIENT-12.* When a server does not respond to requests, the client shall detect the failure, and respond to its request from the end user with failure code <YYYY>. The clients shall initially use the standard response timer values ($T_{TIMEOUT}$) and retry counts (MaxRetryCount). The clients shall keep track of the typical response time of their server and the maximum number of retries required. The clients can lower $T_{TIMEOUT}$ from the standard value to <X> times the typical response time (whichever is lower), and reduce MaxRetryCount to the maximum number previously sent, plus one (whichever is lower). <X> shall be provisionable.

  The YYYY failure code should trigger the end user to reregister with another cluster. The response timer and retry adaptations in this requirement are useful if the server is using active–active or load-shared redundancy. They are not as useful for active–standby servers, since it is likely that the servers will take longer to failover than the clients. The adaptations can reduce the timer value and retry counts from the standard, but they should not be increased above the standard values. The value of X depends on how aggressively the enterprise is willing to lower $T_{TIMEOUT}$. A typical value of X would be 5. $\mu_{TIMEOUT}$ (defined in Chapter 6) is $1/[(1 + \text{MaxRetryCount}) \times T_{TIMEOUT}]$.

- *REQ CLIENT-13.* When a server responds to a request with failure code(s) <XXXX>, then the client shall respond to its request from the end user with failure code(s) <YYYY>. When a server responds with any other failure code, the client shall map the failure code to an appropriate failure code for the end user.

  The XXXX failure code(s) indicates that the server cannot satisfy the request, but another server might. Other failure codes indicate that the request is invalid or cannot be satisfied by any server. The YYYY failure code should trigger the end user to reregister with another cluster.

12.5   OPERATIONAL REQUIREMENTS

The operational requirements in this section apply to the organization that will be responsible for maintaining the target system/solution rather than the organization designing the system/solution.

- *REQ OPERATIONAL-01.* An overall procedure shall be documented that describes all the manual georedundancy activities that must be performed after a complete site failure. This procedure shall reference all the manual procedures required in Section 12.3, "Manually Controlled Redundancy Requirements." It shall also describe:
  - What conditions must be satisfied before performing the manual failover procedures. That is, how should it be determined that the active elements cannot be recovered.
  - Which maintenance engineers should perform each procedure.
  - How the solution should be monitored to check that the failover was successful.
- *REQ OPERATIONAL-02.* The procedure described in OPERATIONAL-01 shall be practiced before deployment, and at least once every <specify number> months thereafter.

13

GEOREDUNDANCY TESTING

Successful execution of a service recovery to an externally redundant element generally requires correct execution of high-quality software and procedures to ensure that recovery time and recovery point objectives are met. As a result, it is important to provide thorough testing at every level to ensure the recovery performance and other requirements are met, and that procedures are accurate and efficient. Georedundancy testing is also a way to gather data on recovery times and verify service impact on new and existing sessions and transactions. All manual, as well as automatic recovery procedures and mechanisms, must be verified for both switchover and switchback. This chapter begins by explaining the different levels of testing that should be performed based on scope and environment, and then provides a suggested set of tests based on the requirements defined in Chapter 12.

13.1 GEOREDUNDANCY TESTING STRATEGY

Georedundancy is tested across several test phases to ensure that each network element, as well as the entire solution, is able to successfully recover from a profound failure and meet its georedundancy requirements. Testing is performed starting in the

Beyond Redundancy: How Geographic Redundancy Can Improve Service Availability and Reliability of Computer-Based Systems, First Edition. Eric Bauer, Randee Adams, Daniel Eustace.
© 2012 Institute of Electrical and Electronics Engineers. Published 2012 by John Wiley & Sons, Inc.

development phases and continues through customer deployment. Each of the following test phases is considered:

- Network element level testing
- End-to-end testing
- Deployment testing
- Operational testing

13.1.1   Network Element Level Testing

The purpose of network element level testing is to ensure that each network element is properly managing its part of the recovery and that interfaces to the network element properly detect the loss of the network element and redirect traffic to the backup network element. Network element level testing should be performed based on a configuration of mated network elements. Network element level testing should verify the manual recovery operations, as well as the system-driven or client-initiated recovery, if provided.

In addition network element level testing is used to gather data on recovery times and characteristics that can be used to validate reliability model parameter values, such as the automatic recovery rate (μ_{CGR}) and the manual recovery rate (μ_{MGR}). For all scenarios below:

- Verify that the recovery time objective (RTO) has been met.
- Verify that the recovery point objective (RPO) has been met.
- Measure the applicable service impact (i.e., active sessions, new sessions, transient sessions, new requests, pending requests)

During testing recovery, times as well as session/call drops are validated to ensure they meet requirements.

For system-driven failover (active/hot-standby):

- Validate that the same configuration (hardware and database) is applied to both the primary and alternate elements, with the possible exception of element location information, such as IP addresses.
- Verify that any state data (generated > RPO minutes) has been successfully replicated.
- If heartbeats are used verify that when the active element fails to send Y consecutive heartbeats, it is considered failed.
- Verify that after X minutes the standby element is activated.

For manual failover (active/cold-standby, active/warm-standby):

- Validate the documented procedures for generating a backup copy of the database on the active element.

- Verify that appropriate alarms are generated when the active element fails.
- Validate documented procedures for restoring the database on the alternate element with the latest backup, or, if synchronized, verify that the synchronization was successful.
- Validate any documented procedures for gracefully shedding traffic from the active component.
- Validate the documented procedure to activate the standby element and take the active element out of service.

For client-initiated recovery:

- Verify that when a server fails, the clients shall detect the failure, and resend requests (or register with) alternate servers.
- Verify that when the failed server recovers, the clients resume using that server.

For switchback:

- Verify the documented procedure that synchronizes the database in the recovering element with the active element.
- Verify the documented procedure that activates the recovering element and puts the alternate element back into the standby state.

13.1.2 End-to-End Testing

End-to-end testing should be configured with all of the network elements located in two sites in order to better emulate a georedundant configuration. Since there are likely to be a team of testers involved, there must be clear roles and responsibilities outlined, including what to look for during the testing. End-to-end solution testing should test scenarios where the solution is running at a high capacity and there is a need to do a manual (or automated if available) recovery of an entire site or cluster. Data should be gathered before and after the failure to compare performance of the primary element versus the backup element. End-to-end testing will be the best place to thoroughly test client-initiated recovery, as it will include a georedundant configuration of all of the Network Elements, and include an environment in which a site or network element failure can be performed that triggers the client to attempt the recovery.

13.1.3 Deployment Testing

Deployment testing is similar to end-to-end testing, but it is done in the actual enterprise's network. The main purpose of deployment testing is to ensure that the behavior within the enterprise's premises is no different from what was verified by the solution supplier in the supplier's lab. Following the documented procedures, the solution should be configured for geographic redundancy, and it should be verified that the solution works properly. A manually controlled switchover should be executed by the staff that will be responsible for taking such an action in the event of a site failure, following the provided procedures to further ensure that the solution has been properly configured and integrated into the customer's network. Just as in the case of end-to-end solution testing, the RTO and RPO values need to be validated, as well as a portion of the applicable network element level tests.

13.1.4 Operational Testing

The main purpose of the operational testing is to ensure that the plans and procedures referenced in Section 1.7, "Disaster Recovery Planning," can successfully provide business continuity in the event of a disaster. By periodically executing the plan, training the staff and gathering results, gaps and areas of improvement can be identified and resolved to provide a means of evolving and improving the procedural reliability of the georedundancy plan. Operational testing is performed by the IT staff to:

- *verify that the plan is robust* by identifying any shortcomings in the plan. By fully reviewing and performing the procedures, gaps may be found or ways to make it more efficient.
- *gather performance data on recoveries* (e.g., recovery time, number of failures) to either baseline results or verify if there are any gaps in meeting customer requirements on recovery time or impact on existing and new traffic. The data will help to identify what can be expected in a controlled environment and identify areas that do not meet customer expectations.
- *provide training for the recovery team* and include a feedback loop on improvements to the plan or procedures. If performed by the team responsible for the recovery, it will give the teams first-hand experience with the process and make them more comfortable with it, as well as provide them a basis to provide input on shortcomings and improvements.

Operational testing shall include a dry run for an actual disaster recovery plan, including a switchback, and is typically tested periodically on the actual system—every quarter or twice a year (as recommended in Gregory and Jan Rothstein [2007])—to ensure that the georedundancy mechanisms are working properly, including the links between the elements and the load balancing services, and that the procedures are clear and correct. As sited in the webinar "Crisis Averted!", a business continuity plan should be reviewed and tested at least annually, more often if the risk is significant. More frequent testing will also enhance the confidence of the staff in handling the recovery.

13.2 TEST CASES FOR EXTERNAL REDUNDANCY

Failure scenarios must be identified and tested, including a total failure of all of the primary network elements, as well as each primary network element individually. Note that some requirements are relatively easy to verify such as the failover time:

- *TEST-SERVICE-01.* Validate that in the event of a failure of any element in the solution, service shall be restored within <Value> minutes by a failover to an alternate element. The automatic failover value will be a key value used in the reliability model to validate the availability for REQ-SOLUTION-01.

Other requirements, such as REQ STANDALONE-01 at the network element level and REQ SOLUTION-01 at the solution level, are verified by inputting FIT rates, MTTR, and results of testing for parameters, such as software coverage and switchover success rate, into a reliability model. The reliability model indicates the likely availability of the network element based on these parameters (and additional information). Testing specifically for availability would take many months of rigorous testing to model long-term behavior of the network element. This is not really practical, so availability modeling is recommended:

- *TEST STANDALONE-01.* The prorated, product-attributable, service availability of the <Name of Network Element> shall be at least <Availability>%. This should be verified through reliability modeling for every network element in the solution.
- *TEST-SOLUTION-01.* The end-to-end, prorated, service availability of the <Name of Service> service shall be <Value>%. In the initial release, the service availability shall be predicted based on modeling (FIT rates, MTTR, coverage factor validated by testing, etc.). After field deployment, the service availability shall be calculated using actual field data.

13.3 VERIFYING GEOREDUNDANCY REQUIREMENTS

The next sections provide guidance on verifying the solution can meet its recovery requirements based on the type of recovery mechanism being implemented. There is a section for each type of recovery—standalone, manually controlled, client-initiated, and system-driven. Some requirements such as the RTO and RPO requirements indicated in SERVICE-01 and SERVICE-02 should be verified for manually controlled, client-initiated, and system-driven recovery.

- *TEST-SERVICE-01.* Validate that in the event of a failure of any element in the solution, service shall be restored within <Value> minutes by a failover to an alternate element. Note that the failover time may vary for each element in the solution, but there should be a maximum time allowed for each.
- *TEST-SERVICE-02.* For each network element in the solution, validate that in the event of a network element failover, the newly active element's persistent data should not be out-of-date by more than <PersistentRPO> minutes, and the session data should not be out-of-date by more than <VolatileRPO> minutes.
- *TEST SERVICE-03.* Validate that in the event of a failure of any element in the solution or of an entire site, that the remaining elements can support the required

services at capacity. This can be done by running a long duration (e.g., 72-hour) capacity load on the remaining elements to ensure that they can support the traffic with required reliability and quality.

13.3.1 Test Cases for Standalone Elements

The purpose of testing standalone elements (no external redundancy) is to establish a performance baseline and to ensure the proper functioning of the standalone elements. Configurations with external redundancy should perform no worse than standalone elements on any of these tests. The following tests should be run with traffic and monitored for impact (e.g., failed components, system downtime).

- *TEST-STANDALONE-02.* Test shall be run to remove and replace every field replaceable unit (e.g., a single blade in a chassis) and verifying that is can be performed on each unit without unacceptable service disruption.
- *TEST STANDALONE-03.* Maintenance operations, such as applying and activating software patches, updates, and upgrades, shall be performed and monitored on each element in the solution to ensure that they do not impact service. This needs to be done with traffic running on the element so that any disruptions in the traffic can be noted.
- *TEST STANDALONE-04.* Tests shall include growing the element with new pieces of hardware or software packages and ensuring that it does not impact service. This needs to be done with traffic running on the element so that any disruptions in the traffic can be noted.
- *TEST STANDALONE-05.* Tests shall include degrowing the element by removing pieces of hardware or software packages and ensuring that it does not impact service. This needs to be done with traffic running on the element so that any disruptions in the traffic can be noted.

13.3.2 Test Cases for Manually Controlled Recovery

Manual recovery is required when automatic mechanisms are not available or not functioning properly. Manual mechanisms can also be used to facilitate planned activities, such as software upgrades. To validate the manual mechanisms, the following tests shall be run:

- *TEST-MANUAL-01.* Validate that a snapshot of the database on the active element is saved periodically and is stored in a different location than the active element.

     The time between snapshots should be less than the Persistent RPO requirement.
- *TEST-MANUAL-02.* Verify that appropriate alarms shall be generated within <MaxAlarmDelay> minutes after the active element fails.

- *TEST-MANUAL-03.* Verify that a procedure for restoring the database on the alternate element with the recovery data is documented. Perform the procedure as documented and ensure that it is successful.
- *TEST-MANUAL-04.* Verify that a procedure for activating the alternate element has been documented. Perform the procedure as documented and ensure that it is successful.
- *TEST-MANUAL-05.* Simulate error recovery scenarios, including network failures, database problems, or single component failures, and attempt to resolve them based on the documented procedures.
- *TEST-MANUAL-06.* Validate that the tools that have been provided to check that the backup element is healthy are fully functional.
- *TEST-MANUAL-07.* Validate that the geographical redundancy failover mechanism is supported between elements whose version number differs by 1 (release N works with release $N - 1$).
- *TEST-SWITCHBACK-01.* Perform and validate the documented procedure to synchronize the database in the recovering element with the active element.
- *TEST-SWITCHBACK-02.* Perform and validate the documented procedure to activate the recovering element and put the alternate element back into the standby state. This value will represent the parameter $\mu_{GRECOVER}$.
- *TEST-SWITCHBACK-03.* Verify that a switchback can be successfully performed with less than <MaxSwitchback> minutes downtime. This value will represent the parameter $\mu_{MIGRATION}$ or the migration disruption rate.
- *TEST-SWITCHOVER-01.* Verify that the documented procedure to synchronize the database in the alternate element with the primary element can be successfully performed.
- *TEST-SWITCHOVER-02.* Verify that if the solution supports a graceful shutdown that new traffic can be directed to the alternate network element(s) while the primary network elements are completing their transactions.
- *TEST-SWITCHOVER-03.* If a documented procedure exists for gracefully shedding traffic from the primary component, verify the accuracy of the procedure.
- *TEST-SWITCHOVER-04.* Verify that taking the primary element out of service can be performed successfully.

13.3.3 Test Cases for System-Driven Recovery

For system-driven recovery (active/hot-standby):

- *TEST-SYSTEM-01.* Provision new parameters or update existing ones. Verify that the changes have been applied or replicated to both elements.
- *TEST-SYSTEM-02.* Verify that state data replication is being periodically performed between the primary and redundant elements (less than <VolatileRPO> minutes between updates).

- *TEST-SYSTEM-03*. Verify that the primary element is sending heartbeats every <HeartbeatInterval> seconds to the <redundant element | monitoring element>. Introduce a failure that is not recovered in the allowed interval. After <MaxMissingHeartbeats> consecutive failed heartbeats, it shall be assumed that the primary element is down. <HeartbeatInterval> and <MaxMissingHeartbeats> shall be configurable.
- *TEST-SYSTEM-04*. Verify that the redundant element is acknowledging heartbeats. Introduce a redundant element failure that is not recovered in the allowed interval. After <MaxMissingHeartbeats> consecutive failed acknowledgments, verify that the primary element reports an alarm.
- *TEST-SYSTEM-05*. Cause a profound failure of an active element. Validate that when the element has failed, the element shall wait (<HeartbeatInterval> × <MaxMissingHeartbeats>) + <StandaloneRecoveryWaitTime> minutes before activating the redundant element. StandaloneRecoveryWaitTime shall be configurable.
- *TEST-SYSTEM-06*. Disable automatic failover and verify that it functions properly by invoking a failure that should normally result in an automatic failover. Re-enable the mechanism and invoke the failure again ensuring that the failover does occur.
- *TEST-SYSTEM-07*. Verify that the active–standby redundancy failover is successful on at least <AutomaticSuccessRate>% of the failover attempts. This will require a reasonable number of attempts (e.g., 100 to verify that at least 90 pass) to verify the success criteria of <AutomaticSuccessRate>%. As clarified in the requirement a "successful" failover is one in which:
  - The previously active element is removed from service.
  - The secondary element takes over service.
  - The clients are redirected to the secondary server.
  - Service context is restored and is out-of-date by less than the RPO requirement.
  - The entire failover completes in less than the RTO requirement.

13.3.4 Test Cases for Client-Initiated Recovery

The following tests will verify the client-initiated mechanism:

- *TEST-CLIENT-01*. Emulate the issuance of invalid requests from a client and verify that the server returns explicit failure code for $<F_{CLIENT}>$% of the failed requests.
- *TEST-CLIENT-02*. In conjunction with TEST-CLIENT-01, validate that when the server cannot satisfy requests for a client, it rejects requests with failure code(s) <XXXX>.

  An example would be if there is an internal problem in the server (e.g., a corrupt database) or a subsequent server that is required to satisfy requests for the client is not available. This failure code would trigger the client to reregister with another server, which might not have the same problem. XXXX could be a list of failure codes. C_{CLIENT} (defined in Chapter 6) is the percentage of the total failure responses that have an XXXX failure code.

The following tests apply to clients that use network element recovery.

- *TEST-CLIENT-03.* Configure and run load tests to verify that clients support load sharing of requests among multiple servers.
- *TEST-CLIENT-04.* In conjunction with TEST-CLIENT-03, monitor the distribution of requests among the servers and validate that the load-sharing mechanism supports an optimal selection of servers (e.g., choosing co-located servers before remote servers).
- *TEST-CLIENT-05.* If the architecture supports client registration with redundant servers, verify the mechanism by performing various failovers and ensuring that the sessions can continue on the redundant server.
- *TEST-CLIENT-06.* Verify that when a server does not respond to requests, the client shall detect the failure and resend its request the redundant servers that it registered with for requirement CLIENT-05. The clients shall initially use the standard response timer values ($T_{TIMEOUT}$) and retry counts (MaxRetryCount). If the clients adopt the mechanism to keep track of the typical response time of their server and the maximum number of retries required in order to reduce the values to lower ones, validate the mechanism.

   Note that the response timer and retry adaptations in this requirement are useful if the server is using active–active or load-shared redundancy.
- *TEST-CLIENT-07.* Create scenarios in which the server responds to a client request with failure code(s) <XXXX>, and validate that the client-initiated recovery to the redundant server it registered with for REQ CLIENT-03. The client shall failover within <$1/\mu_{CLIENT}$> seconds, and failovers shall be successful on <F_{CLIENT}>% of the attempts. When a server responds with any other failure code, the client shall map the failure code to an appropriate failure code for the end user.
- *TEST-CLIENT-08.* While the server is in the failed state, validate that the load-sharing mechanism indicated in REQ CLIENT-03 shall mark the server as unavailable for service until it has fully recovered.
- *TEST-CLIENT-09.* Create scenarios in which the primary server fails, the secondary assumes service, and the primary recovers. Verify that the clients periodically check if the failed server has recovered, and automatically resume using the recovered server.

Note that the tests marked TEST-CLIENT-10, TEST-SERVICE-03, and TEST-SWITCHBACK-02-03 have been added to calculate or validate the values used in the client-initiated recovery model detailed in Section 6.5.3, "Practical Modeling of Client-Initiated Recovery."

- *TEST-CLIENT-10.* Execute numerous server failover scenarios and validate that the client successfully recovers onto the alternate server on at least <ClientInitiatedSuccessRate>% of the failover attempts.

    ClientInitiatedSuccessRate should be in the range of 95–99%. This requirement applies to all types of failures (timer expiry, failure response, etc.). A "successful" failover is one in which:

- The client recognizes that it should fail over.
- The client chooses a valid alternate server.
- The client successfully registers with the new server.

The following requirements apply to clients that use cluster recovery.

- *TEST-CLIENT-11.* While validating client-initiated recovery, verify that clients always send requests to a local server.
- *TEST-CLIENT-12.* Validate that when a server does not respond to requests, the client shall detect the failure, and respond to its request from the end user with failure code <YYYY>. The clients shall initially use the standard response timer values ($T_{TIMEOUT}$) and retry counts (MaxRetryCount). If the clients implement the mechanism to keep track of the typical response time of their server and the maximum number of retries required and lower $T_{TIMEOUT}$ from the standard value to <X> times the typical response time (whichever is lower), and reduce MaxRetryCount to the maximum number previously sent, plus one (whichever is lower), this mechanism should be validated.
- *TEST-CLIENT-13.* Validate that when a server responds to a request with failure code(s) <XXXX>, then the client shall respond to its request from the end user with failure code(s) <YYYY>. When a server responds with any other failure code, the client shall map the failure code to an appropriate failure code for the end user.

13.3.5   Test Cases at the Solution Level

The following test shall be performed to verify the robustness of the solution-level redundancy. Note that there are other solution-level tests indicated below in Section 13.3.6, "Test Cases for Operational Testing," that should be tested in the customers' network in order to ensure it can meet performance and capacity requirements.

- *TEST-REDUNDANT-01.* Verify that for each redundant network element in the solution a failure of one of the network elements results in the recovery of traffic to the other network element.

In order to validate that the service availability requirements are met the following end-to-end solution tests must be run:

- *TEST-SERVICE-01.* Validate that in the event of a failure of any active element in the solution, service shall be restored within <Value> minutes by a failover to an alternate element.
- *TEST-SERVICE-02.* Validate that in the event of a network element failover, the newly active element's persistent data should not be out-of-date by more than <PersistentRPO> minutes, and the session data should not be out-of-date by more than <VolatileRPO> minutes.
- *TEST SERVICE-03.* Validate that in the event of a failure of any element in the solution or of an entire site, that the remaining elements can support the required services at capacity. This can be done by running a long-duration (e.g., 72 hour) capacity load on the remaining elements to ensure that they can support the traffic with required reliability and quality.
- *TEST-SOLUTION-02.* Perform an extended (e.g., 72 hour) stability test with the solution running at advertised capacity, and verify that valid service requests fail at a rate of less than <MaxFailureRate> defects per million attempts (DPMs). If a request is satisfied, but takes longer than <MaxTime> seconds, then it shall be counted as a defect.

13.3.6 Test cases for Operational Testing

The following test should be performed before deployment, and at least once every 6–12 months thereafter.

- *TEST-OPERATIONAL-01.* Verify the completeness and accuracy of the documented procedure that describes all the manual georedundancy activities that must be performed after a complete site failure by executing each step as written and taking the following into consideration:
  - What conditions must be satisfied before performing the manual failover procedures. That is, how should it be determined that the active elements cannot be recovered.
  - Which maintenance engineers should perform each procedure.
  - How the solution should be monitored to check that the failover was successful.

The following solution-level tests shall be performed in the field in order to verify the latency and capacity characteristics in the actual network:

- *TEST-REDUNDANT-02.* If recovery realms are used, verify that the failure of any single site results in the elements in the rest of the sites in the same realm being able to provide sufficient capacity to serve the full engineered traffic load with acceptable service quality using an extended stability run (e.g., 72 hours).
- *TEST-REDUNDANT-03.* Operate the solution at full engineered capacity with all elements operational, and validate that the communications links between

sites in the same realm have sufficient bandwidth to support replicating/synchronizing data between *georedundant elements.*

- *TEST-REDUNDANT-04.* Operate the solution at full engineered capacity and validate that the message latency through the communication network between sites in the same realm is less than <Latency> milliseconds.

13.4 SUMMARY

Network element georedundancy testing is generally performed across the development and deployment life and demonstrates how well a particular network element can perform switchovers and switchbacks. Any anomalies reported during testing should be disclosed and monitored for resolution. An example of a test plan summary is:

The network element successfully passed 90% of its georedundancy tests, including:

- A recovery time of 2 minutes (compared with a target of 3 minutes) based on (manually controlled/client-initiated/system-driven recovery)
- A loss of 3 minutes worth of data updates (compared with a target of 5 minutes)
- 5.2 defective user transactions per million (target < 10) on the new network element versus 3.2 defective user transactions per million on the original network element before the failure.

End-to-end georedundancy testing demonstrates how well an entire solution can recover from a site failure, that is, when all of the network elements must failover. Any anomalies reported during testing should be disclosed and monitored for resolution. An example of a test plan summary is:

The end-to-end testing successfully passed 90% of its georedundancy tests, including:

- Experienced a recovery time of 30 minutes (compared with a target of 30 minutes)
- Experienced a loss of 30 minutes worth of data updates (compared with a target of 45 minutes)
- 5.2 defective user transactions per million (target < 10) on the new cluster versus 3.2 defective user transactions per million on the original network elements before the failure.

Deployment testing is a repeat of the end-to-end testing but exercised in the customer's network with their configuration. In this case, the customer must ensure that all tests pass or are at least documented with an acceptable recovery plan from the provider so the summary could be:

- The deployment testing successfully passed 95% of its georedundancy tests, with the one exception to be resolved with 10 days by the provider.

- Verified a recovery time of 30 minutes (compared with a target of 30 minutes).
- Verified a loss of 30 minutes worth of data updates (compared with a target of 45 minutes).
- 5.2 defective user transactions per million on the new cluster versus 3.2 defective user transactions per million on the original network elements before the failure falling well within our SLA requirement of 10 DPMs.

Operational georedundancy testing demonstrates how well the customer can perform the site switchover and switchback within their network following the documented procedures. The report back to management (and possibly the vendor) could include:

- Accuracy of the documentation provided for site switchover (e.g., number of issues found during execution)
- Accuracy of the documentation provided for site switchback (e.g., number of issues found during execution)
- Experienced a recovery time of 30 minutes (compared with a target of 30 minutes)
- Experienced a loss of 30 minutes worth of data updates (compared with a target of 45 minutes)
- 5.2 defective user transactions per million (target < 10) on the new cluster versus 3.2 defective user transactions per million on the original network elements before the failure.

As mentioned above, operational testing should be performed periodically—every quarter or twice a year—to ensure that the georedundancy mechanisms are still working properly despite element growth/degrowth, software updates, or changes in the network, staff, or procedures.

SOLUTION GEOREDUNDANCY CASE STUDY

This chapter connects the recommendations presented earlier in this book by providing a case study of the hypothetical georedundant solution described in Section 9.1, "Understanding Solutions." This sample solution is built from a web server frontend and a database server backend. The chapter begins by describing the hypothetical solution, and briefly analyzes the standalone, nongeoredundant configuration before considering the georedundant solution configuration. The georedundant solution is analyzed incorporating some of the recommendations given in Chapter 11, "Maximizing Service Availability via Georedundancy." The chapter concludes with requirements and testing the georedundant deployment of the hypothetical solution.

14.1 THE HYPOTHETICAL SOLUTION

This case study considers an e-commerce web solution that is assumed to have the same hypothetical architecture that was depicted in Chapter 9, "Solution and Cluster Recovery"; Figure 14.1 (similar to Fig. 9.3) illustrates the hypothetical solution. The hypothetical solution offers a web-based interface for users to access and manipulate critical enterprise information (e.g., purchase products from the web site) stored in the database server per business policies and rules.

Beyond Redundancy: How Geographic Redundancy Can Improve Service Availability and Reliability of Computer-Based Systems, First Edition. Eric Bauer, Randee Adams, Daniel Eustace.

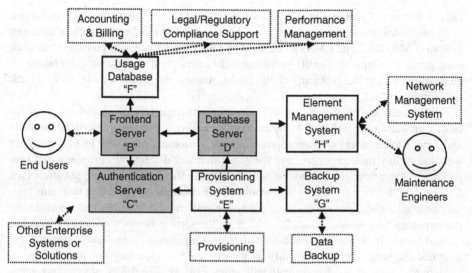

Figure 14.1. Hypothetical solution architecture.

In our e-commerce solution example, product information is provisioned via Provisioning System "E" into Database Server "D." An end user can view this data on their web browser by sending HTTP queries to Frontend Server "B." When the user finds products they would like to buy, they can place them into a virtual shopping cart. When the user is finished shopping, they need to supply a credit card number and shipping address to purchase the products. To avoid reentering this data every time a user shops at the web site, users can register at the web site and create a user profile. The login IDs and passwords to access these profiles are stored in the Authentication Server "C," and the profiles are stored in the Database Server "D."

When the user purchases products, the order is stored in the Usage Database "F." This database could also store user statistics, such as how many users accessed the system and how many users viewed each product. The usage database will be accessed by:

- The shipping department (Other Enterprise Systems or Solutions) to find out which products need to be shipped and their destinations.
- Accounting and Billing systems to send bills to the users or to charge their credit cards.
- Legal and Regulatory systems to ensure taxes are paid, products are only sent to customers who are legally allowed to buy the products, etc.
- Performance Management systems to generate reports that indicate which products are selling well, which elements in the solution are being overloaded, etc.

Periodically, all the elements in the solution will backup their data through the Backup System "G," so that the data can be manually recovered in the event of a major failure. When any element in the solution detects a failure, either internally or on one of its interfaces to another system, it should report an alarm to the element management system (EMS) "H." The EMS can be used by either maintenance engineers or network management systems to identify problems and resolve them (for example, by taking an element out of service, replacing circuit packs, running diagnostics, and putting it back into service).

While service unavailability will not compromise safety of customers, staff, or others, unavailability will impact the enterprise's ability to deliver time-critical products and service to end users with appropriate quality (customers can easily go to some other web site to buy their products, and the enterprise will disappoint customers and lose revenue). Therefore, this could be considered an efficiency-critical application (see Section 1.1, "Service Criticality and Availability Expectations") and thus demands high service availability. The other critical enterprise systems and solutions that interact with the hypothetical solution are assumed to have the same efficiency critical expectation as end users. It is also assumed that the legal/regulatory compliance systems are assigned the same service criticality as the end user service they are monitoring, so compliance support is also deemed efficiency critical. The EMS offers convenient management visibility and control for maintenance engineers, but this service is deemed merely essential because loss of convenient management visibility does not impact end user service; maintenance engineers can temporarily work around this by interacting directly with key systems via console interfaces. Assuming that provisioning is performed by enterprise IS/IT staff rather than directly by end users, provisioning service can be deemed essential rather than efficiency critical because occasional modest delays in execution of provisioning orders should be acceptable. Servicing the network management system is essential to good operation of the enterprise's IS/IT infrastructure and applications, but as unavailability of information to the network management system does not directly impact the efficiency critical services, the network management system is deemed essential rather than efficiency critical. Assuming accounting and billing is an offline service (e.g., producing monthly bills) and does not directly affect users' quality of service, accounting and billing can be deemed routine because offline work can easily be rescheduled around planned or unplanned outages. Likewise, performance management and data backup are deemed routine because they do not directly impact user's quality of experience, and they can be easily postponed to accommodate planned and unplanned unavailability events. Service criticality by user type is summarized in Table 14.1.

14.1.1 Key Quality Indicators

The enterprise naturally wants users to be satisfied by their experience with the solution. Therefore, the enterprise should quantitatively specify requirements for key quality indicators (KQIs) such as:

- *Latency or Response Time.* When a user clicks on a link, the corresponding web page should be displayed on their web browser within a certain amount of time. The transmission time of the HTTP request and response and the performance

TABLE 14.1. Service Criticality by External Solution Interface

Solution User or External Interface	Service Criticality
End user	Efficiency critical
Other enterprise systems or solutions	Efficiency critical
Legal/regulatory compliancy support systems	Efficiency critical
Maintenance engineers	Essential
Network management	Essential
Provisioning	Essential
Accounting and billing	Routine
Performance management	Routine
Data backup	Routine

of the web browser are outside of the control of the web server, so the response time of the server should be measured from the time the frontend server receives an HTTP request until the frontend server sends a response. Some requests will be more complex than others, so several response time requirements may be needed. Typically, 95th percentile service latency is specified (meaning 95% of the transactions complete in no more than the specified time). In addition, one can also specify and measure 50th percentile (median) latency (meaning half of the responses are faster and half are slower). As a practical matter, it may be easier to compute or estimate arithmetic average latency rather than median latency.

- *Success Rate* specifies the percentage of properly formed and authorized transactions that complete successfully within the maximum acceptable latency. Five 9's (99.999%) success rate or probability is a common expectation, which translates to no more than 10 properly formed and authorized transactions failing per million attempts when the system is operating at or below engineered capacity.

The enterprise might also specify service latency and success rate requirements for individual elements within the solution. For example, the enterprise might specify response time and success rate requirements for the authentication server transactions used by the frontend server. The response time requirements for individual elements should be short enough, and the success rate requirements high enough, to support the overall response time and success rate KQI's measured at the end user's interface to the frontend web server.

14.2 STANDALONE SOLUTION ANALYSIS

Before considering the georedundant configuration of a solution, one should complete basic analysis of the standalone (nongeoredundant) solution configuration. The basic steps of this standalone solution analysis are:

1. Construct reliability block diagrams
2. Determine the nominal configuration of the elements of the standalone solution
3. Estimate the nominal service availability of service offered by the standalone solution

If the estimated service availability does not meet target, then one can change the solution configuration of elements and/or the elements themselves to boost the predicted solution availability. Each of these steps is considered below.

14.2.1 Construct Reliability Block Diagrams

The first step in solution reliability analysis is to construct reliability block diagrams for each of the service critical service threads. Reliability block diagrams were introduced in Section 3.1.3, "Single Point of Failure," and reliability block diagrams for some service threads of the hypothetical solution were given in Section 9.2, "Estimating Solution Availability." Figure 14.2 (same as Fig. 9.4) gives the reliability block diagram (RBD) for end users, and Figure 14.3 (same as Fig. 9.5) gives the RBD for enterprise IS/IT provisioning staff. Note that although elements in an RBD are arranged in a sequential daisy chain, the order of elements is not relevant because the loss of any critical component in the chain renders service unavailable. Note also that network infrastructure like WANs, LANs, firewalls, and routers that are in the actual service delivery path between the client element and the solution elements are omitted for simplicity. That network infrastructure is, of course, required, but it is not considered in this analysis.

Reliability block diagrams of the service delivery threads that are at least deemed "essential" for all user and external interface types should be constructed.

14.2.2 Network Element Configuration in Standalone Solution

Broadly speaking, individual elements supporting enterprise information systems/information technology (IS/IT) applications support one of two general configurations:

Figure 14.2. Reliability block diagram for end user service of hypothetical solution.

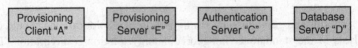

Figure 14.3. Reliability block diagram for user provisioning service of sample solution.

- *Simplex*, in which elements are built with good quality components with no internal redundancy. Simplex systems typically have product attributable availability ratings of 99.9–99.97%; this study will assume a nominal availability rating of 99.95% for network elements with a simplex configurations.
- *Fault tolerant*, in which elements are built with good quality industrial-grade components with at least some internal redundancy and high-availability infrastructure to permit failures to be automatically detected, isolated, and recovered with minimal service disruption. Fault tolerant systems typically have product attributable availability ratings of 99.99–99.999%.

Based on solution service availability expectations, network elements in the solution can be targeted for either simplex or fault-tolerant configurations, as shown in Table 14.2.

14.2.3 Service Availability Offered by Standalone Solution

Having set product availability targets for individual elements, one can overlay those availability targets onto solution RBDs from Section 14.2.1 to estimate the solution's service availability rating for each type of user or external interface. Figure 14.4 (same as Fig. 9.6) gives estimates of service availability experienced by end users; similar analyses can be completed for other users and interfaces. Note that these RBDs omitted IP networking infrastructure (e.g., routers) and facilities (e.g., cables and fiber optic links), and thus the estimated availability is for the hypothetical solution itself, rather than the end-to-end availability likely to be experienced by any particular solution user. End-to-end availability can be estimated by including applicable networking infrastructure, facilities, security appliances, and user elements in RBDs and availability estimates.

14.2.4 Discussion of Standalone Solution Analysis

Ideally, the service availability estimates of Section 14.2.3 meet the enterprise's expectations; if not, then one should consider the following:

1. Improve the service availability rating of individual elements in the solution (e.g., replace standalone element configurations with fault tolerant configurations) to reduce expected service downtime. For example:
   - Frontend servers could be set up as $N + K$ load shared to scale to meet customer needs.
   - Authentication servers could be active–active to provide high availability to the frontend servers.
   - Database servers can be active–active or active–standby. Active–active provides a slightly higher level of availability, but active–active has more complex data update resolution mechanisms.

TABLE 14.2. Availability Expectations for Hypothetical Solution Elements

Element	Configuration	Rationale	Unplanned Service Availability Expectation	Annualized Unplanned Service Downtime Expectation (in Minutes)
Frontend server	Fault tolerant	Highest availability expectations apply to elements that directly impact end user service	99.999%	5.3
Authentication server	Fault tolerant	Highest availability expectations apply to elements that directly impact end user service	99.999%	5.3
Database server	Fault tolerant	Highest availability expectations apply to elements that directly impact end user service	99.999%	5.3
Provisioning system	Simplex	Occasional unavailability of provisioning can be tolerated by the enterprise.	99.95%	250
Usage database	Fault tolerant	Loss of data will result in missed shipments or bills to users.	99.999%	5.3
Backup system	Simplex	Occasional unavailability of the backup system can be tolerated by the enterprise.	99.95%	250
Element management system (EMS)	Simplex	Maintaining management visibility and controllability of elements in the solution is essential to maintaining high service availability. However, since EMS failure does not impact end user service, EMS does not require the same service availability as frontend, authentication, database and usage servers.	99.95%	250

2. Rearchitect the solution to eliminate some elements from the critical service delivery thread, thereby eliminating their expected service downtime from the downtime experienced by users.

3. Lower solution availability expectations.

4. Rearchitect the solution to increase the redundancy and reduce service downtime via client-initiated recovery.

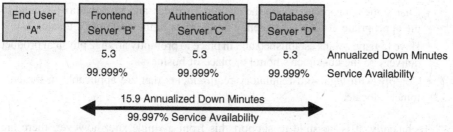

Figure 14.4. Estimating service availability experienced by end users.

Note that all of these mitigation actions can be considered in the context of a standalone solution deployment. In this case study, we will use the first option above to improve end user service availability.

14.3 GEOREDUNDANT SOLUTION ANALYSIS

For operational simplicity, enterprises will typically install all core solution network elements in a single data center. Since locating all solution elements in a single data center on a single site creates a risk of indefinite unavailability of solution service following a site failure, business continuity considerations drive enterprises to create disaster recovery plans, including georedundancy for critical solutions. Solution georedundancy strategy can be analyzed using the methodology given in Section 10.7, "Recommended Design Methodology," via the following steps:

1. Identify the factors constraining recovery realm design.
2. Define recovery realms.
3. Define recovery strategies.
4. Setting recovery objectives.
5. Architect site redundancy.

Each analysis step is discussed in a section below.

14.3.1 Identify Factors Constraining Recovery Realm Design

If we want our solution to sell products worldwide, then based on the location of the customer, it must:

- Deliver web pages in the customer's preferred language.
- Display prices in the customer's preferred currency.
- Provide products that are appropriate for the customer's country. For example, electronic products must come with plugs that work in the type of electrical power socket that is commonly used in the customer's country.

- Charge the appropriate tax on the customer's order, and send the tax payment to the appropriate government agency or agencies in the customer's locale.
- Have logistics plans established and in place to promptly arrange physical product delivery to the customer's home or place of business.
- Comply with legal and regulatory requirements that are applicable in the customer's locale.

Technically, it is possible to support this from a single site; however, there are several practical advantages to serving customers from different service realms supported by sites in the different regions that customers are located in:

- A single site might not provide acceptable performance for users. The latency for HTTP messages might be several seconds if the customer and server are in different parts of the world (e.g., on different continents).
- The locale-specific currency, taxation, regulatory, and logistics in each realm could be simpler, since it would only have to support the data for its local region.
- Each site could be provisioned and maintained by local personnel, who are more knowledgeable about regulations and practical details in their regions.

14.3.2   Define Recovery Realms

Recovery realms are fundamentally driven by the geographic distribution of users. If most or all users are in a single region and there are no compelling reasons to adopt multiple recovery realms, then a single recovery realm is simplest. For our hypothetical solution, we will assume that the enterprise is supporting users scattered across the globe, and thus will serve these users from three recovery regions or realms:

- North and South America;
- Europe, Africa, and the Middle East; and
- Eastern Asia and Australia.

14.3.3   Define Recovery Strategies

Different recovery realms can support different recovery strategies and thus have different recovery objectives. Different recovery strategies can be a pragmatic way to reduce costs by not supporting more aggressive and expensive redundancy and disaster recovery strategies in markets and regions where the customers do not demand it. For example, while customers in some markets may demand consistently high-quality and continuously available service, other markets may accept less robust service. For simplicity, this case study will assume that the enterprise wants to maintain a global brand and reputation, and thus each region will use multiple solution sites with sufficient redundancy that efficiency critical service can be delivered with acceptable service quality to users following catastrophic or planned unavailability of one site. In addition, recovery mechanisms will be automatic: client-initiated recovery for those elements that support efficiency critical services (e.g., frontend, authentication, and database elements) and system-driven for the EMS. Manual recovery mechanisms will be supported but only used for services with routine criticality (billing, performance, data backup), when the automatic mechanisms fail, or to support planned maintenance activities.

14.3.4 Set Recovery Objectives

The next step is to set recovery time objectives and recovery point objectives for each recovery realm. Solution disaster recovery architectures are driven by the recovery time objectives (RTO) and recovery point objectives (RPO) of the different users of the solution. The following sections consider solution RTO, solution RPO, and the architectural implications of those objectives. Since all three recovery realms are assumed to use the same recovery strategies, we'll assume the same RTO and RPO requirements for all three realms.

14.3.4.1 Solution Recovery Time Objectives. The criticality of solution service exposed to different types of solution users and systems drives the recovery time objective expectations of those solution services. The following entities are likely to have the highest (i.e., fastest) recovery time objective:

- *End users* expect rapid service recovery, and hence tight solution service RTO. In the event of a catastrophic failure of the frontend server, database server, or authentication server, service to end users will be lost. Most of the users will give the enterprise a second chance if the solution can recover quickly, so the RTO will be only a few minutes.
- *Other enterprise solutions or systems* may require rapid RTO to meet their service quality, reliability, and availability targets. If the usage database is unavailable, products cannot be shipped.
- *Legal and regulatory compliance systems* may require the same RTO as end user service, depending on applicable legal and regulatory requirements. For example, legal considerations might require end user service recovery to be delayed if it is illegal or otherwise prohibited to deliver service to end users before all legal and regulatory compliance systems are operational.

The following entities are likely to tolerate more relaxed (i.e., slower) recovery time objectives:

- *Maintenance engineers* will want to retain (or restore) management visibility to the recovery systems so they can monitor service recovery and promptly take any necessary manual actions. This implies a prompt RTO for EMSs. Note that maintenance engineers expect high availability for management visibility to critical elements, but this does not necessarily mean that every EMS that provides management visibility needs to have tight RTO requirements because system consoles may provide acceptable management visibility in emergency situations.

- *Network management systems* will tolerate a longer recovery time objective than for end user and other efficiency critical services. If the enterprise uses the network management system in conjunction with EMSs to troubleshoot and recover critical failures, then the network management system might need the same RTO as the EMSs.

- *Accounting and billing systems* often have lower RTO expectations because it may be cheaper to postpone generation of bills than to invest more to aggressively shorten the RTO. Note that RTO for an accounting system represents the unavailability of *access* to usage records rather than the actual *loss* of usage records, assuming systems within the solution are configured to buffer records for an extended period while the accounting system recovers. If the accounting systems are unavailable for so long that buffers for usage records on individual elements are filled, then it is possible that usage records will be discarded. Thus, solution architects must consider both the capacity of elements to buffer usage records, as well as the business impact of lost usage records when setting RTO requirements for the accounting system.

- *Provisioning systems* often support a slower RTO because adding and changing user and product information and other planned provisioning actions can be safely deferred until emergency disaster recovery actions have been successfully completed. Enterprise disaster recovery plans may even assign staff who would normally execute provisioning orders to work-specific (nonprovisioning) tasks from the business continuity plan following a disaster until critical services are fully restored. Thus, it is possible that there is minimal value to recovering the provisioning server interfaces before at least some of the provisioning staff is released from their emergency assignments executing business continuity plan activities.

- *Performance management systems* might support a slower RTO because it is more important to get service restored than it is to collect and analyze traffic statistics. While usage data typically drives organizational revenue/funding via billing or chargeback arrangements, performance data and statistics do not generally affect customer revenue. Thus, most enterprises will deem performance management data and service to be less critical to the business and therefore set a less stringent RTO for performance management systems than for accounting systems. Hence, unlike accounting data, performance management data may actually be lost during the time window after end user service is restored but before performance management system is operational.

- *Backup System.* While it is crucial to enable rapid restoration of backed up data to support prompt service recovery, the ability to perform backups on the impacted elements, site, or solution is less important and may even be explicitly disabled until service has been fully recovered on the redundant site. After all, consuming disk I/O, compute cycles and network bandwidth to take a backup competes with the resource needs of service restoration. Thus, data backup systems might support a slower RTO on the premise since it is more important to restore service than to run backups of partially recovered systems. Note that read/restore access to electronic vaults of backup data is required very quickly to perform recovery actions, but capturing backups from the redundant system(s) that is the recovery target should typically be deferred so that the recovery system and supporting networking resources and staff effort can be focused on rapidly recovering service. After service is recovered and systems have stabilized, regular backups can resume.

14.3.4.2 *Solution Recovery Point Objectives.* Just as the recovery time objectives of different solution interfaces vary based on business needs, the recovery point objectives of elements and datasets within the solution may vary. The following solution users are likely to expect tight (i.e., short) recovery point objectives (RPOs):

- End users expect that when they have properly ordered a product, paid for it, and received a confirmation, they will receive the product. The solution could be designed to update two geographically redundant usage databases before sending the confirmation, but then a failure is possible that causes the database to think the order has completed although the confirmation was never sent. The customer might try to purchase the product again later, and be upset when he/she receives (and is charged for) two of the products. Therefore, the timing of the writes to the redundant databases must be designed to support a very short RPO.

  It is not so important to preserve shopping carts over a failure since it represents a more transient state before order completion. If a failure occurs, the customer will have to login to an alternate system and so he/she should not be surprised that he/she has to refill the shopping cart.
- Other enterprise solutions and systems may require short RPO to avoid compromising their data and service quality. Note that the RPO requirement of the target solution should be aligned with the RPO expected by other enterprise solutions and systems so that if a disaster occurs, then the other enterprise solutions and systems are prepared to recover any work lost in the RPO period.
- Statutory or regulatory requirements may mandate that legal and compliance systems have the same RPO behavior as the user service that is offered by the solution.
- Maintenance engineers will want to recover (or rebuild) the most recent alarm and system status to assure that they have a complete view of solution service status which is essential in driving service recovery.

The RPO for network management systems may be comparable with that expected by maintenance engineers if the network management systems are proactively used by enterprise maintenance engineers to troubleshoot and recover from failures. Otherwise, the network management system will probably have a longer RPO.

The RPO requirement for accounting and billing data is generally easy to analyze because the business value of any lost records can be quantitatively estimated based on typical usage patterns. Lost usage records typically compromise the enterprise's ability to generate correct billing/accounting records. Enterprises can generally estimate the billable financial value of each minute of usage records during both busy periods and typical usage periods. One can then estimate the cost to the business for different RPO values if a disaster occurs during a busy period and if a disaster occurs during a typical usage period. Business leaders can then compare the costs associated with deploying and operating each recovery option to the expected loss of revenue and the overall risk of disaster during the solution's useful service life.

The following entities may tolerate a relaxed (i.e., longer) RPO:

- Provisioning systems because it might simply be cheaper to reexecute the manual provisioning actions that were lost due to longer RPO than to invest heavily to shorten the RPO. While it may be cheaper to re-execute manual data entry operations like user provisioning actions than' to implement backup and recovery mechanisms that assure a short RPO, in some cases, the provisioning changes themselves are more valuable to the business than simply the labor cost to execute the changes. For example, changes to security policies (e.g., locking out user accounts) or grade of service configurations for individual users may have far higher value to the enterprise than simply the cost to reprovision the data, and these considerations might drive some provisioned data to have a short RPO.
- Performance management systems because network and capacity planning activities can easily tolerate moderate data gaps.

The data backup and replication strategy must be designed to meet the RPO requirements of the target systems, and thus it is generally unhelpful to consider the RPO of the data backup system itself. However, the redundant electronic vault of other system(s) that host the backup and/or replicated data must be geographically separated from the systems they protect and must promptly make saved data available for recovery.

14.3.5 Architecting Site Redundancy

Having decided that sufficient geographic redundancy will be deployed in each region so that the expected volume of users can be served with acceptable service quality following catastrophic or planned unavailability of a single site per region, the element redundancy arrangement and configuration of each site must be architected to meet those needs. DNS will be configured to the permit end users' web clients to access any site in their recovery realm, and thus web clients will execute client-initiated recovery. Client-initiated recovery will also be used between the frontend server and the authentication server and usage database.

We expect that there will be a large amount of traffic between the frontend servers and the database servers, so if a database server fails, it would be better to tell the client to switch to a frontend server that has an operational local database server to avoid too much traffic between sites. Therefore, cluster recovery will be used for database failures as described in Section 9.4, "Element Failure and Cluster Recovery Case Study."

The EMS is less critical and can use system-driven recovery mechanisms. The provisioning, network management, and backup systems are even less critical and can use manual recovery.

Table 14.3 summarizes the nominal redundancy arrangement for each site, where "N" represents the number of elements required to serve the engineered load, and "K" represents the spare capacity engineered into the solution. Since the enterprise plans use best practice operational policies, including prompt repair of failed equipment, only a single unit of spare capacity (i.e., $K = 1$) will be engineered. The second column indicates whether manual, system-driven, or client-initiated recovery will be used on the interface between the clients and the element. The third column indicates the client will recover from failures by switching to an alternate element (network element recovery) or by telling the end user to switch to another site in the realm (cluster recovery). It also indicates whether the element redundancy is active/standby, active/active, or $N + K$ load shared.

14.4 AVAILABILITY OF THE GEOREDUNDANT SOLUTION

Client-initiated recovery across a georedundant solution deployment can significantly improve the service availability estimated in Section 14.2.3, "Service Availability Offered by Standalone Solution." One can apply the techniques of Section 9.6, "Modeling Cluster Recovery," to estimate the service availability of georedundant solution deployment.

14.5 REQUIREMENTS OF HYPOTHETICAL SOLUTION

This section tailors the requirements of Chapter 12, "Georedundancy Requirements," to apply to our sample solution.

14.5.1 Internal Redundancy Requirements

An instance of requirement STANDALONE-01 is needed for each of the elements in the solution with the availabilities in Table 14.2, such as:

- *REQ STANDALONE-01A.* The prorated, product-attributable, service availability of the frontend server shall be at least 99.999%.
- *REQ STANDALONE-01B.* The prorated, product-attributable, service availability of the authentication server shall be at least 99.999%.

An instance of requirement SOLUTION-01 is needed for every service supported by the solution (as listed in Table 14.1). These requirements should be interlocked with the standalone network element requirements and should reflect the feasible service availability based on the solution's architecture (e.g., analysis from Section 14.2.3, "Service Availability Offered by Standalone Solution"), for example:

TABLE 14.3. Redundancy Schemes for the Solution Elements

Element	External Recovery Strategy	Network Element versus Cluster Recovery	Notes
Frontend server	Client-initiated recovery	Cluster recovery to a frontend server ($N + K$ load shared) in another site.	N might be different for each realm, depending on the amount of traffic in each realm; N will typically, it will be 2 to 5. K will typically be 1, but might be more if our sites are too close to each other.
Authentication server	Client-initiated recovery between frontend server and authentication server	Network element recovery to a redundant authentication server (active/active) in another site.	The frontend server can query either authentication server. Authentication information should be stored on both servers so that data replication is not needed.
Database server	Client-initiated between frontend server and database server	Cluster recovery to a frontend server in another site. Databases are active/active.	The frontend server will always query the closest database. If that database fails, then the frontend server should tell the user to switch to an alternate frontend server that uses the other database. Data should be replicated between the database servers every 10 seconds to meet the RPO requirement.
Provisioning system	Manual recovery	Element recovery to a redundant provisioning system (active/standby).	If the primary provisioning system fails, manual procedures can be used to activate the alternate system.
Usage (accounting) database	Client-initiated recovery between frontend server and usage database	Element recovery to a redundant usage database (active/active).	The accounting data should be written to both usage databases within 10 seconds to meet the RPO requirement.
Network Management System	Manual recovery	Element recovery to another network management system (active/standby)	If the network management system fails, manual procedures can be used to activate the alternate system.

TABLE 14.3. *Continued*

Element	External Recovery Strategy	Network Element versus Cluster Recovery	Notes
Backup system	Manual recovery	Element recovery to another backup system (active/ standby)	If the primary backup system fails, manual procedures can be used to activate the alternate system.
Element management system	System-driven recovery	Element level recovery to another element management system (active/ standby)	Since the RTO only 5 minutes, automatic failover is required. A heartbeat should be sent every 60 seconds from the active to the standby element, and the standby element should make itself active if 3 consecutive heartbeats are lost. Other elements should always attempt to send alarm information to both elements.

- *REQ SOLUTION-01A.* The end-to-end, prorated, product-attributable, service availability of the end user service of the georedundant solution deployment shall be 99.999%.
- *REQ SOLUTION-01B.* The end-to-end, prorated, product-attributable, service availability of the provisioning service of the georedundant solution deployment shall be 99.99%.

Requirements for solution KQIs for each key user or interface should also be defined, such as:

- *REQ SOLUTION-02A.* When the solution is operating at advertised capacity, valid end user service requests shall fail at a rate of less than 40 defects per million attempts (DPMs). If a request is satisfied, but takes longer than 5 seconds, then it shall be counted as a defect.
- *REQ SOLUTION-02B.* When the solution is operating at advertised capacity, valid maintenance requests shall fail at a rate of less than 40 DPMs. If a request is satisfied, but takes longer than 5 seconds, then it shall be counted as a defect. Note that some maintenance activities can take much longer than 5 seconds, but the solution should at least respond that the activity is in progress within 5 seconds.
- *REQ SOLUTION-02C.* When the solution is operating at advertised capacity, valid requests for accounting data shall fail at a rate of less than 200 DPMs. If a request is satisfied, but takes longer than 10 seconds, then it shall be counted as a defect.

- *REQ SOLUTION-02D.* When the solution is operating at advertised capacity, valid provisioning requests shall fail at a rate of less than 200 DPMs. If a request is satisfied, but takes longer than 10 seconds, then it shall be counted as a defect.
- *REQ SOLUTION-02E.* When the solution is operating at advertised capacity, valid requests for performance management data shall fail at a rate of less than 2000 DPMs. If a request is satisfied, but takes longer than 30 seconds, then it shall be counted as a defect.

14.5.2 External Redundancy Requirements

The following general redundancy requirement is needed:

- *REQ REDUNDANT-01.* The solution shall support redundant instances of each network element. If an element fails, it shall be possible to transfer its workload to a redundant element.

Georedundancy needs to be supported, so the following requirements are needed:

- *REQ REDUNDANT-02.* The solution shall allow its network elements to be distributed among multiple sites in the same realm. If any single site fails, the elements in the rest of the sites in the same realm shall have sufficient capacity to serve the full engineered traffic load with acceptable service quality.
- *REQ REDUNDANT-03.* Communications links between sites in the same realm shall have sufficient bandwidth to support replicating/synchronizing data between georedundant elements when operating at full engineered capacity with all elements operational.
- *REQ REDUNDANT-04.* The solution shall operate properly if the message latency through the communication network between sites in the same realm is less than 500 milliseconds.

Since the world has been divided into three realms, it should be technically feasible to meet requirement REDUNDANT-04.

Requirements are needed for the RTO and RPO objectives per service that were determined in Section 14.3.4, "Set Recovery Objectives":

- *REQ SERVICE-01A.* In the event of a failure of any single element in the solution, a failure of an entire site, or a partial IP network failure, end user service shall be restored within 5 minutes by a failover to an externally redundant element.
- *REQ SERVICE-01B.* In the event of a failure of any single element in the solution, a failure of an entire site, or a partial IP network failure, maintenance of the solution shall be restored within 5 minutes by a failover to an externally redundant element.

- *REQ SERVICE-01C.* In the event of a failure of any single element in the solution, a failure of an entire site, or a partial IP network failure, accounting shall be restored within 8 hours by a failover to an externally redundant element.
- *REQ SERVICE-01D.* In the event of a failure of any single element in the solution, a failure of an entire site, or a partial IP network failure, provisioning shall be restored within 8 hours by a failover to an externally redundant element.
- *REQ SERVICE-02.* In the event of an external network element failover, the newly active element's usage database should not be out-of-date by more than 10 seconds. This applies to failover of a single element, an entire site, or a partial IP network failure.
- *REQ SERVICE-03.* In the event of a failure of any single element in the solution, a failure of an entire site, or a partial IP network failure, the surviving elements must be able to provide required services with quality until the failed element(s) have fully recovered. This applies to the efficiency critical elements.

14.5.3 Manual Failover Requirements

Table 14.3 indicated that manual failover is sufficient for the provisioning, network management, and backup systems. An instance of each of the requirements in Section 12.3, "Manually Controlled Redundancy Requirements," is needed for each of these elements. They are also needed for the EMS, in case the automatic failure detection and recovery fails. They are not needed for the other elements, because since they all run active/active or load shared, a failover is not needed.

Here are the requirements for the active/standby provisioning systems. Similar requirements would be required for the other elements.

- *REQ MANUAL-01.* A snapshot of the database on the primary provisioning system shall be saved periodically so that the redundant provisioning system can be recovered in the event of a failure of the primary. The recovery data shall be stored in a different location than the primary provisioning system.
- *REQ MANUAL-02.* Appropriate alarms shall be generated by the EMS within 3 minutes after the active provisioning system fails.
- *REQ MANUAL-03.* A procedure for restoring the database on the redundant provisioning system from the recovery data shall be provided and documented.
- *REQ MANUAL-04.* A procedure for providing a manual failover to the redundant provisioning system shall be provided and documented.
- *REQ MANUAL-05.* The documented procedures shall precisely detail all of the operations that must be performed, as well as a clarification on errors that might be reported and how to resolve them.
- *REQ MANUAL-06.* Tools shall be provided to verify that the redundant provisioning system is healthy.

To minimize the cost of the solution, we can choose not to specify MANUAL-07. This requires that when we upgrade the software version for the provisioning system, we must make the same upgrade for the redundant provisioning system within a few days, because failover will not be supported while the elements are running on different versions.

Since a loss of the provisioning system does not affect end user service, we do not need to support graceful switchover (without any downtime). If it is necessary to switchover to the alternate provisioning server in order to do maintenance on the primary provisioning server, then we can follow the normal manual procedures. Again, similar requirements are needed for the network management, backup, and EMSs.

- *REQ SWITCHBACK-01.* A procedure to synchronize the database in the recovering provisioning system with the active provisioning system shall be provided and documented.
- *REQ SWITCHBACK-02.* A procedure to activate the recovering provisioning system and put the alternate provisioning system back into the standby state shall be provided and documented.
- *REQ SWITCHBACK-03.* When the recovering provisioning system is activated, the service unavailability during the switchback shall be less than 60 minutes.

14.5.4 Automatic External Recovery Requirements

The only element that will use system-driven recovery is the EMS. Client-initiated recovery will be used:

- Between the customer web browsers and frontend server
- Between the frontend servers and authentication servers
- Between the frontend servers and the usage database

Cluster recovery will be used for database server failures.
Therefore, we have the following instances of AUTOMATIC-01:

- *REQ AUTOMATIC-01A.* The interface between all the network elements and the EMS shall utilize an automatic system-driven recovery strategy.
- *REQ AUTOMATIC-01B.* The interface between the end user web browsers and the frontend servers shall utilize an automatic client-initiated recovery strategy.
- *REQ AUTOMATIC-01C.* The interface between the frontend servers and the authentication servers shall utilize an automatic client-initiated recovery strategy.
- *REQ AUTOMATIC-01D.* The interface between the frontend servers and the database servers shall utilize an automatic client-initiated recovery strategy.
- *REQ AUTOMATIC-01E.* The interface between the frontend servers and the usage database shall utilize an automatic client-initiated recovery strategy.

14.5.4.1 System-Driven Recovery. The following requirements from Section 12.4.1, "System-Driven Recovery," are needed for the EMS:

- *REQ SYSTEM-01.* A mechanism shall be provided to ensure that the same service configuration is applied to both the primary and redundant EMSs. Any provisioning updates shall be applied to both EMSs.
- *REQ SYSTEM-03.* The primary and redundant EMSs shall exchange heartbeats every 60 seconds. After 3 consecutive failed heartbeats, the redundant EMS shall check that it still has connectivity to the network. If this check passes, it shall be assumed that the primary EMS is down/unavailable. The HeartbeatInterval and MaxMissingHeartbeats parameters shall be configurable.
- *REQ SYSTEM-04.* The redundant EMS shall acknowledge the heartbeats it receives from the primary EMS. If the primary EMS does not receive 3 consecutive acknowledgments, it shall be assumed that the redundant EMS is down/unavailable and generate an alarm.
- *REQ SYSTEM-05.* When a primary EMS has failed, the redundant EMS shall wait 1 minute before activating the alternate EMS. The StandaloneRecoveryWaitTime shall be configurable.
- *REQ SYSTEM-06.* A mechanism shall be provided to disable automatic system-driven recovery.
- *REQ SYSTEM-07.* Automatic system-driven failover shall be successful on at least 99% of the failover attempts.

Note that requirement SYSTEM-02 is not needed for the EMS, since data replication between the EMSs is not required. However, it is needed for the database servers and usage databases.

- *REQ SYSTEM-02A.* An automatic data replication mechanism shall be provided for the database servers to periodically synchronize their data (less than 10 seconds between updates).
- *REQ SYSTEM-02B.* An automatic data replication mechanism shall be provided for the usage databases to periodically synchronize their data (less than 10 seconds between updates).

14.5.4.2 Client-Initiated Recovery.

The solution has $N + K$ frontend servers to process requests from the customer's web browsers. We are using client-initiated recovery for this interface—if a frontend server fails, the web browsers should detect that it is not responding and failover to another frontend server. We cannot write requirements for the web browsers since we cannot dictate which browser is used by the customers. However, commonly used web browsers should behave properly.

Therefore, the requirements from Section 12.4.2, "Client-Initiated Recovery," are only needed for the frontend server when it is interacting with the authentication servers, database servers, and usage databases. The server requirements apply to the frontend, authentication, database servers, and usage databases. The network element recovery requirements apply to the frontend server when it is interacting with the authentication servers and usage databases, and the cluster recovery requirements apply for the database server interface.

- *REQ CLIENT-01.* When a frontend server, authentication server, database server, or usage database receives an invalid request from a client, it shall return explicit failure code for 95% of the failed requests.
- *REQ CLIENT-02.* If a frontend server, authentication server, database server, or usage database cannot satisfy requests for a client, then it shall reject requests with failure code 503 `Service Unavailable`.
- *REQ CLIENT-03.* The frontend server shall support a mechanism to load share its authentication requests to both authentication servers and load share its usage reporting to both usage databases.
- *REQ CLIENT-04.* The load-sharing mechanism shall support a means of optimally selecting the authentication server and usage database (e.g., choosing co-located servers before remote servers).

Requirement CLIENT-05 should not be needed because the frontend server does not need to authenticate with either the authentication server or the database server.

- *REQ CLIENT-06.* When an authentication server or usage database does not respond to requests, the frontend server shall detect the failure, and resend requests to a redundant authentication server or usage database. The frontend server shall initially use a 2-second response timer and attempt three retries. The frontend server shall keep track of the typical response time of each authentication server/usage database and the maximum number of retries required. The frontend server can lower the response timer from 2 seconds to $<X>$ times the typical response time (whichever is lower), and reduce the number of retries to the maximum number previously sent, plus one (whichever is lower). $<X>$ shall be provisionable with a default of 5.
- *REQ CLIENT-07.* When an authentication server or usage database responds to a request with failure code 503 `Service Unavailable`, the frontend server shall initiate recovery to the redundant server. The frontend server shall failover within 2 seconds, and failovers shall be successful on 99% of the attempts. When an authentication server or usage database responds with any other failure code, the frontend server shall pass the failure code to the end user.
- *REQ CLIENT-08.* While an authentication server or usage database is in the failed state, the load-sharing mechanism indicated in requirement CLIENT-03 shall mark the server as unavailable for service until it has fully recovered.
- *REQ CLIENT-09.* Clients shall periodically check if a failed authentication server or usage database has recovered, and automatically resume using a recovered server when practical.
- *REQ CLIENT-10.* When the frontend server determines that it should failover to alternate authentication server, it shall be successful on at least 99% of the failover attempts.
- *REQ CLIENT-11.* The frontend server shall always send its database requests to a local database server.

- *REQ CLIENT-12.* When a database server does not respond to requests, the frontend server shall detect the failure, and respond to its request from the end user with failure code 503 `Service Unavailable`. The frontend server shall initially use a 2-second response timer and attempt three retries. The frontend server shall keep track of the typical response time of the local database server and the maximum number of retries required. The frontend server can lower the response timer from 2 seconds to $<X>$ times the typical response time (whichever is lower), and reduce the number of retries to the maximum number previously sent, plus one (whichever is lower). $<X>$ shall be provisionable with a default of 5.
- *REQ CLIENT-13.* When a database server responds to a request with failure code 503 `Service Unavailable`, then the frontend server shall respond to its request from the end user with failure code 503 `Service Unavailable`. When a database server responds with any other failure code, the frontend server shall pass the failure code to the end user.

14.5.5 Operational Requirements

The following requirements are needed for the enterprise's maintenance engineers:

- *REQ OPERATIONAL-01.* An overall procedure shall be documented that describes all the manual georedundancy activities that must be performed after a complete site failure. This procedure shall reference all the manual procedures required in Section 14.5.3, "Manual Failover Requirements." It shall also describe:
  - What conditions must be satisfied before performing the manual failover procedures. That is, how should it be determined that the active elements cannot be recovered.
  - Which maintenance engineers should perform each procedure.
  - How the solution should be monitored to check that the failover was successful.
- *REQ OPERATIONAL-02.* The procedure described in OPERATIONAL-01 shall be practiced before deployment, and at least once every 6 months thereafter.

14.6 TESTING OF HYPOTHETICAL SOLUTION

This chapter provides a suggested set of tests based on the requirements defined in Section 14.5, "Requirements of Hypothetical Solution."

14.6.1 Testing Strategy

Various levels of testing should be performed to validate that each network element can feasibly meet the availability and reliability requirements expected, and that the solution can provide the required service availability and reliability. This includes testing that the failure of any individual network element or of the entire site can be successfully recovered and meet defined RPO and RTO requirements. The requirements lay out the basis for the testing. Each testable requirement must be validated using appropriate fault insertion or stability tests. Some requirements are not specifically testable, such as the availability numbers, but various parameters can be tested (e.g., recovery time) to provide input to reliability models that can verify the feasibility of those availability numbers.

14.6.2　Standalone Network Element Testing

In order to validate each instance of REQ STANDALONE-01 as defined for each of the elements in the solution with the availabilities in Table 14.2, reliability models should be built to determine whether it is feasible and likely that the associated availability can be met based on testing some key reliability parameters, such as failover time and failover success rate.

An instance of requirement STANDALONE-01 is defined for each of the elements in the solution with the availabilities in Table 14.2, and should therefore be verified thru modeling using test results that indicate key parameters such as software coverage, hardware coverage, failover times, etc.:

- *TEST STANDALONE-01A.* The prorated, product-attributable, service availability of the frontend server shall be at least 99.999%.
- *TEST STANDALONE-01B.* The prorated, product-attributable, service availability of the authentication server shall be at least 99.999%.

The following tests should be run with traffic and monitored for impact (e.g., failed components, system downtime) on each of the elements in the solution.

14.6.2.1　*External Redundancy Testing.* Each network element (unless otherwise specified in the requirement) must be tested to ensure it meets the following requirements:

- *TEST REDUNDANT-01.* Validate that when an element fails, it can successfully transfer its workload to a redundant element.

    This applies to all elements except the performance management system.

The following tests verify geographic redundancy requirements:

- *TEST REDUNDANT-02.* Validate that if a single site fails, the elements in the rest of the sites in the same realm shall have sufficient capacity to serve the full engineered traffic load with acceptable service quality. The tests shall include a baselining of the proper engineering guidelines to ensure that this requirement can be met.

- *TEST REDUNDANT-03.* Verify that communications links between sites in the same realm have sufficient bandwidth to support replicating/synchronizing data between georedundant elements when operating at full engineered capacity with all elements operational. The tests shall include a baselining of the proper engineering guidelines to ensure that this requirement can be met.
- *TEST REDUNDANT-04.* During load testing of TEST REDUNDANT-02 and TEST REDUNDANT-03 configure message latency to be < 500 milliseconds and validate that the solution shall operate properly with that latency.

14.6.2.2 *Manual Failover Testing.* As indicated in Section 14.5.3, "Manual Failover Requirements," the following are tests associated with the requirements for the active/standby provisioning systems. Similar requirements would be required for the other elements.

- *TEST MANUAL-01.* Verify that a snapshot of the database on the primary provisioning system is saved periodically so that the redundant provisioning system can be recovered in the event of a failure of the primary. The recovery data shall be stored in a different location than the primary provisioning system.
- *TEST MANUAL-02.* During failure testing of the network element, verify that appropriate alarms are generated by the EMS within 3 minutes after the active provisioning system fails.
- *TEST MANUAL-03.* Execute and verify for accuracy the procedure for restoring the database on the redundant provisioning system from the recovery data.
- *TEST MANUAL-04.* Execute and verify the procedure as documented for manual failover to the redundant provisioning system.
- *TEST MANUAL-05.* Execute and verify the documented procedures for all of the operations that must be performed. When encountering errors during failure testing, verify the clarity and completeness of the reporting, execute the given resolution, and verify that it resolves the error.
- *TEST MANUAL-06.* Using the tools provided, verify whether the redundant provisioning system is healthy. Introduce some failures into the system to ensure that the tools properly detect and report the failures.

14.6.3 Automatic External Recovery Requirements Testing

The only element that will use system-driven recovery is the EMS. Client-initiated recovery will be used:

- Between the customer web browsers and frontend server
- Between the frontend servers and authentication servers
- Between the frontend servers and the usage database

Cluster recovery will be used for database server failures.

Therefore, the following instances of AUTOMATIC-01 must be tested:

- *TEST AUTOMATIC-01A.* The interface between all the network elements and the EMS shall utilize an automatic system-driven recovery strategy.
- *TEST AUTOMATIC-01B.* The interface between the end user web browsers and the frontend servers shall utilize an automatic client-initiated recovery strategy.
- *TEST AUTOMATIC-01C.* The interface between the frontend servers and the authentication servers shall utilize an automatic client-initiated recovery strategy.
- *TEST AUTOMATIC-01D.* The interface between the frontend servers and the database servers shall utilize an automatic client-initiated recovery strategy.
- *TEST AUTOMATIC-01E.* The interface between the frontend servers and the usage database shall utilize an automatic client-initiated recovery strategy.

14.6.3.1 *System-Driven Recovery.* The EMS must be tested for the following:

- *TEST SYSTEM-01.* Perform a series of provisioning updates and ensure that updates are applied to both elements.
- *TEST SYSTEM-03.* Cause the failure of the primary element and verify that the redundant element detects the failure within the detection time as configured through the HeartbeatInterval and MaxMissingHeartbeats parameters.
- *TEST SYSTEM-04.* Cause the failure of the redundant element and verify that when the primary element does not receive three consecutive acknowledgments verify that an alarm is issued concerning the failure of the redundant element.
- *TEST SYSTEM-05.* Initiate a failure of the primary element and verify that the redundant element waits 1 minute (or as configured) before activating the alternate element. The StandaloneRecoveryWaitTime shall be configurable.
- *TEST SYSTEM-06.* Verify that the mechanism provided to disable automatic system-driven recovery functions correctly by activating the mechanism, causing the failure of one of the elements, and noting that the recovery does not occur.
- *TEST SYSTEM-07.* Verify that automatic system-driven failover is successful on at least 99% of the failover attempts by running a large number of failover attempts and calculating the percentage of successful recoveries.
- *TEST SYSTEM-02A.* Verify that state data replication is being periodically performed between the database servers (less than 10 seconds between updates).
- *REQ SYSTEM-02B.* Verify that state data replication is being periodically performed between the usage databases (less than 10 seconds between updates).

14.6.3.2 *Client-Initiated Recovery.* Since the requirements from Section 12.4.2, "Client-Initiated Recovery," are only needed for the frontend server when it is interacting with the authentication servers, database servers, and usage databases, the following tests shall be performed:

- *TEST CLIENT-01.* Validate thru fault insertion testing that when a frontend server, authentication server, database server, or usage database receives an invalid request from a client, it shall return explicit failure code for 95% of the failed requests.
- *TEST CLIENT-02.* Validate that when a frontend server, authentication server, database server, or usage database cannot satisfy requests for a client, then it shall reject requests with failure code 503 Service Unavailable. This test can be run in conjunction with TEST CLIENT-01.
- *TEST CLIENT-03.* Verify that the frontend server supports load sharing of their requests among multiple authentication servers and usage databases by executing a capacity load of customer service requests and measuring the distribution of requests across the servers.
- *TEST CLIENT-04.* Verify that the load-sharing mechanism does support a means of optimally selecting servers (e.g., choosing co-located servers before remote servers) by configuring the selection criteria as recommended and observing the behavior. It would be also useful to configure in a less ideal situation and observe the behavior.

Requirement CLIENT-05 should not be needed because the frontend server does not need to authenticate with either the authentication server, the database server, or the usage database.

- *TEST CLIENT-06.* Validate that when an authentication server or usage database does not respond to requests, the frontend server shall detect the failure, and resend requests to a redundant authentication server or usage database. The frontend server shall initially use a 2-second response timer and attempt three retries. The frontend server shall keep track of the typical response time of each server and the maximum number of retries required. The frontend server can lower the response timer from 2 seconds to <X> times the typical response time (whichever is lower), and reduce the number of retries to the maximum number previously sent, plus one (whichever is lower). <X> shall be provisionable with a default of 5.
- *TEST CLIENT-07.* Validate that when an authentication server or usage database responds to a request with failure code 503 Service Unavailable, the frontend server shall initiate recovery to the redundant server. The frontend server shall failover within 2 seconds, and failovers shall be successful on 99% of the attempts. When a server responds with any other failure code, the frontend server shall pass the failure code to the end user.
- *TEST CLIENT-08.* Validate that when an authentication server or usage database is in the failed state, the load-sharing mechanism indicated in requirement CLIENT-03 shall mark the server as unavailable for service until it has fully recovered.
- *TEST CLIENT-09.* While running a scenario in which an authentication server or usage database fails and then later recovers, validate that the clients eventually automatically resume using a recovered server.

- *TEST CLIENT-10.* Run various failovers of the authentication server and usage database in order to verify that when the frontend server determines that it should failover to alternate server, it is successful on at least 99% of the failover attempts.
- *TEST CLIENT-11.* While running loads on the redundant solution, verify that the frontend server shall always send its database requests to a local database server.
- *TEST CLIENT-12.* While running database server failure scenarios, verify that the frontend server detects the failure, and responds to its request from the end user with failure code 503 `Service Unavailable`. The frontend server shall initially use a 2-second response timer and attempt three retries. The frontend server shall keep track of the typical response time of the server and the maximum number of retries required. The frontend server can lower the response timer from 2 seconds to <X> times the typical response time (whichever is lower), and reduce the number of retries to the maximum number previously sent, plus one (whichever is lower). <X> shall be provisionable with a default of 5.
- *TEST CLIENT-13.* Create scenarios in which the database server responds to a request with failure code 503 `Service Unavailable`, and ensure that the frontend server shall respond to its request from the end user with failure code 503 `Service Unavailable`. When a database server responds with any other failure code, the frontend server shall pass the failure code to the end user.

14.6.4   End-to-End Testing

End-to-end testing involves the verification that the solution level requirements can be met. These include:

- *TEST SOLUTION-02A.* Run the solution at engineered capacity for at least 72 hours and verify that valid customer service requests fail at a rate of less than 30 DPMs. If a request is satisfied, but takes longer than 5 seconds, then it shall be counted as a defect.
- *TEST SOLUTION-02B.* Run the solution at advertised capacity for at least 72 hours and verify that valid maintenance requests fail at a rate of less than 40 DPMs. If a request is satisfied, but takes longer than 5 seconds, then it shall be counted as a defect. Note that some maintenance activities can take much longer than 5 seconds, but the solution shall at least respond that the activity is in progress within 5 seconds.
- *TEST SOLUTION-02C.* Run the solution at engineered capacity for at least 72 hours and verify that valid requests for accounting data fail at a rate of less than 200 DPMs. If a request is satisfied but takes longer than 10 seconds, then it shall be counted as a defect.
- *TEST SOLUTION-02D.* Run the solution at engineered capacity for an extended period of time (e.g., 72 hours) and verify that valid provisioning requests fail at

a rate of less than 200 DPMs. If a request is satisfied but takes longer than 10 seconds, then it shall be counted as a defect.

- *TEST SOLUTION-02E.* When the solution is operating at engineered capacity for an extended period of time (e.g., 72 hours), verify that valid requests for performance management data fail at a rate of less than 2000 DPMs. If a request is satisfied but takes longer than 30 seconds, then it shall be counted as a defect.
- *TEST REDUNDANT-04.* While running the various service request scenarios above (i.e., customer service requests, accounting data requests, and maintenance requests), measure the message latency through the communication network between sites in the same realm and verify that it is less than 500 milliseconds.
- *TEST SERVICE-01A.* Initiate various failure cases, such as the failure of each individual network element in the solution, a failure of an entire site, or a partial IP network failure, and verify that customer service is restored within 5 minutes by a failover to an externally redundant element.
- *TEST SERVICE-01B.* Initiate various failure cases, such as the failure of each individual network element in the solution, failure of an entire site, or a partial IP network failure, and validate that maintenance of the solution is restored within 5 minutes by a failover to an externally redundant element.
- *TEST SERVICE-01C.* Initiate various failure scenarios, such as a failure of each individual network element in the solution, failure of an entire site, or a partial IP network failure, and ensure that accounting is restored within 8 hours by a failover to an externally redundant element.
- *TEST SERVICE-01D.* Initiate various failure cases, such as the failure of each individual network element in the solution, a failure of an entire site, or a partial IP network failure, and verify that provisioning is restored within 8 hours by a failover to an externally redundant element.
- *TEST SERVICE-02.* For each network element, execute an external network element failover and verify that the newly active element's order database is not out-of-date by more than 10 seconds. This applies to failover of a single element, an entire site, or a partial IP network failure.

    It is not necessary to preserve shopping carts over a failure.
- *TEST SERVICE-03.* Validate that in the event of a failure of any element in the solution, failure of an entire site, or a partial IP network failure that the remaining elements can support the required services at capacity. This can be done by running a long-duration (e.g., 72 hour) capacity load on the remaining elements to ensure that they can support the traffic with required reliability and quality.

14.6.5 Deployment Testing

Deployment testing is similar to end-to-end testing but it is done in the enterprise's production network. The main purpose of deployment testing is to verify that the web-based online shopping solution works properly in the enterprise's network. Following the documented procedures, the solution shall be configured for geographic redundancy and verified that the solution works properly during normal operation, as well as during failure situations across realms. Normal operations, such as provisioning for new products, generation of bills and data backup, shall be performed to make sure they are working properly. A manually controlled switchover should be executed for each network element, as well as for the entire site by the staff that will be responsible for taking such actions in the event of a site failure, following the provided procedures to further ensure that the solution has been properly configured and integrated into the customer's network. Just as in the case of end-to-end solution testing, the RTO and RPO values need to be validated, as well as a portion of the applicable network element level tests.

14.6.6 Operational Testing

The main purpose of operational testing is to ensure that the online shopping solution architecture, documentation, and procedures provide business continuity even in the event of a disaster. By periodically executing the plan, staff can gain comfort with the procedures, and any gaps can be identified and resolved before an actual disaster were to happen. As indicated in Section 13.1.4, "Operational Testing," testing is performed by the IT staff to:

- *Step thru and execute the disaster plan to make sure that it is accurate, robust,* and efficiently manages all of the elements in the solution. If there are any gaps in the procedures or inefficiencies in the plan or associated tools, improvements should be made at this time.
- *Gather performance data on recoveries* (e.g., recovery time, number of failures, accuracy of billing data) of each of the elements as well as of the solution to either baseline results or verify if there are any gaps in meeting the online customer requirements on recovery time or impact on existing and new customer requests or billing records.
- *Provide training for the recovery team* and include a feedback loop on improvements to the plan or procedures.

Since continuity of service is critical for the online shopping solution, operational testing should include a dry run for an actual disaster recovery plan, including a switchback, and be tested at least twice a year to ensure that the georedundancy mechanisms are working properly, including the links between the elements and the load balancing services, and that the procedures are clear and correct.

More specifically, the following tests shall be performed:

- *TEST OPERATIONAL-01.* The documented procedure referenced in REQ OPERATIONAL-01 shall be executed, monitored, and verified by the assigned maintenance engineers.
- *TEST OPERATIONAL-02.* The procedure described in OPERATIONAL-01 shall be practiced before deployment, and at least once every 6 months thereafter.

SUMMARY

Redundancy is designed into a system to enable prompt service recovery following inevitable system failures. The most basic recovery strategy relies on humans to detect and troubleshoot the failure to the appropriate repairable or recoverable module, and then manually switchover to a redundant unit or take other repair action to recover service. High-availability mechanisms and middleware are written to automate failure detection, failure isolation and activation of recovery action to restore service much faster than a human could. Engineering redundancy internal to a system with appropriate high-availability middleware (e.g., duplicating hard disk drives within a RAID array) is generally a cost-effective way to boost service availability beyond that of nonredundant configurations (e.g., nonredundant hard disk drives).

While internal (i.e., intrasystem) redundancy is effective at mitigating, most product-attributed software and hardware failures that might cause service outages, even the most robust internal high-availability mechanisms are subject to some "sleeping" or "silent" failures that are undetected by the system itself for minutes or longer, thereby resulting in service downtime. Failed recovery actions or other duplex failures will occasionally occur and thus accrue further service downtime. External redundancy can provide an additional layer of failure detection and recovery to mitigate some of this service downtime. While another system in the same location using external redundancy mechanisms could potentially mitigate some service downtime without any service performance penalty by detecting the system failure and directing traffic to the other system, a co-located redundant system does not mitigate downtime due to catastrophic external threats, such as fires, floods, earthquakes, and other *force majeure* events that could impact an entire site. To assure business continuity following disasters or total site failure, many enterprises and organizations will deploy redundant systems on two or more sites that are geographically separated. The geographic separation should be sufficient (e.g., hundreds of miles or kilometers) to assure that no single disaster would affect both sites yet take into account other practical, business, technical, and regulatory factors that assure both sites can lawfully serve users with acceptable

Beyond Redundancy: How Geographic Redundancy Can Improve Service Availability and Reliability of Computer-Based Systems, First Edition. Eric Bauer, Randee Adams, Daniel Eustace.
© 2012 Institute of Electrical and Electronics Engineers. Published 2012 by John Wiley & Sons, Inc.

service quality. As with internal redundancy, the most basic strategy for geographically separated systems is a manually controlled recovery. Manually controlled recovery procedures fit well into typical organizational disaster recovery plans and are generally only activated in cases of site disaster or total system failure. At the highest level, after a major event has occurred, a team assesses the damage and a designated manager makes a formal decision to declare a disaster and thereby to activate the enterprise's formal disaster recovery plan. Part of the formal disaster recovery plan typically involves recovering service onto a redundant system that is geographically separated from the site of the disaster.

Manual control of georedundancy in the context of a formal disaster recovery plan is certainly essential for business continuity, but service outage durations are inevitably long since humans must first assess the situation and then consciously decide to activate georedundant recovery before manual georedundant recovery processes can even begin. While taking hours to recover service following a true disaster may be expected, it is unlikely to be acceptable for more common product and human attributable failure events. In these cases, faster automatic recovery mechanisms should be used. Automatic georedundant recovery mechanisms can generally identify system failures and recover traffic onto the georedundant system following failure of the primary faster than manually controlled recovery, thus improving overall service availability. Automatic georedundant recovery mechanisms fall into two broad categories:

- *System-driven recovery* (described in Section 5.5, "System-Driven Recovery") in which the systems monitor the health of each other, and if one system detects a profound failure of the other, then the operational system automatically assumes the traffic for the failed system.
- *Client-initiated recovery* (described in Section 5.6, "Client-Initiated Recovery") in which the system's client elements monitor the health of the system they are communicating with, and if the client detects a critical system failure or unavailability of the primary system, then the client redirects service to a redundant system instance. Following the generic system redundancy model depicted in Figure S1 (originally described in Section 4.1, "Generic External Redundancy

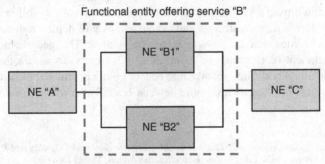

Functional entity offering service "B"

NE "B1"

NE "A"   NE "C"

NE "B2"

Figure S1. Generic high availability model.

Model"), client element "A" receives service from server element instance "B1." When "B1" fails, client "A," is responsible for:

- Detecting failure or unavailability of "B1," either explicitly via a failure response return code or implicitly via nonresponse to original and retried requests.
- Identifying an alternate server element instance offering service "B," such as "B2."
- Contacting "B2" to recover service, which could include recovery of session context and perhaps even transactions that were pending when "B1" failed.

A good example of client-initiated recovery is the domain name system (DNS), which is discussed in Chapter 8, "Case Study of Client-Initiated Recovery." When a DNS client finds a particular DNS server instance is deemed nonresponsive or it returns RCODE 2 "Server Failure," the client simply retries its request to an alternate DNS server instance. In this way, highly available DNS service can be delivered by a pool of standard (rather than high availability) DNS server instances.

Much of the product-attributed service downtime accrued by individual high-availability system instances comes from "uncovered" failures, that is, failures that are not automatically detected and thus not automatically recovered by the failed system itself. Unfortunately, system-driven recovery mechanisms are often ineffective at detecting these uncovered/undetected failures because the system instance experiencing the uncovered failure is, by definition, unaware of the failure, and the redundant system instance may not be effective at detecting the uncovered failure either. For the example depicted in Figure S1, in the event of an "uncovered" failure of instance "B1," instance "B1" will continue to report to the external redundant system "B2" that it is operational. An automatic system-driven recovery action is unlikely to be executed as a result, since "B2" may then believe that "B1" is truly operational. Another problematic scenario for system-driven recovery occurs when the systems are unable to communicate with each other and try to assess the situation independently. In this case, a "split brain" situation may occur, resulting in both systems believing they are active and assuming the other system is not operational. In contrast, client-initiated recovery mechanisms have an independent perspective on the service availability of systems they interact with based on the responses (or nonresponses) returned by those system instances. Thus, client-initiated recovery can potentially mitigate system failures that are undetected (or uncovered) by the system "B1" itself. For some state- and context-driven systems in which key data may be lost in the switch to another system instance, the client may make additional checks to ensure that the primary system has truly failed rather than merely experiencing a momentary or transient issue (e.g., network congestion) before attempting to recovery to the alternate system.

Chapter 6, "Modeling Service Availability with External System Redundancy," presented a generic mathematical model that quantitatively compared the service availability benefit of external recovery strategies to standalone configuration. Figure S2 summarizes the modeling results of Chapter 6 as a comparison of predicted service

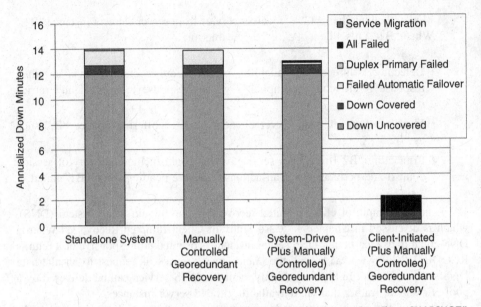

<u>Figure S2.</u> Visualization of sample generic modeling results. From "Bar Chart SNAPSHOT" worksheet of "GR Availability Mode—0_01.xls."

downtime based on the recovery mechanism. As Figure S2 illustrates, manually controlled georedundancy is likely to mitigate a portion of the duplex downtime of the primary system in which neither automatic nor manual recovery of the primary system can be completed promptly. Since "Duplex (Primary) Failed" downtime is typically a very small contributor to overall service downtime, the product-attributable service availability benefit of manual georedundant recovery is likely to be negligible. Assuming timing parameters are set appropriately, automatic system-driven recovery can mitigate some downtime associated with failed automatic internal failovers, as well as duplex (primary) failures, and thus offers a modest reduction in product-attributable service downtime relative to both standalone system deployment and manually controlled georedundant recovery. Client-initiated recovery offers the potential to mitigate most service downtime of the primary system by automatically recovering service to a redundant (external) system as soon as a failure is detected by the client.

As explained in Section 6.1, "The Simplistic Answer," the theoretically maximum feasible service availability of a pair of elements is defined as:

$$\text{Availability}_{\text{Pair}} = 2 \times \text{Availability}_{\text{Element}} - \text{Availability}_{\text{Element}}^2.$$

This equation implies that a pair of 99.9% elements (each with almost 9 hours of annualized unplanned service downtime) will have a service availability 99.9999% (six 9's), which is 32 seconds of service downtime per year. This service availability can be approached if a client ("A") maintains active sessions with both systems ("B1" and "B2"), sends each request to both systems in parallel, and uses the first correct response returned by one of the systems. While simultaneous parallel use of a pair of servers is simple to manage when both systems return the same response, if the two systems return different values because of an inconsistency between the two systems or a failure has occurred on one of the systems, then it may be challenging to promptly determine which of the two responses is correct. This ambiguity will inevitably lead to additional service downtime, thus preventing parallel systems in the real world from achieving this theoretical availability. The practical client-initiated recovery model presented in Section 6.5.3, "Practical Modeling of Client-Initiated Recovery," addresses the primary real-world limitations of external redundancy arrangements. A case study of the client-initiated recovery model is presented in Chapter 8, "Case Study of Client-Initiated Recovery," for DNS. Although the case study client-initiated recovery model does predict that service availability of DNS across a pool of redundant DNS system instances is significantly better than traditional $N + K$ load sharing models predict, it is far more realistic than the simplistic results of the equation above, which does not take into account real-world considerations like noninstantaneous, imperfect failure detection and imperfect failure recovery. Also note that DNS has a higher potential for high availability due to the fact that a client can easily choose another DNS server without the burden of maintaining context from another DNS server or the need to reauthenticate with the alternate DNS server.

Many critical solutions are comprised of a set of network elements that interwork to deliver service to users. Following site failure, it is generally feasible to execute disaster recovery for each of the network elements individually; however, disaster recovery times can sometimes be shortened by recovering clusters of elements. Chapter 9, "Solution and Cluster Recovery," compares cluster and element-level recovery and provides a model for cluster recovery.

Chapter 10, "Georedundancy Strategy," introduces the notion of recovery realms, that is, determining the appropriate recovery location assignment based on practical, business, technical, and regulatory factors. A recovery realm can define the geographic region that can lawfully serve users with acceptable service quality. Systems or solutions deployed in each recovery realm can then be configured to meet the specific customer, legal, regulatory, and other constraints applicable when serving users in that particular recovery realm. Recovery strategies and policies can then be assigned to each recovery realm as appropriate to meet the enterprise's needs. The sites should be engineered and architected to implement the recovery strategies and policies. The possible recovery strategies discussed in the Chapter 10 are:

- Rapidly recover normal service for all users.
- Limp along with degraded functionality (e.g., some services temporarily suspended), limited user support (i.e., some classes of users denied), or degraded quality of service (i.e., longer service latencies) until failure is repaired.
- Service is unavailable to users until failure is repaired.

The insights from the recovery realm analysis should be instrumental in creating the appropriate georedundancy design across sites.

Chapter 11, "Maximizing Service Availability via Georedundancy," synthesizes the analyses from the earlier chapters and makes concrete recommendations to enable systems to maximize their product-attributable service availability. A summary of the recommendations is as follows:

- *Use client-initiated recovery* to maximize the service availability benefit of external redundancy. As a separate entity, a client is often effective at quickly detecting and initiating recovery from failures that might not be automatically detected and recovered by the system itself. Clients should detect both critical failures explicitly indicated via return codes and failures implicitly indicated via expiration of timeouts and exceeding maximum number of retries.
- *Use active–active redundancy to provide faster failover times*. Since "active" systems are already initialized and running, client-initiated recovery is not delayed while a redundant system is made "active."
- *Optimize timeout and retry parameters* to shorten failure detection latency without incurring false positives for transient failure events that can be mitigated by retries or occasional service delays that can be mitigated via generous timeouts.
- *Enable rapid session (re)establishment*, so that (if required) identifying, authenticating, and authorizing a client's session to another server instance is very fast, thus adding minimal incremental latency to service recovery.
- *Enable rapid context restoration*, such as by maintaining user data in a common and replicated data store that is accessible to redundant system instances. For example, web server applications often use cookies to reference context data that can easily be retrieved by whichever server instance handles a particular service request.
- *Enable automatic switchback* to return the system quickly to its optimal configuration (e.g., traffic load balanced across server instances) with negligible service impact after recovery. Thus, if another failure occurs shortly after the first failure, then the redundancy mechanisms are fully operational and able to mitigate service impact.
- *Implement overload control* to prevent floods of primary and retried client-initiated recovery requests to the alternate system crashing the alternate server moments after a failure of the primary has been detected. Overload control mechanisms are often configured to shed traffic or defer noncritical tasks in order to prevent the system from critically failing or crashing as a result of greatly increased traffic.

Chapter 12, "Georedundancy Requirements," offers verifiable requirements that should be considered for any element, cluster, or solution that supports external redundancy, especially georedundancy. The chapter provides requirements for a standalone element with internal redundancy, as well as for the externally redundant solution based on manual procedures and on automatic recovery.

Chapter 13, "Georedundancy Testing," provides test plans that can be used to verify the requirements in Chapter 12 at both the network element, as well as the solution level. It also recommends levels of testing including deployment testing within the enterprise's network, as well as operational testing to ensure that the enterprise staff is well trained in the execution of the procedures and that the procedures accurately fulfill the business needs and service requirements of the enterprise.

Chapter 14, "Solution Georedundancy Case Study," provides a case study of a hypothetical solution configured with a web server front end and a database server backend. The chapter begins by framing the context of the solution, then reviews the service availability expectations of the solution and captures the high-level requirements of the solution. Based on the high-level requirements the redundancy strategy is defined, followed by architecture, high-level design, detailed requirements, and an associated test plan. The goal of this chapter is to show how the guidance provided in this book can be used in a real-life example.

By following the architecture and design techniques described in this book, it is possible for many applications to leverage client-initiated recovery to significantly improve service availability offered by a georedundant system configuration.

As described in Section 2.2, service availability can be measured from data for a large population of systems operating for a long time. Unfortunately, engineers who are designing systems need practical models of system availability to evaluate architectural options and design tradeoffs long before systems are actually built and deployed. Fortunately, continuous time Markov chains enable one to estimate the probability of being in a particular state based on rates at which each state is entered and left. By creating states for fully operational (i.e., "up") and various appropriate failure detection and recovery states (typically "down") with appropriate transition rates between these states, one can estimate the probability of being in "up" states. The probability of being in an "up" state is an estimate of service availability.

Andrey (Andrei) Andreyevich Markov (1856–1922; Fig. A1) was a Russian mathematician who invented Markov chains. A Markov chain is a random process in which the next state depends only on the current state, meaning that the history that led to the current state is ignored. The chain consists of a number of discrete states. Continuous-time Markov chains enable one to estimate the probability of being in a particular state. A Markov chain is typically illustrated as a directed graph in which states are represented as circles and arrows between these states represent logical transitions.

Figure A2 illustrates the simplest state transition diagram for system availability which includes only two states: "UP" and "DOWN." P_{UP} represents the probability of the system being in the "UP" state; P_{DOWN} represents the probability of the system being in the "DOWN" state. Since all probability must sum to 1 in a state transition diagram:

$$P_{UP} + P_{DOWN} = 1.$$

Beyond Redundancy: How Geographic Redundancy Can Improve Service Availability and Reliability of Computer-Based Systems, First Edition. Eric Bauer, Randee Adams, Daniel Eustace.
© 2012 Institute of Electrical and Electronics Engineers. Published 2012 by John Wiley & Sons, Inc.

Figure A1. Andrey Markov (1856–1922).

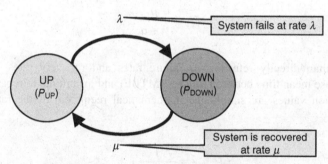

Figure A2. Simple availability transition diagram.

When the system is "UP" it is vulnerable to failures, which transition the system to the "DOWN" state. This transition rate is modeled as λ. Systems that are "DOWN" are repaired, and then the system transitions back to the "UP" state at the rate μ. Over the long term, we expect system availability to be stable so that the rates of entering and leaving each individual state are equal:

$$\text{EntryRate}_{\text{StateI}} - \text{DepartureRate}_{\text{StateI}} = 0.$$

For the "UP" state to be stable, the following equation must be true:

$$P_{DOWN} \times \mu - P_{UP} \times \lambda = 0.$$

Similar equations can be constructed for each state in a transition diagram. Since Figure A2 has only two states, the DOWN state equation is logically identical to the UP state equation; more sophisticated models generally have unique equations for each state.

Thus, the model of Figure A2 has two variables of interest—P_{UP} and P_{DOWN}—and two simultaneous equations:

$$P_{UP} + P_{DOWN} = 1$$
$$P_{UP} \times \lambda - P_{DOWN} \times \mu = 0.$$

One solves for P_{UP} as follows:

$$P_{UP} \times \lambda = (1 - P_{UP}) \times \mu$$
$$P_{UP} \times \lambda = \mu - P_{UP} \times \mu$$
$$P_{UP} \times \lambda + P_{UP} \times \mu = \mu$$
$$P_{UP} \times (\lambda + \mu) = \mu$$
$$P_{UP} = \frac{\mu}{\lambda + \mu}.$$

Rather than directly referring to failure rates and recovery rates, it is more common to use mean time between failures (MTBF) and mean time to repair (MTTR). These common values are simply the mathematical reciprocal of the rates used in Figure A2:

$$\lambda = \frac{1}{MTBF}$$

$$\mu = \frac{1}{MTTR}.$$

One solves P_{UP} for MTBF and MTTR as follows:

$$P_{UP} = \frac{\mu}{\lambda + \mu} = \frac{\dfrac{1}{MTTR}}{\dfrac{1}{MTBF} + \dfrac{1}{MTTR}}$$

$$P_{\mathrm{UP}} = \left(\frac{\mathrm{MTTR}}{\mathrm{MTTR}}\right) \times \frac{\frac{1}{\mathrm{MTTR}}}{\frac{1}{\mathrm{MTBCF}} + \frac{1}{\mathrm{MTTR}}} = \frac{1}{\frac{\mathrm{MTTR}}{\mathrm{MTBF}} + 1}$$

$$P_{\mathrm{UP}} = \left(\frac{\mathrm{MTBF}}{\mathrm{MTBF}}\right) \times \frac{1}{\frac{\mathrm{MTTR}}{\mathrm{MTBF}} + 1} = \frac{\mathrm{MTBF}}{\mathrm{MTTR} + \mathrm{MTBF}}.$$

P_{UP} is more commonly referred to as simply "Availability," and thus we have derived the familiar equation:

$$\mathrm{Availability} = \frac{\mathrm{MTBF}}{\mathrm{MTTR} + \mathrm{MTBF}}.$$

Practical system reliability models, such as those used in Section 3.2 "Modeling Availability of Internal Redundancy," generally have significantly more than 2 states and thus are solved using more sophisticated linear algebraic techniques, but the principle is the same.

Further information on Markov modeling of service availability is available in numerous references, including Pukite and Pukite, (1998), Telcordia (2007), and Trivedi (2001).

ARP	address resolution protocol
ASAP	as soon as possible
ATM	automated teller machine
CDMA	code division multiple access
CPU	computer processing unit
DNS	domain name system
DPM	defects per million operations/attempts
DR	disaster recovery
EMS	element management system
EU	European Union
FIT	failures in time
FQDN	fully qualified domain name
FRU	field replaceable unit
GR	geographically distributed redundancy
GUI	graphical user interface
HA	high availability
HTTP	hypertext transfer protocol
ICT	information and communication technology
IETF	Internet Engineering Task Force
IP	Internet protocol
IS	information systems
ISP	Internet service provider
IT	information technology
ITU	International Telecommunications Union
KQI	key quality indicator
LAN	local area network

Beyond Redundancy: How Geographic Redundancy Can Improve Service Availability and Reliability of Computer-Based Systems, First Edition. Eric Bauer, Randee Adams, Daniel Eustace.
© 2012 Institute of Electrical and Electronics Engineers. Published 2012 by John Wiley & Sons, Inc.

LTE	long-term evolution (a fourth-generation wireless standard)
MTBF	mean time between failures
MTD	maximum tolerable downtime
MTTR	mean time to repair
NE	network element
NMS	network management system
PC	personal computer
QoS	quality of service
RAID	redundant array of inexpensive disks
RBD	reliability block diagram
RFC	request for comments
RNC	radio network controller
RPO	recovery point objective
RTO	recovery time objective
SNMP	simple network management protocol
SIP	session initiation protocol
VoIP	voice over IP
WAN	wide area network
WCDMA	wideband code division multiple access

REFERENCES

"Adopting Server Virtualization for Business Continuity and Disaster Recovery." 2009. Available at: http://www.ca.com/files/whitepapers/hyper-v-protection-whitepaper_206948.pdf. May.

Balaouras, Stephanie. 2009. "How the Cloud Will Transform Disaster Recovery Services." Forrester Research, July 24.

Bauer, Eric. 2010. *Design for Reliability: Information and Computer-Based Systems*. Wiley.

Bauer, Eric, Xuemi Zhang, and Doug Kimber. 2009. *Practical System Reliability*. Wiley.

Billinton, Roy, and Ronald N. Allan. 1992. *Reliability Evaluation of Engineering Systems: Concepts and Techniques*. Springer.

"Crisis Averted! A Proactive Approach to Mitigating Disaster." Web seminar sponsored by Quest Business.

Dolewski, Richard. 2008. *Disaster Recovery Planning*. MC Press.

Gregory, Peter, and Philip Jan Rothstein. 2007. *IT Disaster Recovery Planning for Dummies*. John Wiley & Sons.

"High Availability and Disaster Recovery for Virtual Environments." Available at: http://www.virtualizationadmin.com/articles-tutorials/general-virtualization-articles/high-availability-disaster-recovery-virtual-environments.html.

IEEE. 1991. *IEEE Standard Glossary of Software Engineering Terminology*. January.

Internet Engineering Task Force. 1987a. "Domain Names: Concepts and Facilities." November. Available at: http://www.ietf.org/rfc/rfc1034.txt.

Internet Engineering Task Force. 1987b. "Domain Names: Implementation and Specification." November. Available at: http://www.ietf.org/rfc/rfc1035.txt.

Internet Engineering Task Force. 2002. "SIP: Session Initiation Protocol." June. Available at: http://www.ietf.org/rfc/rfc3261.txt.

Internet Engineering Task Force. 2003. "Diameter Base Protocol." September. Available at: http://www.ietf.org/rfc/rfc3588.txt.

ISO/IEC 24762. 2008. "Information Technology—Security Techniques—Guidelines for Information and Communications Technology Disaster Recovery Services."

ISO/IEC 27001. 2005. "Information Technology—Security Techniques—Information Security Management Systems—Requirements."

ISO/IEC 27002. 2005. "Information Technology—Security Techniques—Code of Practice for Information Security Management."

Khnaser, Elias. 2009. "Final Frontier: Leveraging Virtualization for BC/DR." Information Week Analytics Report, December.

Pukite, Jan, and Paul Pukite. 1998. *Modeling for Reliability Analysis*. IEEE Press.

QuEST Forum. 2006. *TL 9000 Quality Management System Measurements Handbook Release 4.0*. Quality Excellence for Suppliers of Telecommunications Forum. December 31. Available at: http://www.tl9000.org.

Rauscher, Karl F., Richard E. Krock, and James P. Runyon. 2006. *Eight Ingredients of Communications Infrastructure: A Systematic and Comprehensive Framework for Enhancing Network Reliability and Security*. Bell Labs Technical Journal, 10.1002. John Wiley & Sons.

SHARE. Available at: http://www.share.org/.

"Seven Tiers of Disaster Recovery." Available at: http://www.redbooks.ibm.com/abstracts/tips0340.html.

Singh, A., and G. W. Hannaman. 1992. "Human Reliability Assessment and Enhancement During Outages." June.

Snedaker, Susan. 2007. *Business Continuity and Disaster Recovery for IT Professionals*. Syngress.

Telcordia. 2007. "Methods and Procedures for System Reliability Analysis." SR-TSY-001171 Issue 2, November.

Toigo, John William. 2003. *Disaster Recover Planning: Preparing for the Unthinkable*. Prentice Hall.

Trivedi, Kishor. 2001. *Probability and Statistics with Reliability, Queuing, and Computer Science Applications*. John Wiley & Sons.

U.S. Federal Aviation Administration. 2008. "Reliability, Maintainability and Availability (RMA) Handbook." FAA-HDBD-006A. January 7.

Wikipedia. "Seven Tiers of Disaster Recovery." Available at: http://en.wikipedia.org/wiki/Seven_tiers_of_disaster_recovery.

ABOUT THE AUTHORS

ERIC BAUER is reliability engineering manager in the Solutions Organization of Alcatel-Lucent. He currently focuses on reliability of Alcatel-Lucent's IMS solution and the products that comprise the IMS solution. Before focusing on reliability engineering topics, Mr. Bauer spent two decades designing and developing networked operating systems and applications. He has been awarded more than a dozen U.S. patents, authored *Design for Reliability: Information and Computer-Based Systems* (ISBN 978-0470604656), coauthored *Practical System Reliability* (ISBN 978-0470408605), and has published several papers in the *Bell Labs Technical Journal*. Mr. Bauer holds a BS in Electrical Engineering from Cornell University, Ithaca, New York, and an MS in Electrical Engineering from Purdue University, West Lafayette, Indiana. He lives in Freehold, New Jersey.

RANDEE ADAMS is a consulting member of technical staff in the Applications Software Division of Alcatel-Lucent. She originally joined Bell Labs in 1979 as a programmer on the new digital 5ESS switch. Ms. Adams has worked on many projects throughout the company (e.g., software development, trouble ticket management, load administration research, software delivery, systems engineering, software architecture, software design, tools development, and joint venture setup) across many functional areas (e.g., database management, recent change/verify, common channel signaling, operations, administration and management [OAM], reliability, and security). Currently, she is focusing on reliability for the products in the Applications Software Division. She has given talks at various internal forums on reliability. Ms. Adams holds a BA from University of Arizona and an MS in Computer Science from Illinois Institute of Technology. She lives in Naperville, Illinois.

Beyond Redundancy: How Geographic Redundancy Can Improve Service Availability and Reliability of Computer-Based Systems, First Edition. Eric Bauer, Randee Adams, Daniel Eustace.
© 2012 Institute of Electrical and Electronics Engineers. Published 2012 by John Wiley & Sons, Inc.

DANIEL EUSTACE is a distinguished member of technical staff in the Solutions Organization of Alcatel-Lucent. He originally joined Bell Labs in 1982 as a software developer for the 4ESS toll switch, working on call processing, routing, ISUP signaling, and call detail recording software. Mr. Eustace also did Intelligent Network and SIP signaling software development on the 5ESS and LSS switches, and systems engineering for the LSS and 5060 MGC-8 products. Currently, he is a systems engineer/solution architect in the IMS Solution Management department, focusing on reliability, performance, and geographical redundancy issues across the Alcatel-Lucent IMS Solution. Mr. Eustace holds a BS in Electrical Engineering from Case Western Reserve University and an MS in Electrical Engineering from the California Institute of Technology. He lives in Naperville, Illinois.

INDEX

Printed in the United States
By Bookmasters